W0254200

# State, Violence, and Legitimacy in India

'This unusual book asks an unusual question—how and why do people find state violence acceptable and even desirable, even when that violence is turned against them? Khanikar finds her answers in the lived experiences of ordinary people which embody a curious mix of repulsion, resignation, a need to incorporate state power to their own ends, and a craving for respectability. This fascinating book will challenge all those interested in questions of state power, policing and democracy to rethink their concepts and strategies.'

—Nandini Sundar, professor of sociology,
Delhi School of Economics, New Delhi, India

'This is a rigorous ethnographic account of violence which is authorized by the state and gives it legitimacy. Focusing on people's memories of state violence, and violence imbricated in law and order functions of the state, the author crafts a vivid account of the everyday state and the diverse imaginations of the political community.'

—Anupama Roy, professor of political science,
Jawaharlal Nehru University, New Delhi, India

'The book relies on rich ethnographic research to ask difficult questions about the place of state violence in a constitutional democracy. The locations that it chooses—a 'peripheral' village in Assam and the heartland that is the capital of Delhi—allows for a remarkable study in the contrasts and collusion between the extraordinary armed violence of armed militancy and the Indian army and the more everyday violence of the Delhi police. Such a study has not been attempted before and is therefore a singularly important contribution towards understanding the inextricability of state violence and constitutional democracy in contemporary times.'

—Sanghamitra Misra, assistant professor, Department of History,
University of Delhi, New Delhi, India

'What is the threshold of state violence that leads to a loss of its legitimacy? Santana Khanikar's wonderful book reminds us of the urgency to study state violence, policing practices, and legitimacy of political authority as central problems in political theory, and contemporary scholarship on India. Khanikar brilliantly dissects the distinction between police violence in routine contexts and army violence in conflict areas pointing to the centrality of violence in everyday lives of people across India. Through powerful ethnographic work, and insightful textual analysis, Khanikar both details the foundational violence and chillingly explains how political authority gets legitimized in conditions of normalized violence.'

—Jinee Lokaneeta, associate professor, Drew University, USA

# State, Violence, and Legitimacy in India

Santana Khanikar

OXFORD
UNIVERSITY PRESS

Oxford University Press is a department of the University of Oxford.
It furthers the University's objective of excellence in research, scholarship, and education by publishing worldwide. Oxford is a registered trademark of Oxford University Press in the UK and in certain other countries.

Published in India by
Oxford University Press
2/11 Ground Floor, Ansari Road, Daryaganj, New Delhi 110 002, India



First Edition published in 2018



ISBN-13 (print edition): 978-0-19-948555-0
ISBN-10 (print edition): 0-19-948555-0

ISBN-13 (eBook): 978-0-19-909202-4
ISBN-10 (eBook): 0-19-909202-8

Typeset in Dante MT Std 10.5/13
by Tranistics Data Technologies, Kolkata 700 091
Printed in India by Rakmo Press, New Delhi 110 020

# Contents

# Contents

# Map and Figures

## Map



## Figures

# Acknowledgements

The journey through this work, which began as a doctoral project, had allowed me to gather several friendships, and a lot of debts which I would never be able to repay. I want to thank the Sonowal family in Laupoti village, Deepak Gogoi from Pandhowa, Sewali Neog, Durga Dutta, members of the Digboi regional committee of the Moran Chatro Santha, Lalit Chandra Gogoi, and the numerous other people in and around Lakhipathar who I have failed to name here but who hosted me warmly at their homes, who agreed to reopen and narrate their difficult pasts to me, who often took my work as seriously as if it is their own, and trusted me enough to tell their life-stories.

The fieldwork in Delhi too was possible because of the cooperation of various people. I thank the Deputy Commissioner of Police of the North West district of Delhi for permitting me to observe the daily working of a police station very closely. The numerous officers, men and women, of various ranks serving in different police stations of Delhi, whom I cannot acknowledge by name due to requirements of anonymity, took me as a friend despite not being sure what I am going to write about them. The families and acquaintances of custody death victims, and other sufferers of police violence, had spoken to me, a stranger that I was, letting me peep into their private lives, which many of us would guard very fiercely.

I am thankful to the newspapers, *The Assam Tribune* and the *Dainik Asam* for permitting me to use cartoons originally published in their newspapers and for making arrangements for me to access them.

I thank Sunil Sejwal, cartographer in the School of International Studies, Jawaharlal Nehru University, who has beautifully recreated a faded map that I collected from Assam State Archives.

Journalist and democratic rights activist Ashis Gupta had shared with me his vast knowledge of the political history of Assam and introduced me to several people in Assam whom I interviewed for this work. Pranjit Saikia contributed right from the beginning of the work, helping me to choose Lakhipathar as one of my field-sites, through discussions on various aspects of politics in Assam, and with logistics until the final preparation of the work. Utpal Tahbildar has helped with collection of material from Guwahati. Debajit Nath took me to Lakhipathar for the first time. The community of friends at Peoples Union for Democratic Rights (PUDR) has been a guidance and support in many ways.

I discussed my work at various stages with Nandini Sundar, Nivedita Menon, P.K. Datta, Anupama Roy, and Jinee Lokaneeta and received very helpful feedback. I thank them for their constant encouragement.

Parts of the work were presented at seminars and workshops at Political Science department of Delhi University, at Gadjah Mada University, at Indraprastha College, Delhi, the CSSS cultural studies workshop, at a symposium and a conference of LASSNet, the BIARI workshop at Brown University, and at the University of Liverpool. I benefitted from the interactions and feedback received at all these places.

I thank the staff of the following libraries for their support: Political Science Departmental Library, Delhi University; Ratan Tata Library, DSE; Central Reference Library and the South Campus Library of Delhi University; Nehru Memorial Museum and Library; District Library at Guwahati; library of the Omeo Kumar Das Institute of Social Change and Development, Guwahati; the library of the *Sadin* newspaper group; Central Library JNU; Sydney Jones Library at the University of Liverpool; and the British Library, London. The staff at the Assam State Archives was also very helpful.

The research fellowship received from University Grants Commission and the UTA-ship provided by the University of Delhi, gave me the much needed economic independence to focus on this research and to complete my PhD. A postdoctoral fellowship, which I availed briefly from the Institute of Economic Growth, Delhi, and my stint as an India

Fellow at the University of Liverpool also helped by offering time and resources for research and writing.

Friendships of both academic and personal nature have played an important part in sustaining me through the difficult journey of doing a PhD and preparing the dissertation for publication. I thank Anusha, Anushka, Indrajit, Kamal, Kasturi, Mithilesh, Neelam, Preeti, Shefali, Subarta, Tarangini, and Vikas.

Ujjwal Kumar Singh, my doctoral supervisor, has been a tower of support throughout and beyond my PhD research. Apart from being a great teacher and guide, his humility, friendship and encouragement, and the very fact that he listened to me with so much patience and attention every time I had to tell a story, gave me the courage to write.

My sisters Juri and Mamun have given me immense love, support, and encouragement. My brothers-in-law Utpal and Pranjit have not only offered brotherly love, but have also saved me from many familial concerns while burdening themselves with those. I thank my parents for their faith in me, and for teaching all three of their daughters through example to be courageous and perseverant. I thank my parents-in-law, aunt-in-law Bhani *piti*, and sister-in-law Hironmoyee for their encouragement in my academic endeavours. I thank Abhigyan, Misi, Emon, Jun, Dhan, and Dhunu for their love. My husband Shantanu has shared the pains and happiness throughout the process of what at times seemed to be a never-ending project, and often bore with my seven-days-a-week work schedules. Without his unflinching love and friendship, the pleasure of writing this book would have been much less.

Last but not the least, I extend my gratitude to the team at Oxford University Press for their support at various stages of the manuscript and for seeing it through to the end.

# Abbreviations

| | |
|---|---|
| AASU | All Assam Students Union |
| ACP | Assistant Commissioner of Police |
| AFSPA | Armed Forces Special Powers Act |
| AGP | Asom Gana Parishad |
| ASI | Assistant Sub Inspector |
| ASTC | Assam State Transport Corporation |
| ATO | Anti Terrorist Operations Officer |
| BC | Bad Character |
| CCTV | Closed-circuit television |
| CP | Commissioner of Police |
| CPI (M) | Communist Party of India (Marxist) |
| CrPC | Criminal Procedure Code of 1973 |
| CRPF | Central Reserve Police Force |
| DCP | Deputy Commissioner of Police |
| DD | Daily Diary |
| DDA | Delhi Development Authority |
| DO | Duty Officer |
| FIR | First Information Report |
| IO | Investigating Officer |
| IOC | Indian Oil Corporation |
| IPC | Indian Penal Code |
| LP School | Lower Primary School |
| MCD | Municipal Corporation of Delhi |
| ME School | Middle English School |
| NAGP | Natun Asom Gana Parishad |

| | |
|---|---|
| NCRB | National Crime Records Bureau |
| NHRC | National Human Rights Commission |
| POTA | Prevention of Terrorist Activities Act |
| PLP | Purbanchalio Loka Parishad |
| PS | Police Station |
| PSI | Probationary Sub Inspector |
| PSU | Public Sector Undertaking |
| PUDR | Peoples Union for Democratic Rights |
| SHO | Station House Officer |
| SI | Sub Inspector |
| SP | Superintendent of Police |
| SULFA | Surrendered ULFA |
| TADA | Terrorist and Disruptive Activities (Prevention) Act |
| UAPA | Unlawful Activities (Prevention) Act |
| ULFA | United Liberation Front of Assam |
| URMCA | United Reservation Movement Council of Assam |

# Introduction

## Probing State-legitimacy in the Context of Violence

Territorial nation states have become the inevitable fate of organizing all societies in present times. Regardless of the specific form of the government, all states claim that they protect and nurture a given population, within a defined territory and from outside enemies. Within such a theoretical discourse, our imaginations find it difficult to grasp the reality of a state that destroys or violates a part of the community, which it is supposed to protect. In the case of a state with a democratic form of government, where the state is run by elected representatives of the ruled, it might seem improbable that the state would act violently against those very people on whose mandate it stands. This is particularly the case when this violated group does not have a sustainable difference of identity laid out in principle with the rest of the citizens. Even if we accept the possibility of a state acting violently against its citizens as an interim measure, most often we like to believe that there cannot be a durable rule, based on consent, which uses continual violence as a *regular* technique, and not as a last resort, on its own citizens.

However, despite such apparent contradictions of an inwardly violent state, what we see in the context of many official democracies is that in a routine manner the armed, paramilitary, and police forces of the state are employed against their own people.

My attempt in this work is to look into the lived experiences of people, with authority and its (capacity for and actual) violence. The point of attention is how the wielding of violence by a power shapes peoples' notions of belongingness, security, and freedom and how these processes construct or affect the legitimacy of a given power. The focus is upon two different violent manifestations of the Indian state and how people, over time, have related and responded to it, enhancing or depleting its legitimacy.

In the context of the secessionist struggles in Assam, an ex-member of the rebel organization United Liberation Front of Assam (ULFA) narrated a story to author journalist Sanjoy Hazarika, about the perception of freedom of some cadres from another rebel group of a geographically contiguous area:

> ... they were astonished by the size of the towns, the quality of the roads, the bright lights of the shops and homes and the relative affluence that was visible ... 'But what are you fighting for, ... You have electricity, drinking water and cars—you are already free'. (Hazarika 1994 [2011], pp. 180–1)

ULFA, on the other hand, constructed the notion of freedom as secession of Assam from India, and self-rule by the ethnic Assamese in their homeland. Their stated attempt was to fight an armed war for independence by organizing the common 'exploited' masses (ULFA 1989). A major element of organizing the common masses was to explain to them the reality of their 'un-freedom' and thus delegitimize the Indian state on that count.

In Lakhipathar where the ULFA had its central camp, however, when no state official dared to venture into Lakhipathar and engage with the rebel organization, a villager said that, 'it felt as if we already had independence' (Mr J. Koch, 2012, pers.com, 22 May). Once the hold of the Indian army had consolidated in the region, the rebel cadres had stopped frequenting the area and people wanted 'things to remain that way' (Ms A. Gogoi, 2012, pers.com, 9 April).

An ethnographic peep into the practices of policing in Delhi, offering a varying perspective, shows that the marginal sections of the city are the ones who are 'policed' in a restrictive sense so that law and order can be maintained. Despite that, people from various marginal sections invite the police into their lives, in instances of neighbourhood quarrels or of children's fights, apparently incidents which are not of serious urgency.

Evidence from the comparative study of these two field-sites suggests that the lived experiences of suffering, of violence, and living under the threat of it may not lead to delegitimation of power. Instead, at times authority is found to be valued for its capacity to respond, despite its violent form. On many occasions, people may look forward to one power structure to keep another power structure at bay, or just to be able to live their everyday lives. In the process, the state re-establishes and justifies its requirement to act violently. I argue that this process of legitimation of power-holders, who act violently, is intricately connected to a dominant vision of political rule, that is, territorial–national. While drawing on the historical–sociological and deconstructionist genres of literature (Benjamin 1999; Derrida 1999; Giddens 1985; Mann 1988; Sarat and Kearns 1995; Tilly 1975) which show that the state, and more specifically the modern nation state, is intricately bound up with practices of violence, this work takes up the further task of exploring how the inherent and continuous inward violence of the state affects its legitimacy, in the specific context of the Indian state.

If we look at the history of the democratic state in postcolonial India, many of its developmental moments are marked by violence towards its own people. Violence of partition at the birth of the Indian state as well as some early violent developmental moments—such as offensives against the princely state of Hyderabad and the Telangana movement, against aspirations of the Nagas—led to give the present shape to the Indian state. Since then, the state in India has been using violence in various forms ranging from direct physical force and killing, to violence in the forms of deprivation of people of their means of livelihood. There are numerous examples: from the national emergency of mid 1970s, army operations in Punjab in mid 1980s, army and paramilitary operations against peasant and tribal populations and ethnic groups in the north-eastern provinces, in Kashmir and in the central and eastern parts of India in the name of suppressing rebel groups, to the more routine and mundane violence towards sections of urban poor.

The democratic procedures in India seem to have, however, survived despite all such use of force. It is intriguing to see if this stability of democratic procedures also represents a successful generation and maintenance of legitimacy on the part of the state, despite sustained and prolonged use of coercive methods, and if so, what accounts for such legitimacy of states.

The state's violence has been continual in India in various forms and at diverse locations. For the purposes of conducting an ethnographic research one has to pick up one or two such moments keeping in view the form of violence, spatial and temporal location, and the social, political, economic, and cultural contexts. Raising questions about social structures and processes concretely situated in specific times and places, this work follows a historical-sociological approach (Skocpol 1984a, 1984b) to understand interplay of meaningful actions and structural contexts. The two moments that this study focuses upon are: first, violence of the police towards people from margins—both socio-economic and spatial—in the capital city of Delhi in the process of keeping it 'safe' and 'secure'; and second, a study of armed violence in the context of conflict between a rebel group and the Indian state's army and central paramilitary forces, which impacted and shaped lives of tribal and ethnic peasant groups in a remote cluster of villages, collectively known as Lakhipathar, in the Tinsukia district of the northeast Indian state of Assam.

These two instances are broadly separated along a few criteria. One is the rough classification in terms of routineness and extraordinarity. The study of policing in Delhi and violence involved therein appears to be of routine nature in a sense that it happens on an everyday basis in day-to-day circumstances, and is meted out specifically to the urban poor who live in slums and depends on irregular or informal occupations. The army and paramilitary violence in a peripheral location appears to have more extraordinarity built into it, though the separating line between what is routine and what is extraordinary or non-routine is a fuzzy one, affected by temporality, geography, and social relations. There are instances when the everyday violence of police in Delhi veers into moments of extraordinarity, the infrequent, such as in cases of custodial death. Similarly, an event, if repeatedly performed/emerge in a specific location, the very fact of familiarity with it can transmute it to be perceived as a routine. The long-lasting armed surveillance of daily life in Lakhipathar has become a part of their everyday.

Apart from the form of violence in both the instances, there are a few other criteria for selecting these two specific instances for study. The foremost reason for choosing Delhi as the field-site for studying policing practices is that the city of Delhi is one of the most prominent of Indian metropolitan cities, with the added qualification of being the seat of political power. The most powerful state structures of the country including the offices of the heads of the state and government are located here. According to the *Crime in India* report for the year 2013 of National Crime Records Bureau, the city of Delhi accounts for 13 per cent of the total crimes reported from 53 mega cities, which is the highest share among all these mega cities (NCRB 2013). The average rate of IPC crimes in the city of Delhi is 441.9 in comparison to the all India average of 215.5 (NCRB 2013). As given in the Annual Review of Delhi Police, during the year 2013 (up to 15 December), a total of 73,958 IPC crimes were registered in Delhi (Delhi Police 2013).

In this context the police in Delhi is portrayed as one of the most advanced and people-friendly police forces in the country, which is also subject to constant media surveillance. Given this scenario, policing in Delhi is about a minute balancing of acting to political and social pressure of solving crimes as well as of respecting rights of those who are policed. Despite this, however, police custodial violence and deaths thereof are not rare in the city. According to data provided by a report of the People's Union for Democratic Rights (PUDR), between 1980 and 2006, there have been at least 128 deaths in custody of Delhi Police, out of which conviction has taken place in only five, at the lower courts (PUDR n.d.). How does violence seep into the practices of a police force which is one of the best maintained in the country, coming directly under the Ministry of Home Affairs of the central government structure, and how such practices of violence influence the image of institutions, are pressing questions to be asked.

The very foundation of a constitutional democracy is that institutions like the police or the army do not work outside the laws of the land. In a normative understanding, the legitimacy of a constitutional democracy should be based on that very principle. The reality of the routine occurrence of violence by state institutions, however, raises questions about the place of legally under-defined violence in the practices of the state and brings into view the spaces where the law cannot look at, or enter, despite it being an arena that is open to wide public view. How do such public viewings find meanings and interpretations in the larger question of the legitimacy of the state?

Another factor that makes an ethnographic study of policing in Delhi promising is existence of sharp divisions amongst the people that are inhabitants of the city in terms of their location along lines of caste, religion, community, ethnic and social background, political affiliation, occupation, habitat, standard of living, level of education, etc. The presence of centres and margins within the space of a capital city brings into fore the questions of boundaries—social and territorial—that define the nation state.

Boundaries in the context of the field-site in Assam, on the other hand, offers a scenario which is both similar and different. Lakhipathar, a cluster of forest-villages in the district of Tinisukia in the north-eastern peripheries of the Indian national territory, is peripheral to the centralized space of Delhi in several respects. The most apparent difference is the geographical remoteness and cultural distinctness. Further, the city of Delhi is the central space of the state in India, with major seats of political and administrative power, at the beginning of the temporal period that comes within the scope of this research, experience of the state in Lakhipathar was only in the form of the forest department. Thus, it presents itself as a space where authority itself is under contestation and consolidation.

Further, the police in Delhi is a body to maintain law and order and its acts of violence are in the process of maintaining everyday security of life and property. On the other hand, the practices of violence in Lakhipathar are (most of the time) from national armies, such as contingents of the Indian army or ULFA's independence army, largely meant for fighting external wars. However, both are manifestations of the claimed 'legitimate monopoly of violence' by states, and hence crucial facets to study the effects of violence by power-holders on its legitimacy.

While these two are the sites of research, the nature of the field work also contributes to how and what arguments and conclusions are arrived at in the work. The fact that versions of people who are targets of violence from state institutions are studied and analysed not only in the context of narrating past events of violence but also while talking of or living out their everyday lives, allows us to estimate the ways the state has seeped into the lives of these people, making it inevitable for them. The fact that we see a woman who lives in a slum wants the police to fight her quarrels through ways that are not officially sanctioned, or the fact that the Indian army which is stationed in Lakhipathar to fight insurgency is actively welcomed and involved in the social, cultural, and familial life of the villagers, indicate a belief in the legitimate place of these institutions in the larger schema of people's everyday living. The fact that a custodial violence victim begins thinking that the wielders of state violence deserve a different and lesser form of punishment for their misdeeds or the fact that they end up collaborating with those same institutions of violence indicates towards people's keenness in being included in the figure of power. The inclusion that theories of democracy talk of, is acted out in a very different way here, where the inclusion to the side of the powerful, the one who can keep you safe, is a constant struggle, and this struggle requires acceptance of authority in every form as an entry fee.

## Methods and Sources

The question of how one studies the state is dependent on one's understanding of the state. The state can be understood both as a historical reality and as a concept, and both aspects of the term seem to be important. Understood as a specific historical reality, the state is composed of a 'differentiated set of institutions and personnel ... embodying centrality ... to cover a territorially demarcated area over which it exercises ... some degree of authoritative, binding rule making, backed up by some organized physical force' (Mann 1993, 55). The state as a concept on the other hand is imagined as an embodiment of sovereignty condensed in the Hobbesian covenant, as a source of social order and stability, producing citizens as well as subjects, 'as an agency capable of creating a definite and authorized nation-space materialized in boundaries, infrastructure, monuments, and authoritative institutions' (Blom Hansen and Stepputat 2001, 2). Blom Hansen and Steputtat (2001) consider this as a 'myth' of the state that is prevalent in various degrees in diverse contexts, in the face of everyday experiences of often profoundly violent and ineffective governments.

These two aspects are seen within this work not as unrelated, but rather, as influencing and shaping each other. This research views the state as a set of concrete, local, and personified institutions, and studies some of these institutions as experienced at the everyday level through their practices of coercion and violence. Such a research agenda calls for an examination of various ways in which the state attempts to make itself tangible, and also studying it from ethnographic sites: how does it appear to those who present/perform the state as well as to those who face the state in their daily practices?

Observing people in their daily lives, listening to their accounts of happenings, memories of past, strategies of everyday survival, and so on, are tools through which this work is developed. I draw upon unstructured interviews and informal conversations apart from observation of people in their everyday contexts. Through analysis of such interactions an attempt is made to make sense of the commonsense assumptions behind the localized social worlds under study.

Being based on two field-sites, the study amounts to an engagement with what George E. Marcus calls a 'multisited imaginary' (Marcus 1998). It studies people's perceptions of authority from two different geographical–cultural sites. In contemporary times, when culturally bound communities completely separated from the outside no longer exist, field sites are no longer only geographical locations, but could be *other locations*, other aspects crisscrossing various geographical–cultural sites. I take social, political, and territorial marginality and suffering of physical violence in the hands of state institutions as my criteria here.

The more concrete form of the research shaped by these methodological approaches involved intense on-site participant–observation for a period of thirteen months from October 2011 to October 2012, covering both field sites. While listening to 'remembered pasts' was a major route, an attempt was also made to grasp the day-to-day practices of people and their sense of 'governance', and the location and understanding of authority in their life-worlds.

The work relies heavily on orality and memory as sources. While the very nature of the work—requiring to gauge popular beliefs and perceptions—make oral sources crucial, the use of orality and memory becomes important here also because the narratives from the field are many times about events that happened in the past. I take recourse to orality both in the form of narratives about past events and in the form of depictions of the present lives of the interviewees. My familiarity with the native languages of both the field sites—as a native speaker of Assamese, the language of Lakhipathar, and a proficient speaker-reader-writer of Hindi and its various versions that are used in Delhi—was immensely helpful in using oral narratives as sources.

Use of oral sources in researching into the present, at times provides invaluable resources for uncovering and exploring experiences which have been marginalized from the mainstream sociological writing based on documented sources. My research into the contemporary policing practices in Delhi relies on orality, as the recording of practices, procedures, and beliefs by official sources are most often limited to either the legal–normative assertions or the dominant voices.

When the oral sources are in the form of memory of past events, they are of an additional value for a social science researcher, as it not only reconstructs a past event, but reconstructs it in light of the subsequent experiences and future expectations of the subjects. Reliance on memory not merely helps us in cases where written or documented sources are unavailable, but, as Perks and Thomson (1998, 3) write: '… the subjectivity of memory provided clues not only about the meanings of historical experience but also about the relationships between past and present, between memory and personal identity, and between individual and collective memory'.

The task of this research in inquiring into past events through memory is not to recover the past as it happened in its exactitude. Any form of history, no matter whether it claims to give a full picture or not, is always written from some vantage point. The task here is to understand through the analysis of the act of recollection, 'how people make sense of their past, how they connect individual experience and its social context, how the past becomes part of the present, and how people use it to interpret their lives and the world around them' (Frisch 1990, 188). How things from the past are recollected in the present is an indicator of people's current attitudes towards the things, institutions, and people they talk about. Thus, in an attempt to understand the place of the state, or the authority of the institutions and their acceptance in the present as shaped through their experiences with them, memory acts both as a subject as well as source.

The manner in which the events of the past are recollected in itself is a crucial tool for analysis. While some memories are maintained within a community as collective memories through continuous story-telling and formalized narratives, others remain personal memories. However, even collective memories acquire individual specifications when narrated by different people, due to a deep personal involvement of the subjects in a variety of ways. Apart from variations in experiencing a collective event, other factors like how a narrator is placed within the social structure of a given society produce varied narratives, which draw one's attention for their political implications.

The oral sources that I use in this work are acknowledged in the text and in footnotes, wherever possible. I stay away from providing a list of interviews, as, while there are interviewees who wanted to be named and identified in the work, there had been others who preferred to talk 'off-the-record', while offering crucial information for the research. There are a few respondents, whose names have been withheld/changed due to the sensitive nature of information provided by them. Likewise, the real name of the specific police station in Delhi in which in-depth and continuous participant observation was conducted is not revealed.

Following a practice that has become standard in academic writings by now (S. Baruah 1999 [2008]; Goswami 2014), in the sections of the book with narratives from Assam, I have used the letter 'x' to represent the Assamese velar fricative. The sound of the 'x' here is similar to the 'ch' sounds in German 'acht' and Scottish 'loch' (Baruah 1999 [2008], ix). In case of Assamese proper nouns, however, where the English spelling with an 's' has broad usage, I have not used the letter 'x'. Also, not all the sounds conventionally represented by 's' is a velar fricative, and in certain cases, the letter 's' is an accurate representation of the Assamese sound (Baruah 1999 [2008], ix).

Apart from field-based resources, some other primary sources also contributed to the development of this work. One important source was government documents secured through applications under the Right to Information Act, 2005. Other primary sources include scheduled interviews with resource persons, literary works, written memoirs, government documents and archives (including archives of the record rooms in various police stations), pamphlets, audio-visual media, and internet resources such as blog spaces, and social networking sites. Newspapers, both old and contemporary, are used. Chapter 5 extensively draws on news reporting of the Lakhipathar incident in the state and national media, to provide a background to the field narratives in the following chapters and to supplement them in the absence of any other scholarly work focusing on the episode.

## The Study of the State in this Work

It is helpful for this work to mark out at the beginning the understanding of the state that it works with. As a social science concept the meaning of the state is highly contested, and if at one extreme of argument it is identified with one or more highly specific features such as organized police power or defined territorial boundaries, at the other end of the spectrum it is regarded simply as the institutional aspect of political interaction, without specifying any concrete structure and hence making it coterminous with society. My purpose in this section is not to do an exhaustive survey of literature on the concept, but to show the conceptual location of the state as taken up in this work.

First, I look at the state in terms of its role and functions. While probing the question of the role of the state vis-à-vis various other social categories like class, caste, and gender, I attempt to tease out into view the spaces where the state acts or retains the potential to shape social relations and political imaginations. Following from this, I also proceed with the understanding that state–society relations cannot always be read simply in terms of legitimating capital, but by dint of having an autonomous presence, could generate acceptance or rejection on its own terms. Within this framework, it is possible to see acceptance of the state, at the same time when bourgeois value-structures, market economy or normativity of capitalism are rejected. Saying this does not, however, dismiss the interactions between the state and the society, and the ways in which both shape and influence each other. Such an understanding is based on a set of historical–institutional and Weberian literature on the state, where the state is studied as an 'actual organization', consisting of 'a set of administrative, policing, and military organizations headed, and more or less well coordinated by, an executive authority' and having more or less autonomy to act independent of any of the social classes (Skocpol 1979, 29). Such theories predict that all actors in the society are constrained by existing political institutions. Institutional statism believes that 'states are essentially ways in which dynamic social relations become authoritatively institutionalized ... States institutionalize present social conflicts, but institutionalized historical conflicts then exert considerable power over new conflicts—from state as a passive place (as in Marxian or pluralist theory) to state not quite as actor (as in true elitism) but as active place' (Skocpol discussed by Mann 1993, 52). Michael Mann (1993) and Joel Migdal (2001) modifies this understanding by looking at the state as less centralized and in theorizing a 'state-in-society' approach where the state as a myriad of institutions is crystallized by the dominant and transient forces active in society.

At the second level, and inspired by works of Abrams (1988), Mitchell (1999), and Nettl (1968), I understand the state as produced by an interaction of various institutions (such as police, army, legislature, and judiciary), and various ideas of the state. For Nettl (1968), the state has a 'conceptual existence', 'incorporated in the thinking and actions of the individual citizens', and which can vary corresponding to important empirical differences between societies, such as differences in legal structure or party system. Phillip Abrams (1988) advanced this line of thinking by arguing that there is only the *idea* of the state, and that there is no material object like state whether concrete or abstract. There only exist state-systems as material objects. He conceives of the state as an idea, an ideological power which creates effects of its own influence, thus making it appear as if the state is a material reality. Thus, the state too is a part of the effect, a part of the mirage that the idea of the state produces. He argues that, in this way of seeing the 'state' as an ideological construct allows one to see the actual disunity of political power, as opposed to the projected unitary locus of the power of the state.

Timothy Mitchel (1999), arguing further, shows that the state ideas and state institutions, or state systems as Abrams calls them, are not two distinct entities, one non-material and the other material. Rather, the material forms of incoherent state practices in totality produce the effect of something larger than them—a metaphysical form—and that is the abstraction of the state. For example, through drill, uniform and other minutely disciplined practices, the entity of the army is created which appears as something greater than the sum of the total members of the army. The state-idea and the state-system are better seen as two aspects of the same process.

I benefit from these engagements with the conceptual and material aspects of the state, yet find that this debate leaves some questions unanswered. For example, when Abrams talks about a 'state-idea', which is projected and believed differently in different societies, does he also leave space for multiple 'state-ideas' within the same context? If the dominant state-idea of our time is that of a territorially defined unit of rule with internal and external sovereignty, an organized administrative system and claimed monopoly of violence inside its borders, then is it possible for people to nurture alternate ideas of state? On the other hand, is there a possibility of a difference between the projected state-idea and the perceived state-idea? Given that the 'state-system' is fragmented and that people experience different institutions thereof in a variety of ways, is it possible for the same people to develop several fragmented state-ideas simultaneously? Taking the notion of 'state-effect' given by Mitchell, does the working of an institution of the state-system, the army or the police, to take an example, generate a variety of state-effects? Alternatively, is it merely the singular effect of producing the perception of reality of an entity called the state which further effects a perceived separation between economy and state and society and state?

My attempt in this work has been to see if the experiences of the state lead to alternative imaginations or ideas of the state, separate from the dominant imaginations. I try to examine how the experiences of violence from the state-institutions affect the imaginations of acceptable and possible political communities. The state is experienced by common people through their everyday interactions with institutions like the police, the panchayat, the forest department, the village headman, the army contingent stationed in the village, the government school, various welfare schemes, etc. In the localized social world of Lakhipathar, for example, the presence of the state in certain and specific forms could reorganize a society itself. Similarly, in the case of Delhi, a given way of policing, which is shaped by the influences of society and economy upon it, does not succeed in creating the effect of a separation between state and society or state and economy. However, despite that, it can shape the attitudes and behaviour of a people subject to dealings with it. If the experiences of the state thus affect attitudes and behaviour, what are the impacts of experiences of state-violence? Do they legitimize the state, or lead to a rejection of or withdrawal from the state?

## The State as a Temporally-spatially Located Territorial Political Community

Though the concept of the state seems to be ahistorical in various strands of political thought, historical literature on political organizations elaborates that the state or the modern nation state form that is dominant today is only one of the developmental phases of the political organization of society. In Europe, where the modern territorial state form originated, it was preceded by about six other political organizations, that is, the Greek city-state or polis, the tribute taking Roman Empire, feudalism, the Holy Roman Empire, the Polity of Estates, and the Absolutist states (Hall 1984, 1–8; also, Held 1992). What is generally defined as the 'modern state' today developed as an empirical reality in the context of Western Europe from sixteenth century onwards for four centuries to assume the present form.

The trajectory of the development of the modern state has been subject to historical interpretation of various kinds. All interpretations, however, mark that there is some linkage between the capacity for violence of the nation state as a political organization and its survival amongst many other forms of political organizations (von der Dunk 1997; Finer 1975; Giddens 1985; Held 1992; Mann 1988; Poggi 1990; Tilly 1975, 1992).

While preparation for wars led to development of a bureaucracy, fighting wars consolidated and strengthened control, and print-capitalism facilitated the spread of the ideas of oneness, Jordan Branch argues that another contribution to the specific form of modern state that we see today came from the developments in the technique of cartography. As the lands that were under control came to be represented in maps, with boundaries clearly demarcating an inside and outside, the state came to be visualized and conceptualized as a control over a specific territory, rather than over places, things, and people (Branch 2014). Such territorialized imagination placed the nation state in distinction from an outside, an 'other' to the space that is national, which then came to be construed as a threat.

As the structure of the nation state succeeded in immensely and unprecedentedly enhancing the European societies' capacity in terms of mutually reinforcing factors of military might and economic prosperity, so the venture of these European states to colonize other parts of the globe came as a sequel to this. These European states entered their colonized world with an arrogance propelled by military and economic superiority, and indulged in experimenting *their* ideas and institutions in the non-European lands to 'civilize' the people here. As a result, ideas and institutions of the modern nation-state were implanted in the form of colonial administrative organs. However, what is more important is that, even after decolonization, these institutions and ideas of modern territorial nation-state were accepted enthusiastically in the postcolonial societies.

## State-violence, 'Necessary' Force and Legality: Seeing through the Definitional Project

The major focus of this study is the internal violence of the liberal democratic state in India. The modern state, as a definition, claims for itself the possession of a monopoly of legitimate 'force'. The term violence with an 'excessively negative moral loading' (Coady 1998, 615), however, does not seem to go well with the idea of the state. Especially in the case of liberal democracies, the portrayed image of a benevolent state seems to be an antithesis to the notion of internally directed violence. The modern states themselves often deny that their acts constitute violence, torture, or terror, preferring to characterize them as necessary measures to ensure order and respect for the law. The task attempted in this work, however, is an examination of this very phenomenon which seems to be so unconceivable apparently.

To understand how we see the two phenomena of the state and violence as linked to each other, we first need to clarify what is considered as violence within the scope of this work. While not denying the fact that social injustices and structural inequalities could be validly seen as forms of violence, the focus of the present study is narrowed down to acts where the infliction of force harms the bodily integrity of a person. Taking up the more commonsensical definition of violence as physical injury sharpens the case for the research. A physical injury or harm is more readily seen as violence, and thus makes a more powerful case to look for the impact of violence.

When acts of physical violence or potential threat of it emanates from the state, such violence can be termed state-violence. Though modern states often deny that their acts constitute violence, and state leaders everywhere claim respect for universal human rights, frequently states are seen to be the instigators of violent cycles of human rights abuses suppressing opposition movements which challenge the legitimacy of the state. The Indian state is no exception here. In fact, violence has occupied an important place in the theories and practices of state in India, beginning from the pre-colonial times until the present.

While the principle of *Danda* had a crucial place in the Arthashastra tradition of statecraft literature (Troutman 1979), more historically, superior military capacity played a major role in establishment and stability of the extensive Mughal empire between the sixteenth and the eighteenth centuries (Rudolph and Rudolph 1987, 52). Coming to colonial times, superior military technology, and a superior bureaucratic organization were two pillars that held up the colonial state against and above all pre-colonial forms of political authority (Boyes 1993; James 1997; Marston and Sundaram 2007; Sherman 2010; Sundaram 2002). The postcolonial Indian nation state has not shown any substantive break in terms of practices of violence, and the violence coming out of the state is often projected as necessary force/action, not unlike many colonial justifications of the use of violence. Such necessary 'force'/violence is often wrapped in legislations like the Armed Forces Special Powers Act 1958 (AFSPA) and other laws termed extraordinary, but used often in ordinary situations.

The question of what constitutes violence is closely linked to the legitimacy of the acts. Violence perpetrated by the state is often legitimized in the name of the need of societies to modernize, in the name maintaining law and order, or in the name of strengthening unity and integrity. And violence is seen as violence *by definition* only if the perpetrators fail to establish the legitimacy of their acts against claims of others that it is illegitimate. Therefore, when the state uses force it is very often projected as use of legitimate physical force, not as violence (Nagengast 1994; Riches 1986).

A crucial element here is the invocation of the 'reasons of state'. While the existence of restrictions and limitations on governmental powers is a fundamental attribute of democracy, the concept of 'reasons of state' as elaborated by Bakunin, advocates the exercise of unrestricted panoply of measures by the state when faced with 'existential challenges'. In the name of sustaining the state, acts that are commonly considered as crime are from the standpoint of the 'reasons of the state' seen as justified acts that are done for the 'greater glory of the state'. According to this logic, no matter how repugnant an act may seem to people in their individual capacities, as members of state, people are required to do it for the sake of the survival of the state.[1]

Thus the question of legitimate force/illegitimate violence is posed with a normativist distinction in mind where a just state uses legitimate

[1] Discussed by Ujjwal Kumar Singh (2007, 17), from Michael Bakunin, *Federalism, Socialism and Anti-Theologism.*

force. But in practice, what is legitimate force is decided by the state itself, in an ad hoc manner, by proclamations of 'national interest', 'reasons of state', and 'exceptional conditions'. In this way, it is a vicious circle, where the standards of justice are contingently decided by the very institution/entity that is judged. Paddy Hilyard, by critiquing such a distinction, talks of the 'violence of jurisprudence' refusing to see law as an antithesis to abuse of power and violence. Legal use of force is rather one way of organizing state violence, shrouded under the legitimizing discourses of 'national security' and 'democracy'.[2] A classification made by Upendra Baxi is relevant in this context: first, what he says to be the '… state's weak commitment to the rule of law values (or substantial justice values) …' (Baxi 1982, 21); and second is the aspect of 'governmental lawlessness' (Baxi 1982, 21–2). The distinction between these two types of violence and a third category that one could visualize through this understanding, that of violence in accordance with rule of law, however, gets blurred when we look at it through a Derridean and Benjaminian understanding of law as mythical violence, simply violence founded on itself, later defined as justice (Benjamin 1999, 57–69; Derrida 1999, 77–83).

Following such an understanding, I avoid a distinction between legitimate force/illegitimate violence of the state, and consider any physical violence emanating from the state-institutions, whether legal or illegal, as state-violence. Quite often, such attempts at renaming violence as legitimate force fail too, and the acts are indeed recognized by the people, both sufferers and onlookers, as violence. However, despite the acts being seen as violence, the right of the state agents to act in such ways is not questioned. While violence, when it is upon the poor and the marginal, is often received with a muted response by onlookers, for the sufferers themselves it becomes a part of their everyday life.

As a study of legitimacy of the state, I also leave out in the present work the aspect of legality/illegality of action as a marker of legitimacy. This follows from an apprehension to recognize any valid distinction between legal/legitimate 'force' and illegal/illegitimate 'violence', as discussed above. There, however, is a more sociological ground too, for dismissing the fact of legality as marker of legitimacy,

[2] Paddy Hilyard (1993), discussed in Singh (2007, 15–16).

which is developed through field observations. It was observed several times that rather than legality bringing legitimacy to the state, a creative manipulation of laws, blurring the line between legality and illegality often legitimizes the state. Here the legitimacy that the state derives is not for/of its laws, but of the official positions, and of the personnel in their official capacity.

Thus, there are instances when the laws are seen as illegitimate, but the state may be seen as legitimate. This apparently contradictory statement makes sense, when it is kept in mind that the state is understood in this work as institutions and personnel who are available for daily interaction to the people.

## Routineness/Extraordinarity of State-Violence

The two moments of violence that are picked up for study in this work are broadly divided as a routine and an extraordinary moment. However, while using the terms 'routine' and 'extraordinary', I am aware that 'routine' is not something that stands in a dichotomous opposition to what is called 'extraordinary'. The categories of routineness and extraordinarity are not seen here as non-porous watertight compartments, but as with fuzzy borders marked by liminality.

Academic literature in the context of India studying the legal violence of the state, has argued that the moments of extraordinarity and routineness in legal definition are weaved together in a way that a distinction between the two is blurred. Singh (2007) in his work shows how the provisions allowing violence or torture in various laws of extraordinary nature like Terrorist and Disruptive Activities (Prevention) Act 1985 (TADA) and Prevention of Terrorist Activities Act 2001 (POTA) impact the proceedings under ordinary laws, thus marking the 'interlocking between the extraordinary and the ordinary' (2007, 71). Lokaneeta (2011) shows how the tensions—between the law's/state's *need* to be violent and its *promises* of a liberal democratic rule—that are experienced in enacting day to day laws, help constitute the contours of the extraordinary laws in a more coercive manner, thus pushing the fulfilment of the inevitable need of violence to a zone that is seen/termed as out of the ordinary.

A look at literature dealing with the modern state and role of violence in its formation, literature on various forms of political violence like in a civil war situation, in situations of so-called normalcy, violence targeted at the state and violence emanating from the state, etc., shows that the notions of 'extraordinary' and 'routine' are not clearly definable in dichotomous ways. Violence is practised by the modern states in unexceptional conditions, as much as in extraordinary situations. So, ordinary and extraordinary, state-violence and its absence, war and peace, are not dichotomous and exclusive 'events', though we may be able to make strict separations between them conceptually. Rather they appear to be fluid categories that spill over into each other.

Further, when we argue about continuation of violence in times of so-called 'normalcy'—in routine forms that people generally tend to overlook, we also need to remember, that this line of divide between violence and non-violence, between war and peace is not so clear-cut even in the conditions of apparent conflict or violence. Rather peace often starts in the midst of war in the front lines, in the actions of resourceless common people, whereas aspects of war may be present stealthily even in conditions formally declared as 'peace'. In Carolyn Nordstrom's ethnographic work we find the story of how Angolan street children in Luanda created a peacefully functioning community, living in storm drains under the city streets, in conditions of extreme poverty, when the country was engaged in a civil war; and the contrary examples of how people cannot find peace even after the formal end of war, as violent practices that get institutionalized do not go away so easily (Nordstrom 2004).

Das and Poole (2004) also show that the 'everyday' is not dissociated from the 'spectacular', and that the 'spectacular' is grounded in the routines of everyday life. Critical events shape large historical questions as well as everyday life. There is a mutual absorption of the violent and the ordinary. As the memories of such moments of horror get folded into ongoing relationships, the men and women who have seen and endured such moments of violence on their bodies, make her believe that the everyday itself is eventful. The events are experienced not only on one's body but also in the fragility of the social where one ceases to trust. This produces a fear that is 'virtual and potential', one that is real but not necessarily actualized in events; and this comes to constitute the '... ecology of fear in everyday life' (V. Das 2007, 7–9).

Das argues that the potentiality of violence makes even the everyday imbued with violence. But, turning the thread of argument in the reverse direction, we may see that the everyday may become so routinely imbued with violence, that a potential 'event' can also become transmuted to be a part of the 'everyday'. Talking of infant death in an urban slum of Brazil, Nancy Scheper-Hughes discusses its 'routinization' as the outcome of an average expectable environment of child death, as the product of a set of conditions '... that place infants at high risk, accompanied by a normalization of this state of affairs in both the private and public life ... What is created is an environment in which death is understood as the most ordinary and most expected outcome for the children of poor families' (Scheper-Hughes 1993, 20).

In the present work, police violence and torture, which may not seem to be a part of 'everyday' for many, is understood as a 'routine everyday practice' in a similar sense. The context here is of the urban poor again, mostly of the streets and slums of Delhi, where torture or harassment at the hands of the police becomes a most ordinary and most expected thing. Such things may seem to be extraordinary to the 'respectable' citizens, to use Michael Taussig's terms, those usually shielded from state, especially police terror; but for the popular classes, the everyday is 'terror as usual' (Taussig 1989). What makes outbreaks 'extraordinary' is not inherent in the nature of the acts, but when violence that is normally contained to the social space of the marginal sections suddenly explodes into open violence against the 'less dangerous' social classes.

On the other hand, the events of Lakhipathar can qualify as extraordinary—at least at the first chronological moment of Lakhipathar's experience with the Indian army—as these were events entirely dissociated from their social lives. Lakhipathar was governed by the rebel ULFA cadres, but the Indian state in its violent face was never before experienced so closely and so bluntly. It is remembered by the people as the 'event', in contrast to all subsequent years of army and paramilitary presence in the vicinity.

However, apart from differentiation made on the basis of context and familiarity, there is another aspect of extraordinarity built into both the moments of violence taken up in this study, in a more politico-philosophical sense. Drawing on the idea of exception and sovereignty articulated by Giorgio Agamben (1998) where sovereign is defined as the one who can decide the exception, the exception itself is understood as the ability to produce 'bare lives' / *homo sacer*, lives that could be taken without any legal repercussions. This is a theory of sovereignty which is both inside and outside the law, as the sovereign itself is not bound by the law, but brings into existence complex legal practices that render some lives bare. And in both the contexts of study in this work, we find that the state or state-like bodies are acting outside the law, in taking lives and also simply in the manner in which power is embodied in the figures of the policemen, the rebel leader, or the army commander (Das and Poole 2004, 11–13).

However, despite such contextual and philosophical reasoning, I still maintain this differentiation because that is a sense that we can gather from the terminologies of the state, and from how the Indian state projects various moments of its use of 'force'/violence. In the context of Delhi, use of force by the police is seen mainly for the purpose of maintaining the regular, day-to-day 'law and order', for keeping people and property safe, and for running the city smoothly on a daily basis. On the other hand, in the context of Lakhipathar and many other places where the forces of the Indian army and other paramilitary installations are employed, the situation is seen as that of extreme urgency, as a situation calling for a President's rule[3] at times, and at other times requiring imposition and operation of extraordinary laws like the AFSPA.

## The Notions of 'Margin' and the 'Other'

While studying state violence, I argue that such violence is most prominent in the margins of the state, and thus I focus on how people in the margins relate to the state. Both the field sites for this work are conceptualized as margins, despite their contrasting locations. The margin that I conceptualize has both spatial and ontological connotations: they are margins of the state in both senses. Das and Poole (2004) talk

[3] President's rule refers to Article 356 of the Constitution of India, which deals with the failure of the constitutional machinery in an Indian state. If the President receives a report from the Governor of the state, or is otherwise satisfied about the fact that there is a breakdown of constitutional machinery in the state, then the President may proclaim President's rule, whereby the state comes under the direct control of the central government. In this scenario, the executive power is exercised through the Governor, instead of a Council of Ministers headed by an elected Chief Minister accountable to the state legislature.

about how the modern state operates through the languages of 'order' and 'reason': administrative and hierarchical rationalities make places and people legible and ordered. This order making function of the state is, however, incomplete, and the spaces where the state is unable to impose complete order upon, spaces that the state has not been able to rationally classify and organize, are the margins. These margins are geographical places with people and ways of being. These margins of the nation state are often at the edges of the territory that is claimed to be owned by the states, but at other times, these margins are illegible or unordered parts in the centre of that territory.

## The Notion of Legitimacy in this Research

While attempting to answer questions about legitimacy, we first need to define how the notion of legitimacy is conceived within the framework of this research. In social and political thought, we can broadly find two groups of conceptualizations about it. One is the normative philosophical notion, which defines conditions and circumstances in which a regime would be legitimate. These theorizations offer universal standards to be matched by regimes to be seen as legitimate. There however, is another strand of work which is more political–sociological in nature. Rather than defining what a state ought to be, to be legitimate, this strand of work looks at existing states, sees whether they enjoy legitimacy, and analyses reasons for their legitimacy or illegitimacy. Whereas political philosophers see legitimacy as a moral and rational principle upon which states' demands of obedience are based, political–sociological literature views it in terms of why people obey a particular state or system of rule. They understand legitimacy as a willingness to comply with a system of rule regardless of how this willingness is achieved.

In this work, legitimacy is understood as the attribute of a political organization in a given social context rather than being a context-independent phenomenon. Further, while talking of legitimacy, the task of this work is not to examine the right of the state to rule / govern based on some normative ideas of governing, but rather to analyse what are the causes and consequences of the relations between a state and the people it governs.

Various competing conceptions of the idea of legitimacy come with various understandings of the nature of the state itself, that is, the political organization concerned. Starting with an understanding of the state as an autonomous actor organizing its domination over society, Max Weber defines legitimacy as the ruled peoples' *belief* in the justifiability of the state. A state is legitimate if the people involved in it believe it to be so (Weber 1978, 1984, 2002). Studies of S. M. Lipset and Dennis Kavanagh on legitimacy, regime stability, and political culture advance conceptions of why people actually obey, within the general framework of their understanding of the state as representative of or neutral to the interests of various groups and people in society (Kavanagh 1972; Lipset 1984, 1994). Lipset's definition of legitimacy talks of legitimacy of a political system as its capacity 'to engender and maintain the belief that the existing political institutions are the most appropriate ones for the society' (Lipset 1959, 86). R. Merelman similarly talks of legitimacy as a *quality* attributed to a regime by a population and that quality as being the *outcome* of the government's capacity to engender legitimacy (1966).

David Beetham (1991), developing a critique of such theorizations of state-legitimacy, argues that taking legitimacy as the *belief* of those who are ruled rids the concept of its position as an actual *characteristic of the system of power* in question. When the beliefs of people could be shaped by various means in an age of propaganda and public relations, he says, the question of legitimacy would thus remain in the hands of the powerful themselves.

Beetham argues that, rather than looking at whether individuals believe in the legitimacy of a regime, what is required to be examined is whether a regime is justifiable in terms of the beliefs and values established in the given society. For this, one has to first see what are the basic normative standards prevalent in a society, and then whether the performance and the goals of a given regime are compatible with that. Apart from this, in Beetham's analysis, to understand the legitimacy of a regime one has to examine whether the regime is valid in terms of the established laws, and whether or not is there demonstrable evidence of consent to the given relations of power from those who are subordinated (Beetham 1991).

Though Beetham attempts to draw a distinction between the subjective beliefs of individuals about the legitimacy of a regime, and the compatibility of the goals and practices of a regime with the accepted norms and beliefs of a society, on a closer look the way he marks the distinction looks problematic. He says: 'a given power relationship is not legitimate because people believe in its legitimacy, but because it can *be justified in terms of* their beliefs' (Beetham 1991, 11).

However, real states and societies are not two entities mutually closed to each other, and thus, the beliefs and normative standards of people are not developed entirely independent of the state in any society. People's values are shaped through their interactions in society and with state and power. The state and society are involved in a two-way process in which both influence and shape each other. Thus to judge the state's legitimacy by taking the accepted beliefs of society as a standard, which are assumed to be completely insulated from the influences of the state, does not appear to be a fruitful task.

One has to keep in mind that the state, while attempting to justify itself in terms of the beliefs of the people, at the same time engages in a constant process of shaping people's beliefs, practices, and life-conditions. In the same process, the state that is available for experience also bends, to make it conform to various norms of the society.

Further, in Beetham's analysis, a conceptual distinction between the notions of hegemony and legitimacy cannot probably be sustained. In his understanding, power is seen as always involving a relation of hierarchy, and the holders of power who are at the superordinate position in the dyadic relation are seen as requiring consent at least from the most important of their subordinates (1991, 1). For legitimation of a regime, he argues, three conditions corresponding to three negative characteristics of power have to be fulfilled. First, the inequality of circumstances between the dominant and the subordinate has to be justified by a principle of differentiation, which *shows* the dominant as specifically qualified, suited, or deserving to possess the resource, pursue the activity, or hold the position which form the basis of their power. Second, the systematic transfer of resources and opportunities from subordinate to dominant is justified when it can be shown to serve not merely the interests of the powerful, but those of the subordinate too. And third, if evidence of consent on the part of the subservient can be proved, then the limitations of freedom for them by the holders of power can be justified (1991, 59–60).

Thus, it appears that his notion of legitimacy is akin to the notion of operation of a 'false consciousness' or 'hegemony' in the Marxist sense and does not hold out possibilities of legitimacy of a regime/power in a liberatory sense. He does not seem to think of legitimacy as an outcome of just and egalitarian state–society relations, rather he talks about prevalence of inequalities, and that the ability to *show* such inequalities as justified, generates legitimacy. Hegemony in Marxist thought has a somewhat similar meaning: it is seen as the product of ideological state apparatuses, which either hide the unequal class relations or provide justifications for them.

Marxists and neo-Marxists who view the state as partisan—working in the interest of only some section(s) of society—however, leave space for a conceptual distinction to be made between the notions of legitimacy and hegemony. They see legitimacy as potentially achievable in hypothetical societies, while critiquing the present, which operates as an effect of ideology or successful hegemony of the dominants. In terms of their concern to show why people accept a specific rule or social system as justified, and why people willingly obey inegalitarian or exploitative systems, these theorists of the partisan-state belong to the political sociological genre of conceptualization, though they have a normative dimension when they talk about the ideal societies.

Such thinkers often tend to dismiss the concept of legitimacy, or dismiss its value, as a concept for analysing the *present* social order and tend to replace the concept of legitimacy with various conceptions of false consciousness, hegemony, or ideology, or equate legitimacy with these conceptions. (Althusser 1971; Marx 1970; Marx and Engels 1932). Goran Therborn, advancing from the classical formulations of Marx, Engels, Althusser, and Gramsci, gives another version of such a view when he says that a political domination is made acceptable to people by various modes of ideological interpellation, that is, different modes of ideological *subject formation*. He expands the Gramscian concept of hegemony to involve/incorporate in varying combinations, the sense of representation, accommodation, deference, and resignation, and thus goes beyond the force/consent or legitimacy/false consciousness dichotomy, by saying that all of them involve ideological domination (Therborn 1980).

Such an understanding follows from the Marxian and neo-Marxian concept of 'relative autonomy of the state', where the state is relatively autonomous from any of the social classes (or fractions of classes) in a social formation *in order to* maintain the class divided capitalist social formation in the long run. Poulantzas argues that, the relative autonomy of the state enables it to gloss over the primary contradiction between the dominant and dominated classes; and so makes it possible for the state to appear as the political representative of all sections of society (Poulantzas 1980). In this way, it tries and succeeds in generating acceptance in the eyes of most of the people without really representing their interests. In capitalist society, the state maintains an apparent separation from the various economic classes and their fractions so that it can better serve the function of class domination in a masked way[4] (Poulantzas 1980).

People like Miliband and Poulantzas, and Marx himself, however, have discussed this category of 'relative autonomy of the state' in the context of advanced capitalist countries, where the state acts relatively autonomously for *functional* reasons of maintenance of the capitalist formation in the long run. However, there are challenges to this understanding from the point of view of peripheral capitalist societies, where relative autonomy of the state, it is argued, is not for the purpose of creating hegemony of a dominant class. Rather, in these contexts, the logic of state autonomy is more specifically *structural* than functional. As Thomas Bamat (1977) argues, in the post-colonial societies the relative autonomy of the state does not necessarily assure dominant class hegemony *due to* the weak development of the social classes, particularly the bourgeoisie. K.E. Trimberger, through a study of the Japanese transition to capitalism, has argued that the state can assume greater degree of relative autonomy when the mode of production is indeterminate and no one class is assured hegemony (Trimberger 1977). Hamza Alavi, in his study of postcolonial societies (focusing on Pakistan and Bangladesh), argues out the historical condition of continuation of the 'overdeveloped' state bourgeoisie (originally rooted in the metropolitan base) in comparison to the weak social classes in the colony, as the reason of the relative autonomy of the state in these countries (Alavi 1972). Samir Amin similarly argues that the bureaucracy that had been left

[4] Poulantzas, however, goes further to argue that the relative autonomy of the state is dialectical, with a possibility of class struggle within the state apparatus itself. Such an understanding, therefore, identifies the scope for the dominated classes taking over the state for their own purposes (Poulantzas 1980).

over from colonial times enjoys the traditional prestige of state power, and was further strengthened by the experience of absolute colonial power together with the monopoly of modern education and technical skill in the hands of the petty bourgeoisie, from which the bureaucracy stems (Amin 1976).[5]

Pranab Bardhan writing in the context of India says that the powerful or 'overdeveloped' colonial state here actually drew upon pre-colonial heritages of Mughal rule. Challenging the society-centric theories, which view the state as to be determined by the material conditions of society, whether of the Marxist, neo-Marxist, the postcolonial, or liberal–pluralist and structural–functionalist variety, Bardhan follows Theda Skocpol in showing the explanatory centrality of the states as potent and autonomous organizational actors. There are of course serious constraints posed by dominant societal and economic interests, but that does not mean absence of choices and autonomy on the part of the state (Bardhan 1987 [2005], 32–9). Therefore, while it is a critique of the theories of overt determinism of third world state structures, it also retains an emphasis on the specifics of post-colonialism. This is in line with the broader argument of the state-autonomy theories as advanced by Skocpol and others, which show that the nature and working of states are to be taken as specific cases and cannot be said once for all through some all-encompassing theories. Rather, states are contextual and we need to see them as that. The autonomy of the state can be understood here by what Weiss and Hobson term as an 'embedded autonomy'—a condition where the state cultivates collaborative strategies with civil society and the uneven and the unequal distributions of power that exist within it, to mobilize and direct it towards given ends (Weiss and Hobson 1995).

Thus, if we can see that there is a possibility of embedded autonomy of a state, it follows that we cannot push the question of legitimacy merely to a future ideal polity. The 'relative autonomy' of the state here

[5] Challenges came to such 'postcolonial' or 'overdeveloped state' theorizations as well. Colin Leys pointed out that the centrality of the state is now a feature of the advanced capitalist countries as well. Further, the colonial states had no need to create powerful bureaucratic law-and-order state structures because the weakness of indigenous social formations in comparison to the states actually preceded colonialism (Leys 1981).

is not for the purpose of producing a false image, but is present as an institutional characteristic of the state. In such a context, the acts of the state may result in production of genuine legitimacy or illegitimacy, and the notion of hegemony may not be operative.

In the present work, the notion of legitimacy is preferred over the use of the notion of hegemony for similar reasons. The performances of the state in India is seen not *merely* as guided by the logic of capital, but as portraying the spaces that are retained for some autonomous state action even within the operations of a so-called liberal–capitalist social order. Along with this belief in potential autonomy of the state, I also argue that the state does not necessarily have to be completely non-partisan or a neutral arbiter, to be autonomous or to be legitimate. The state, acting on its own, may sustain and encourage inequalities, and may not be able to justify or hide such behaviour. However, the people may still accept such behaviour, for their own reasons, and not necessarily through the justifications advanced by the state. The question of legitimacy in this work assumes *relative* autonomy of both the state and the society from each other, none being totally determining of the other as a general principle, but as working in an interactive social set-up.

For this project, thus, we understand legitimacy as marked by two signifiers. The first signifier is about the beliefs and norms of a society. The attempt is to take a middle ground between the Weberian notion of 'belief in legitimacy' and the Beethamian criterion of compatibility of the goals and practices of the state with the prevalent normative standards of a given society. We see the state and the society as two spheres which are mutually influential to each other. Thus, while the state may embark on a propaganda drive to produce a 'belief in legitimacy' of the state in the minds of people, at the same time, values, norms and the material culture of a society may influence the goals and performances of the state. And the society may also, at points in time, find stark discrepancies between its own aspirations and that of the state thus leading to revolutionary change. A continuous working of both these aspects influences the legitimacy of a state.

To study this process, one needs, however, to keep in mind that the norms and beliefs prevalent in society are not only of one order, and there may be multiple and even contradictory norms at the same time. Thus, the question—whose normative standards the state attempts to match in its performances—arises. This aspect also raises questions about the relative agency of various sections like the state, the marginal people, the middle classes, etc.

Second, the expression of consent by the governed is taken here as a benchmark to measure legitimacy. While talking of consent, I do not mean merely the acts of conscious and knowing approval of a given regime or a state by a people, for example, by voting in favour of a particular political party or by talking in support of a state institution.

I rather see consent as expressed also through the ways in which, and the degrees to which, individuals invest themselves in the life of the state. Thus, we note that a particular person may *talk* of the state as illegitimate or corrupt, but the same person, in conducting the affairs of their life, may approach the state rather than any other power-holder that could be availed. Further, when we talk of legitimacy, we do not talk about the legitimacy of a specific regime or government, but of the state-structures as a whole. What is attempted is to examine whether the state-form has acquired legitimacy in the eyes of the people in India, despite it being so routinely violent.

Raising questions about the linkages between state legitimacy and state-violence, this work attempts to re-examine the prevalent theoretical discourses on the issue. It advances a modest claim of mid-level generalizations where the social, economic, political, cultural, geographical, and temporal contexts (among others), and values and perceptions play their roles.

## Organization of the Chapters

The book is divided into two parts, each focusing on one of the two field sites. Both parts have four chapters each, and those eight chapters are followed by a conclusion. The first part is on the policing practices in Delhi. Chapter 1 titled 'Everyday Policing and Legality' discusses the day-to-day routines of police work in Delhi in an attempt to portray how legal requirements are flouted in the practices in the field, and how such creative manipulation of legal provisions allow physical violence to seep in, fortified by the general acceptance of violence in a deeply hierarchical society. The chapter draws on extensive field material, texts of laws and the manuals of Delhi Police. The second chapter brings into focus how practices of torture are viewed by those who engage in them, and the chapter argues that such practices are often justified on various grounds, to themselves and to the larger society. The primary resources used in this chapter are entirely from the field and the chapter draws on day-to-day interactions and observations at Uday Nagar police station in Delhi. The third chapter takes the argument of the second chapter forward, by showing that the justifications offered for police violence are often conditioned by discursive production of some places and some people as filthy and criminal. Such discursive meanings not only legitimize use of violence, but also facilitates the image of a protector state whose violence is required for the peace and security of the citizen self in contrast to a 'criminal other'. The primary sources used in this chapter are texts of various laws, Delhi Police publications and reports of democratic rights organization PUDR, apart from the field narratives that shape the analysis. The fourth and the final chapter of the first part of the book goes on to ask some questions that are central to this work. Building up on the understanding of the institution of police as 'legitimate' wielder of violence beyond legally sanctioned limits to both onlookers and practitioners, in this chapter I specifically look at how those who are targets of police violence relate to them. While the violence of police do not generate affection, I argue that it is often seen as way to exercise agency by those in the margins, and at other times, cooperation and acceptance are seen as best possible strategies within the given framework of governance. This chapter brings into view the ways in which the margins, the outside to the civic space of the nation state attempts to enter this sanctified space of civil citizens, to which I come back in more detail in the conclusion of the book.

The second part of the book focuses on Lakhipathar as a field site. This part of the book is slightly different from the first part in its structure, as it studies the practices of both a movement army trying to form its own independent political territory by fighting the Indian state as well as the Indian state's institution of army, both in their relations with the common people of Lakhipathar. This section has also required a brief socio-political and cultural–historical background of the field-site Lakhipathar, given that it is a relatively unexplored and understudied area. Chapter 5, that is, the first chapter in this section, is where I depict the field site in terms of its history, culture and people drawing on field interviews, a few archival resources and secondary literature, and then go on to recover the details of the first Indian army operation named Operation Bajrang, remembered in Lakhipathar as the first 'war', through a reading of newspapers of that time. The next chapter takes the narrative back to before the Indian army's entry into Lakhipathar. This was the time of ULFA rule, seen as the times of 'fear' or 'freedom', depending on one's specific position with regard to the ULFA army and movement. Field narratives again prove very helpful for this chapter, as the perceptions of different sections of people in and around Lakhipathar about the regime of ULFA give us a unique picture of ways and grounds of authority formation. While this chapter depicts the nature and status of the ULFA regime in pre-Bajrang period, the next chapter goes on to narrate the entry of Indian army through operation Bajrang and the twenty subsequent years of army rule in Lakhipathar. In both this and the previous chapter, where I rely extensively on memory-based narratives, I am aware of the fact that these memories are conditioned by years of living under army rule and the expectations from and experiences with those who rule. The fact that these narratives are seen as thus conditioned, in fact, shows us their helpfulness in understanding the place of authority that is violent in the contemporary society of Lakhipathar. Chapter 8, the last chapter of Part II, takes us to this very question of what makes wielders of violence to be perceived as legitimate authorities. This chapter discusses some striking similarities between the modes of operation of the ULFA and the Indian army, and how these warriors for the two distinctly imagined nation states could both generate acceptance for themselves through a display of their superior capacity for violence and thus as providers of 'freedom' and 'peace' respectively. Whereas an unit of the Indian army meant to fight external wars would be in principle seen as an exception if located and operated in a place like Lakhipathar that is officially a part of India, for people in Lakhipathar, the presence of a powerful army is seen to be leading to 'peace' and 'law and order' albeit of a kind different from the constitutionally sanctioned kind in a democracy. This chapter too, draws heavily on ethnographic fieldwork, including both informal interviews and day-to-day participant observation. The book ends with a conclusion that brings together the insights from both parts of the work, into a larger understanding about how the way our political communities are imagined enables even extreme forms of violence by rulers to be acceptable. I advance two basic arguments in the conclusion: one is that the production of a self versus other distinction in the imagination of our political communities as composed of civic citizens in territorial nation states, constantly works toward legitimation of violence towards the 'other' defined in a specific context. This 'other' is not necessarily outside the limits of the nation state's boundaries, but in the spaces that are not completely ordered, spaces that are in the margins, spaces that are contested. The second argument is that those who are 'othered' in this discourse, are in a continuous attempt to break the divide, and be included in the respectable 'self', which in the process results in acceptance of the norms, institutions and practices of a ruler that is violent towards them. The visible result that is produced is that of a thriving and participatory democratic legitimacy.

# PART ONE

# 1

# Everyday Policing and Legality

In the last two decades, on many occasions, the cruel nature of the police force in Delhi has come to light and has been increasingly noted by the popular media, as we can see from the reporting of custodial death cases.[1] How this facet of the state works out in practice is the subject matter of this chapter. This is done through a study of the everyday practices and arrangements of the force. Studying everyday policing by observing day-to-day operations in police stations and analysing them in the light of the rule books called police manuals that guide police work, in this chapter I try to develop a background to understanding the position of police in the sociopolitical imagination of people, including the police personnel's own socio-political imagination, and more specifically the imagination in the margins, which form the content of

[1] Till the early 1980s, the cases of custodial death in Delhi mostly went unnoticed. In the mid-1980s, the Delhi-based democratic rights organization People's Union for Democratic Rights (PUDR) took cognizance of this issue, investigated every case that came to its notice, alerted the media, and approached the courts and bodies like National Human Rights Commission (NHRC). Such efforts have brought some changes and now we see that cases of custodial crimes are generally reported in the media, though this has not necessarily led to conviction of the guilty, or to much structural change. Guidelines advanced in the *DK Basu vs. State of Bengal* judgment to be followed in case of custody are not practiced till date. As reports of PUDR over a period of three decades show, custodial deaths have continued in the city, and there have been at least 138 deaths in custody of Delhi Police since 1980. See PUDR 2014.

later chapters in this section. Such a background helps us to examine the larger question of the work, that is, the impact of violent practices of the state on popular acceptance or rejection of it. Understanding regular practices based on interpretation of laws in exceptional ways, paves the path for us to see how violence is not deterred by presence of laws and constitutional limits even in cases of serious custodial violence and death.

## The Suspicious 'Outsider' in the Field: Uday Nagar Police Station[2]

Uday Nagar police station is located in the north-west district of Delhi, and is close to a major bus terminal, a wholesale market of fruits and vegetables, some industrial set-ups, a few middle class localities, and a few lower-income localities of migrant labourers.

On my first day of formally being present in the Uday Nagar thana, the station house officer (SHO) asked me to attend the evening briefing at 5 o'clock where he would introduce me to his staff. Before it was 5 pm, I noticed, whoever was there in the thana and was not in uniform, changed to their uniforms. At 5 pm they moved into the SHO's room. Everyone saluted the SHO while entering. I was offered a seat at the front in one of the side rows. Officers in ranks of Assistant Sub-inspectors (ASIs) or Sub-inspectors (SIs) took all the other chairs. Some of these officers were not in uniform, but all the constables and head constables, who were all standing, were in full uniform. No women officers came for the briefing, despite the fact that a couple of women were present in the thana on duty at that time.

When everyone settled down, the SHO first introduced me to his men. He introduced me as a researcher, and said that I was in the thana to see how the police behave with people while doing their work:

> Now that she is here, all of you must take care that you give her a good image of us. You should be in full control of yourselves, so that nothing untoward happens, and we can give her a good impression. Whatever

[2] This is a police station in the north-west district of Delhi, where I got official permission to observe policing practices on a day-to-day basis. I have used fictional names for the police station as well as for all the police personnel mentioned in this work, for purposes of maintaining anonymity.

> she sees will go out as how police behaves. So all of you must pay attention to that, and co-operate with her in every possible way. She is our guest. (Personal observation, 5 March 2012)

The men looked at me and nodded. Some of them had already spoken to me during the day, while others seemed to be curious.

By this time, I had already visited about 20 police stations in various parts of the city, and had been at Uday Nagar too. But this was the first time that I was in a police station, with an official letter from the higher levels, permitting me to be there for in-depth field research: to observe the day-to-day practices of policing. As I was present through an institutionalized way, the pressure they felt about me was tangible in this formal introduction.

However, neither an 'outsider' like me felt very comfortable or welcome in the police station. I was an 'outsider' not merely because I was not a member of the police community, but by several cross-cutting exclusions. While Delhi Police has a policy of having at least one woman personnel in every police station, women in the force are seen more as a cosmetic addition without adding value to police work (Khanikar 2016). In a highly masculinized domain of the police station, a woman studying how police personnel go about their everyday work, appeared to be interpreted scornfully as well as suspiciously. The fact that my Hindi accent was not one of the 'acceptable' Hindi-belt versions but indicative of my north-east Indian roots, which does not go well with my seemingly 'normal Indian' face raised curiosity and generated stereotypical assumptions.

Though they did not question when I said I wanted to look at how policing takes place on an everyday level, the Inspectors and some senior head constables talked of police being corrupt, without me asking anything about corruption, and went on to say that they did not have the option of not being corrupt given the conditions under which they work. It was a time when the Anna Hazare-led 'India Against Corruption' movement was at its peak. In addition, just some time prior to that the infamous Ramleela ground episode where the police lathi-charge on protestors at midnight took place.[3] It was

[3] The 'India Against Corruption' movement started in the month of April 2011 following several earlier campaigns from late October 2010 through late March 2011, under the leadership of Anna Hazare. It developed as a series of

apparent that most of them were assuming that I wanted to see how corrupt the police are.

While the higher-ranked officers like the ASIs, Sis, and the Inspectors generally treated me well, a few male Head Constables showed their contempt of my work quite openly. One of them commented that I would not know anything in a few days and that if somebody should write on police then it should be somebody like him who had seen and had been there for 27 years. This contempt sounded very similar to the widespread contempt of women police personnel that I saw across police stations in Delhi. Another day, when I asked the Daily Diary writer woman constable Pooja if someone is bandh in the lock-up and she said no, the male head constable who was the duty officer commented, 'Why should you trust her, go and check yourself.' While I mostly opted to laugh such comments off, many times such attitudes caused a strong sense of discomfort too. Experiences of this kind, though of a personal nature, point toward the form of authority, the way power operates and the relationship between state institutions and the society at large.

## What Police Does: From *Buddhimaan* to *Pehelwan*[4]

Policing is the most difficult job: I was told by numerous policemen and policewomen that I met. If for one day police goes on strike, then you cannot imagine what will happen. The police is first to reach in case

---

protests and demonstrations across India, intended to establish strong legislation and enforcement against endemic political corruption. The movement developed primarily as non-violent civil resistance, featuring demonstrations, marches, acts of civil disobedience, hunger strikes, and rallies, as well as the use of social media to organize, communicate, and raise awareness. Yoga guru Baba Ramdev joined the movement as a crucial figure raising the issue of repatriation of black money from Swiss and other foreign banks. In June 2011, Ramdev organized a rally in the Ramleela maidan in central Delhi which saw police intervention in the middle of the night, which was widely condemned in the media and by democratic rights groups. The Delhi Police was under fire for this action, and an inquiry was called in to look into the episode.

[4] An officer of the Inspector rank summed up the kind of work police needs to do in these two words. *Buddhimaan* is the Hindi word for intelligent and *pehelwan* is the Hindi word for a wrestler.

of an emergency, whether it is fire, flood, or earthquake. One officer narrated a story of the police being called when a snake entered someone's house. When the police was accused of reaching the spot late, he recalled to have responded to the complainant that the police was 'looking for a snake-charmer's *been* in the *maalkhana*, and hence got delayed'. When someone in the crowd asked if police keeps a *been* too, the officer reportedly responded that if police has to catch snakes then it has to play a *been* too.

The broad understanding presented by officers across Delhi is that without police and the fear associated with it, our society will collapse. It was emphasized that the police was the foundation of a society, a round-the-clock service, as any other service would be possible only when law and order was maintained.

> Any organized human society, even in history, needed police. The role of police has become even more important now, because the primary systems of control are almost eliminated. Earlier family and kin used to control even private behaviour like marriage and property. These institutions have now lost these values. Now people are free, there are fewer regulations; there is only law to control people. In addition, in the criminal justice system, the police are the primary body. Others come into the scene only later. Judiciary can take twenty years in interpreting a simple matter. The primary and immediate role has to be played by police. Tomorrow if there is no police, life would not move. If you leave a road-crossing without police for half an hour, nobody would be going anywhere, as everyone would try to go first. Police has a very important role.[5]

From such portrayals, one immediately receives a picture of an organization which is *mai-baap* to the people, sought after for all kinds of tasks, whether they involve a law-and-order situation or not. The impression received is that while there are several other civic bodies like the municipal corporation or the electricity boards to look after specific issues, the common people remember only the police in any case of urgency. Such a picture entails one to think of a situation where the police is the state institution that is most needed, most acceptable and most trusted by the people.

[5] Personal interaction with an SHO in the north-west district. The conversations took place in English.

If one goes beyond these statements, and looks at documents such as various Acts and manuals related to policing in Delhi, they give a more nuanced and detailed account of the work the police is supposed to do and its stated purpose.

The policing services in Delhi are provided under a Commissionerate system through 11 police districts consisting of 184 Police Stations and other specialized units (The Delhi Police Act, p. 4; India, Delhi Police 2010, II). One can see that the various functions of policing as given in the rules and laws broadly cover the stated major objectives of Delhi Police, that is, maintenance of public order and peace, keeping people safe, and keeping property safe (India, Delhi Police 2010, 1). These goals are supposedly achieved through a four-pronged strategy: regulative, preventive, remedial, and investigative.

According to Manual 1 of the Delhi Police, police stations or police posts are specifically responsible for tasks such as registration of first information reports/non-cognizable reports (FIR/NCR) and investigation of cases, arrest of the accused, recovery of stolen property, challaning of cases and prosecution; depositing unclaimed property under Section 66 of the Delhi Police Act; recording reports regarding missing persons and children and tracing them (investigative); verification of servants/chowkidars and tenants and registration of security agencies; granting permission for loudspeakers, rallies, political/religious functions; checking of banks; providing guards for the transportation of cash, if required, as per police rules (preventive); providing help to senior citizens; providing documents for filing claims in the Motor Accident Claim Tribunal; public hearing for redressal of grievances; helping rape victims and other victims of heinous crimes (Rape Crisis Intervention Centre) (remedial); implementation of the Neighbourhood Watch Scheme; assisting NGOs and involving them in community oriented policing; organizing meetings with Residents Welfare Associations/Mercantile/Traders Associations to sort out their problems relating to their safety, security, and maintenance of peace in their locality. Further, under the provisions of Section 28 of the Delhi Police Act, the Commissioner is empowered to make provisions for issuing licenses for arms and ammunition, eating houses, swimming pools, amusement houses, petrol pumps, press, use of loudspeakers and amplifiers, exhibition and fairs, drugs, setting apart places for slaughtering animals, the cleaning of carcasses or hides, the deposit of noxious or offensive matter and for obeying calls of nature, regulating the conduct of or behaviour of persons constituting assemblies and processions on or along the streets, licensing or controlling in the interest of public order, decency, or morality or in the interest of the general public, musical, dancing, mimetic, or theatrical or other performances for public amusement (The Delhi Police Act, 1978, pp. 11–13) (regulative/ preventive), etc.

As can be read from the police manuals, there are ways in which police try to prevent occurrence of crimes.[6] For example, all the police stations of Delhi Police maintain four registers called Ruffian register Part 1, Part 2, Part 3, and Part 4 respectively. Part 1 maintains the details of 'ruffians' of the area under a specific police station. Part 2 maintains details of 'ruffians' of other areas. Part 3 is about bogus surety, and Part 4 keeps a record of 'budding criminals'. All four of these registers are maintained as per Circular No. 42/2003 (Manual 6, India, Delhi Police). Another register named the Surveillance Register, maintained as per Punjab Police Rules 22.61 (Register No. X, X-A, and X-B), keeps a record of the history sheets of persons 'habitually addicted' to crime. This register is made by police officers of the rank not below Inspectors after receipt of orders from the SP. This register is kept in all police stations and is retained up to two years from the date of the last entry. This is considered a confidential official record (Manual 6, India, Delhi Police).

Further, Manual 6 of the Delhi Police mentions a Crime Record Register maintained as per Punjab Police Rules 22.59 and Punjab Police Rules 22.60 (Register No. IX), permanently in all police stations. In this register, detailed notes on community, persons of doubtful character having been convicted of suspicious and cognizable cases are maintained. The topography of the area population, etc., is also kept. This is considered confidential and unpublished official record, through which surveillance on criminals is maintained (Manual 6, India, Delhi Police). In my interviews with heads of police stations across Delhi, most often SHOs said that this practice of keeping records of communities is a 'thing of the past' and that they 'no longer use it'. However, some

[6] Categorization of people into specific groups by Delhi Police Manuals have a very crucial effect on how the marginal sections of people in Delhi are policed. This is discussed in detail later in the chapter and in Chapter 3.

officers also pointed out that though some of the communities are 'still criminal' they are no longer targeted as a group but as individuals.[7]

The conventional powers and duties of the police force in the field of prevention of crime are: (a) when any person apprehending attack to life or property goes to the nearest police station and reports the matter to the officer in duty, then the officer is supposed to take preventive action to save the life or property; and (b) patrolling: almost all the police reports so far have stressed in their reports about the usefulness of having a beat constable present in any area around the clock. Street patrols on foot, motorcycles, cars, and so on, are essential.

However, these conventional preventive measures seemed inadequate alone, and policing in Delhi have been supplemented by various restrictive powers delegated to police, normally enjoyed by magistrates, through the *Delhi Police Act*, 1978. Section 47 of this Act, through the provision of 'removal of persons about to commit offences', empowers the Commissioner of Police to extern any person, who in the Commissioner's belief poses the danger of committing a crime, out of Delhi for a year or so. Section 48 similarly empowers the Commissioner of Police to extern a person found guilty under Chapters XII, XVI, and XVII of the *Indian Penal Code*; under the *Delhi Public Gambling Act*, 1955; *Immoral Traffic in Girls and Women Act*, 1956; *Arms Act*, 1957, *Customs Act*, 1962; *Excise Act*, 1955; *Opium Act*, 1878; *Dangerous Drugs Act*, 1930; *Drugs and Cosmetics Act*, 1940; *Bombay Prevention of Begging Act*, 1959;

[7] An Inspector in a north-east district police station thus said: 'Doubtful community is a thing of the past. Earlier some people like Meenas, Bawarias, and Pardis were considered as doubtful or criminal. Now you see Meena people become IPS (Indian Police Service, an all India service through which recruitment to higher posts of the force takes place) officers. Bawarias and Pardis are still criminal and doubtful, but now we don't use that category. We take them as individuals, not on the basis of caste.' (Personal interaction on 6 January 2012). Recently, Kiran Bedi, an ex-top ranked cop of Delhi Police, the first female IPS officer of India and the Bharatiya Janata Party's chief ministerial candidate for the February 2015 Delhi polls, commented that she 'did crime prevention saving women from being raped in rural areas on dark nights by *erstwhile criminal tribes*' (*The Times of India*, 16 Febraury, 2015, emphasis added). The addition of the officially required word 'erstwhile' does not change anything here, as the presumption is still about the criminality of these tribes, who purportedly would rape women if she had not intervened.

*The Indian Explosives Act*, 1884; the *Poison Act*, 1919; and under sections 105 and 107 of the *Delhi Police Act, 1978* (*The Delhi Police Act, 1978*).

Further, the police officers have been empowered under sections 107/108 and 116(3) of CrPC to bind any person who is considered a problem for the maintenance of peace.

Coming to solving of crimes once they are committed, according to Manual 3 of the Delhi Police, the process of investigation has to follow the CrPC, where investigation means collecting evidence regarding a crime. The steps followed in the process are: (a) registration of FIR; (b) examination of witness; (c) visit of investigating officer at the scene of offence; (d) collection of evidence; (e) preparation of site plan; (f) arrest of the accused; (g) recording of confessions; (h) obtaining police/judicial custody remands; (i) search; (j) seizure; (k) preparation of case diaries, etc.; and (l) filing of charge sheet. All these steps have to be followed within the level of action and timeframe as prescribed in the CrPC.

In my interactions with the policemen and women, the following set-up of the activities of a thana was presented to me. The two main channels for cases to enter the police domain are the Duty Officer (DO) and the Reader to the SHO. When anyone calls on the police assistance number of 100, the control room forwards the message to the police station concerned as well as to the mobile teams of the 100-number control room operating in the specific area. While the 100-number vehicles reach the place too, the thana concerned handles the case.

People who personally come with their complaints are received at the DO desk. The complaints, both coming over calls and through personal visits are taken down in the Daily Diary (DD) register and if they need further pursuance then the DO asks one of the Investigating Officers (IO) who is on emergency duty at the time, to follow up. The IO decides if FIRs have to be filed after doing preliminary investigations. In other cases which do not need immediate attention, like cases involving property disputes, etc., the complainant is forwarded to the Reader to the SHO, and s/he assigns cases to IOs accordingly. The duties of the policemen and women are allotted by the *chittha munshi*, mostly a constable, who assigns work under the instructions of the SHO.

To maintain law and order and to prevent crime in an area under a specific police station, the police station area is divided into several divisions and divisions are further divided into beats. The work in a division is supervised by officers of the SI rank. Beats are looked after by two to three constables and a head constable. All these officers are generally men, and women are rarely allotted beat duties.

In every station, there are three officers of the Inspector rank. The senior-most is the SHO, the next in line is called the Anti-Terrorist Operations officer (ATO) and the third one is Inspector Investigations, commonly known as Bravo.

Despite such a structured set-up and elaborate procedural rules, first-hand observations and experiences in a police station, however, reveal a complex working of (il)legalities, procedures, and structures of power. A foray into the real world of policing puts legal provisions and officially presented procedures into perspective. Everything from filing of FIRs, prevention of crimes, investigation of cases, managing day-to-day order and public safety, to following up of cases in court, one comes to see, are often pursued in ways which 'use' the legal provisions, interpret, and mutate them in ways that many a time blur the thin line between what is 'legal' and what is 'illegal'.

## Hyper-formalism and Getting around it when the 'Problem is the Law'

The DO desk and the women's help desk are generally the first structures that one encounters while entering a police station. The DO desk is the best place to observe the day-to-day working of a police station, I was told by the SHO of the Uday Nagar thana. Though I had encountered several DO desks in my visits to various thanas, the Uday Nagar station's DO desk was the place where I could sit at the official side of the table and not on the complainant side. The desk was mostly attended by female DOs and DD writers during the day shift from 8 am to 4 pm, and male officers take charge after that, though the DD writer is a female constable even in the evening shift at times, but seldom in the night shift.[8]

[8] The place of women personnel in the profession of policing appears to be full of contradictions, and women personnel are often dismissed as not suitable for 'real' policing work, leading to their engagement in mostly routine record-keeping work and as a 'feminine' public face in the duty desks. See Khanikar 2016.

In a few days I saw that the DO would at times call up an Inspector and ask, if she should enter his *rawangi* (exit) or *wapasi* (return) in the DD at so and so time. Alternatively, at times, an officer would ask the DO to enter his rawangi and *wapasi* at specific times, and not the ones when he actually went out and came in. This was curious, as the formality of entering the exact timings every time you go out of the thana premises was given as one of the various difficulties of hyper-formalism followed in the department. Only a few days back an officer of the Inspector rank emphasized upon this matter several times throughout our discussion:

> There is too much formalism, which influences how well we can work. We have to sign in the DD even if we have to go just outside the *thana* gate ... now, if you have an emergency call, should you wait to fill the DD or should you run for the case? But if we ask somebody to fill it for us, the SHO would say, 'no, you should fill it yourself'.[9]

Interestingly, the calls that come in to the thana were recorded in the duty register with the exact timing; while the rawangis and wapsis were not recorded in the same way. In fact these were often entered with a much different time than the real entry and exit timings, and not infrequently, at fictional times. How did both the things fit in together in the DD, how do they manage to combine true recordings of calls and false recording of entry and exit in the same register that records daily events of the thana in a temporally linear manner? The trick was explained to me by Poonam, a young female constable: All the calls that are received and the complaints that are reported, are first noted down in a register called the rough register, as and when they come, with the exact timings. The task of entering these details into the DD is followed a little behind time, after making the necessary adjustments for rawangis and wapsis. This is important, Poonam said, because once calls are entered in the DD, after that, a back-timed rawangi or wapsi, timed before the last call cannot be entered. For example, if the time now is 2.45 pm, and a call came at 2.30 pm and had already been entered in the DD, then a rawangi for 12.45 can no longer be entered. That is where the rough register helps.

[9] Personal interaction with an Inspector at Uday Nagar police station, 20 January 2012.

Poonam very keenly helped me to understand the procedure, with all the necessary explanations and examples. While she emphasized that it is very important not to have irregularities in the DD, she somehow missed the point that hiding the irregularity in this way by maintaining a 'rough register' itself is something to be hidden. With regularity of use, the practice has almost assumed the position of a valid procedure, and probably has been so routinized that it no longer even appears illegal to those who practice it.

The routine illegalities thus involved in recording the proceedings of a thana also operate along and create paths for other violations regarding the procedures to be followed in custody and interrogation. The law defines custody as 'the detaining of a person by virtue of lawful process or authority, actual imprisonment, safe keeping, protection, charge, care, guardianship'.[10] The law also provides that no person should be kept in police custody without producing them before a magistrate, for more than 24 hours.[11]

When formally interviewed, most of the police officers would say that the rule of not more than 24 hours custody before producing in a court is very strictly followed. Some officers even said that they were so used to this practice that the question of custody beyond 24 hours without production in court does not even arise. If they require custody for longer periods then they can get it from the court for a maximum of 15 days.

In real practice, however, it is not only about the limitations on time, but also the limitations on certain practices of interrogation that decides how custody timings are 'managed'. The laws and various judgements state that the definition of custody extends to include pre-arrest detentions for purposes of interrogation or for any other reason. But, given that the DDs are maintained in a way which allows space

[10] *Code of Criminal Procedure 1973*, sections 167 (2) and 51 (a).

[11] Section 57 of the *Code of Criminal Procedure 1973* says:

> Person arrested not to be detained more than twenty-four hours. No police officer shall detain in custody a person arrested without warrant for a longer period than under all the circumstances of the case is reasonable, and such period shall not, in the absence of a special order of a Magistrate under section 167, exceed twenty-four hours exclusive of the time necessary for the journey from the place of arrest to the Magistrate's Court.

for 'accommodations',[12] there is often no way that one can prove pre-arrest detentions. And this is the space for tweaking the laws. One of the Inspectors at the Uday Nagar thana, after several days of interaction, spoke to me.

> Beatings happen in this *thana* as well ... There are reasons for it: pressure, inadequate salary, low level of education of employees, and expectation of complainants, etc. You are now attached to this *thana*, so you see people are treating you very well. But if you go to another *thana*, and go as a victim ... you will see how difficult it is to lodge a case. All these are reality. We are known for this. These days torture has gone down, if earlier it was 100 per cent, now it is 10 per cent. But though there is talk of scientific interrogation, those are not practical things. In theory, we have lie detector, but we can only use it if the suspect agrees to it in a court. So we need to do all kinds of things. According to laws we have to produce a person within 24 hours of arrest. But before producing we need to give medical report. If there are signs of beating then that would be a problem. So after beating up, we keep them for a week or ten days and then take to the court ... All these things happen. We just try to see that too many laws are not violated while trying to satisfy people. (2012, pers.com, 13 March)

In the comment of the SHO, though there was a confession about violation of the laws and the continuity of brutal methods, at the same time, it condoned the police of these acts by talking of 'trying to satisfy people'. The statement exuded an air as to the police being the real representatives and protectors of the 'people' while the laws are inadequate.

Most of the things that he spoke of—that people are beaten up, and that scientific interrogation is mostly a façade—were casually admitted and even justified by most policemen. Though the media briefings of Delhi Police and other public relation campaigns always claim that such methods are not used, the matter is not even seen as 'unjustified' or 'immoral' enough to be hidden from a researcher who interviews the officers.

Another Inspector who was quite frank about how the laws are 'managed', talked of intervention of 'human rights *walahs* (guys)' as the hindrance in working of police, when I asked if they are unable to

[12] As discussed above, through manipulation of timings.

solve crimes due to the legal restrictions on various methods of interrogation. He replied that crimes are solved despite that: '*tadika hota hain*' (there are ways). He went on to describe:

> ... we somehow ultimately manage things ... just see that marks are not left. And we don't produce them in court in twenty-four hours; that can be managed. Some time back this incident happened: at that time I was in Prashant Vihar police station. The case involved an old woman who lived alone, with tenants living downstairs. In the night two boys came from the terrace, throttled her to death, and took silver *payals* from her feet, some money, and ran away. We kept running after them for seven days. Both went to UP. We caught both of them in UP. But we did not show the arrest in UP, because remand becomes a problem. It is very difficult to explain things to judges in other places. So we brought them here, and then produced here in the court. So this is how it happens.[13]

Though the laws require that no physical and psychological violence is meted out to the detainees, '*thoda tight hona*' (to be a little strict), and arguments that those who are uneducated, dealing with them requires '*thoda mar-pitai*' (a little beating up) and at least a little intimidation was very commonly admitted. To 'successfully' deliver the services of policing, one needs to use all the ways of '*shaam, daan, danda* and *bheda*',[14] I was told. Though the use of force has ended '*rule ke hisab se*' (according to rules), I was told, '*pitai se he log bolte hain*' (people speak only after being beaten up).

## Theft of a Car and Working out Cases

In early March of 2012, the most commonly reported cases in Uday Nagar police station were of petty quarrels and loss of mobile phones and purses. On Saturday, 11 March 2012, however, there came reports of a car and a motorbike being stolen from the area. The SHO looked tense. Instead of sending a lower ranked IO to visit the site, he himself

[13] Personal interaction with an Inspector from the North district, 7 February 2012.

[14] Literally pacification, donation, punishment, and division; these are known as four guiding principles for rulers in Kautilyan thought.

sat in the front seat of the official Gypsy[15] accompanied by two other personnel. I hopped into the back seat too.

A silver-coloured Santro[16] car was stolen between one and two-thirty in the afternoon from a bustling area near the MCD colony where there were several shops, and a lot of other cars parked by the roadside. After talking to shopkeepers in the area and lecturing the owners of the car that police cannot take care of everything and that they should have got CCTV cameras installed, the SHO turned to the constables on beat duty to find out the specifics of barricading and patrolling in the area. On the way back to the police station he told me that his superiors were going to shout at him for this.

Back in the thana, while the SHO went to his room, I sat at the DO's counter. DO Head Constable Omkar Lal was talking to Head Constable Daleep about a cash and jewellery theft in a shopping mall in Gurgaon.[17] He was telling Daleep about the way the detainees should be treated: 'heat them up, they would divulge everything'. After a while, the phone on the DO desk rang and I was called into the Bravo's, that is, the Inspector Investigations' room by the SHO. In the Bravo's room, accompanied by the Bravo, the SHO started speaking to me:

> You see under how much pressure we work ... Now that two vehicles are stolen, we'll have to hear so much from the DCP. But funds are nil, there is no infrastructure ... So no one likes us ... everyone criticises us. This is very frustrating. So we make mistakes, we shout at people ... The DCP is going to shout at me for the MV thefts[18] today. We are going to shout at people whom we can shout at.

In the evening, the SHO called for a briefing for his staff in his room. I too went in, despite the SHO, unlike earlier times, not being very

[15] Gypsies are powerful four-wheel-drive vehicles from the company Maruti. The Police Control Room fleet and other official vehicles of Delhi Police are composed mostly Gypsies, with some recent additions of Toyota Innova cars.

[16] Santro is a small hatchback from the automobile company, Hyundai.

[17] Gurgaon is a commercial hub which falls in the National Capital Region (NCR), and is a city in Delhi's neighbouring state Haryana.

[18] Motor vehicle theft, or MV theft in short, is a group of crimes in the classificatory categories of policing in Delhi.

enthusiastic about my presence there. The focus of the meeting was the MV thefts. The SHO was visibly upset and was telling his men: 'You never realise how much I have to hear from the DCP. So I'm going to be very strict with you, so that you also understand what it is to hear from your superiors.'

After scolding everyone from beat constables to SIs who were in-charge of various beats, and giving them a list of things to do to prevent crimes in their respective areas, especially in view of the upcoming Municipal Corporation of Delhi (MCD) elections, the SHO went back to the issue of the MV thefts. He said, 'From every division, I want five-six boys. All of you have lists of people, just get them in. We need to show to the DCP office that we have taken some action.' He emphasized his instructions with a bit of sarcasm: 'If you can't get in people, then I'll give addresses of my relatives, get them in, because you'll not bring your own relatives. By any means, we need some people in custody.'

Police officials subsequently told me that solving of MV thefts is not within the capacity of thana-level police, and that those cases have to go to the Crime Branch. They, however, needed to be seen as doing their work, which pressurized them to detain and interrogate people. While the police manuals and the laws of the country do not permit custodial violence,[19] it is practised in routine manner in cases that the police hopes to solve as well as those that police knows it cannot solve.

[19] The Indian constitution provides various legal and procedural safeguards against torture. See Chapter 3, section 'Civic Disciplining in a Postcolonial City' for a detailed discussion. There are laws providing rights against self-incrimination, which ideally should prevent custodial torture, as well as laws laying out rules for detention, trial, and prosecution of the guilty which also looks at issues of rights of people in custody. There, however, are some loopholes within the law and the constitution itself with some contravening provisions taking back what it had offered through some other provisions. Further, though the Government of India is a signatory of the *United Nations Convention against torture and other cruel, inhuman or degrading treatment or Punishment* (UNCAT), it has not ratified it yet. The *Prevention of Torture Bill* floored in 2010 too had a lot of problematic provisions and could not be passed till date.

## Regular Processes of Investigation and Policing of 'Suspects'

Violence on 'suspect' detainees is a regular practice involved in the process of crime investigation and crime prevention in Delhi. From my interviews with policemen/policewomen in various Police Stations of Delhi, the common process of investigation comes out to be like this: when a crime is committed, 10 to 15 people who are known Bad Characters (BCs)[20] of the area are brought in and interrogated separately. Each of them is told that somebody else has complained against him or her. The use of slaps and kicks are common. An SHO in the central district said that the suspects are people of a different kind altogether, they do not talk easily, and tough interrogation is needed at times. If the 'criminals' do not confess, then they are told, 'there will be beatings during the night', to put psychological pressure which is deemed essential. A woman constable in the Outer District said that at times the policemen also get irritated and this leads to beatings, 'because they *know* that the person is lying'. An officer of the Inspector rank in charge of investigations in a North West district police station showed me a stout stick and said 'off the record', that 'it doesn't work without thrashing up; criminals are afraid of only two things: beatings and imprisonment'.[21]

While there are procedures laid out in the police manuals for investigation of crimes as discussed in the previous section, they are often flouted while following the shorter route of bringing in a few BCs, interrogating them through custodial torture, attempt for recovery if possible, and occasionally filing an FIR, if that becomes inevitable.[22]

[20] According to the official definitions, a BC or a Bad Character is a person 'habitually addicted to crime'. See Punjab Police Rules 22.61 in Manual 6 (India, Delhi Police n.d.c). The Punjab Police Rules enlist various procedural mechanisms to deal with the BCs. The category of BC is discussed in more detail later in this chapter and in Chapter 3.

[21] Interviews and conversations, period: October 2011–March 2012.

[22] A personal observation, based on Annual Reports of Delhi Police, charts of crimes reported and solved displayed publicly in every police station and the general working of the thanas is that police try to avoid registering FIRs whenever possible, because higher numbers of unsolved registered cases push the thana's reputation down.

In the words of a constable from Uday Nagar: 'Once the stolen item is recovered, no one wants to go for a court case. If somebody has lost a gold chain, they want police to find it, but want to end it there … don't want to fall into the trappings of courts.'

The manuals of Delhi Police talk of specific classes of people, regarding issues of prevention of crimes and investigation of cases, in the four registers called the Ruffian Register Part 1, Part 2, Part 3, and Part 4 respectively. These registers are maintained for the purpose of keeping track of 'ruffians' and 'budding criminals' of their own station jurisdiction and beyond. A category that consistently appears in the manuals guiding police action and also routinely in the narratives about investigating crime is that of a 'history sheeter' or a 'BC'. While official documents define a BC as a person 'habitually addicted' to crime (see footnote 20 above), police personnel more concretely define BCs as 'people with records of committing three or more crimes'.[23] An examination of what constitutes a crime and how one becomes a 'history-sheeter', however, complicates this simple definition.

In this connection, it is helpful to remember some of the colonial laws defining crime, and to notice their afterlife. Chandavarkar (1998) had commented upon how in the colonial period the need to pin down wandering cultivators for the purposes of taxation and policing had led to categorization of some tribes and castes as 'criminal', which still retains some operative value today despite their de-notification (see footnote 7). In a similar way, he argues, the crime of 'dacoity' was brought in to cover a wide range of agrarian conflicts (1998, 226). Commenting upon how ineffective was the police categorization of 'bad characters'—readily identified with the poor, unemployed, and the rural migrants in the context of colonial Bombay—he argued that it did not help in controlling crime (1998, 206). Gooptu (2001, 152) has

[23] This definition of a BC was first given by a Head Constable in a North East district police station, and was supported by many others during my fieldwork. When I asked a clarification about the category of ruffians, I was told that BCs are a grade higher than the ruffians in their criminality. In practice, however, it seemed that the police often conflated between the two categories. Also see Vivek Dhareshwar and R. Srivatsan (1996), where they discuss, how for police, often the two categories of rowdy and history-sheeters are the same for all practical purposes (pp. 206–10).

noted that the continued use of history sheets in colonial north India despite their ineffectiveness in controlling crime and violence, was due to the generalized deterring effect it had—by unleashing fear of surveillance, or of falsely being included in the sheet, combined with the discipline and coercion that comes along.

Writing of postcolonial Andhra Pradesh, Dhareswar and Srivatsan (1996, 208) in their work on the 'rowdy-sheeters' have noted that both the police and the media (which substantively influences the middle-class imagination of who is a rowdy) are clear that 'a rowdy is almost never an upper-caste Hindu. He is either a Scheduled Caste, Backward Class, or Muslim, all belonging to a socio-economic (non-) class which by definition resides in a *basti* or slum'.

Such construction of crime and criminality as associated with particular social groups is reflected in statistics about custodial deaths in Delhi. While custodial deaths have remained an unfailing presence in the records of Delhi Police since 1980,[24] an analysis of who died in custody shows that majority of them come from marginal sections: young men from economically/socially exploited classes such as casual labourer, informal worker, or unemployed people (PUDR 1998, 6). Most often those who die in police custody are not even convicted criminals or offenders. PUDR reports over the years have showed that, during the period between 1980 and 1997, approximately 23 per cent of those who died in police custody in Delhi were without any alleged offence. During the same period only approximately 15 per cent of the dead were *accused* of serious crimes like murder, stabbing, and abduction, who may or may not eventually would have been convicted, had they survived police custody. About 62 per cent of the dead were *accused* of petty crimes like theft, quarrel, bribery/forgery, crimes categorized as others and not known.[25]

The people that the police bring to the thana for interrogation—the BCs—are almost always from a specific socio-economic group, their socio-economic and spatial location being a major decider of their presumed criminality. For the purposes of interrogating such people, often

[24] Refer to note 1 and see PUDR 2014.

[25] Calculated from PUDR 1998. The total number of deaths investigated by PUDR during this period was 93 out of which 21 were people who had committed no known or alleged offence.

a whole mechanism of torture is developed and standardized, which thus assumes a life of its own, beyond legal limits. In Uday Nagar thana, I was introduced to a class of instruments collectively known as *aan milo saajna* (literally, come, meet me my beloved), including things such as smooth rubber strip whips, wooden sticks, hollow iron pipes, fire-extinguishers, revolvers, etc. The extent to which such instruments of torture have been a part of a larger police culture could be gauged from the fact that some of these instruments had the words aan milo saajna neatly written on them. The easy acknowledgement of such tools of policing and the uninhibited description of how rules are manipulated on a daily basis, are indications of what constitutes the regular in a police station. These are the foundations on which events that appear to be extraordinary to many of us: custodial torture and deaths in custody, take place. What we see as extraordinary is intricately bound with the everyday ways of policing and *practices* of law.

Observing nonchalant daily practices of a police station, such as the mundane task of recording calls, engagement with visitors, or briefing of personnel gives us a window to the deeper understandings that the institution nourishes about legality, criminality, and the role of police. When we turn to the next field site Lakhipthar, there also we see how practices of life that appear to be regular and mundane at first glance, have deeper implications in terms of who rightfully belongs and who not, what is acceptable behaviour or not, and about what are legitimate ways of ruling. The routines of the state are often bound with the exceptions of the state. In this chapter we saw how systematic and regularized practices like maintaining a rough register combines with social and institutional biases and opens ways for violence against sections of people. While I would go on to discuss in Chapter 3 how such practices of violence are often targeted against specific spaces and people, in the next chapter, I would focus on how such practices are seen and justified by the police personnel themselves.

2

# Torture, Notions of 'Justice', and Petty Sovereigns

Torture is not a taboo in the sociopolitical discourse of India, despite the fact that we have laws prohibiting torture. In this chapter, I attempt to look into the questions of why and how police personnel engage in torture. Drawing on ethnographic material including long conversations with police personnel, I argue that not only is torture widely prevalent, but it is also seen as a justified act within the discourses of policing, on various grounds. Such an understanding of police violence as a requirement is based on a 'self' versus 'other' division which also reflects the understanding of vast numbers of people who are witnesses to police violence. This chapter, thus, opens up the question of how police violence impacts and shapes the self-understanding of those who enact the state in the institution of police, leading us to examine in the next two chapters how the de facto state understandings of 'right' and 'wrong' penetrate into the popular understanding of 'good' and 'bad', 'legitimate' and 'illegitimate'.

Jinee Lokaneeta opens her book *Transnational Torture* (2011) with a scene from the British/Indian film *Slumdog Millionaire* where a constable beats up a boy from a slum who wins twenty million rupees in a game show, assuming that he is winning by cheating. According to her sources, initially the senior police official was seen as torturing the boy. However, at the request of the Indian government, the producers changed the torturer to the constable. She points that, interestingly, the Indian government did not ask to remove the scene altogether showing that even the government accepts that it is not entirely improbable (Lokaneeta 2011: 1–2).

Such a portrayal of police torture is regular in various Indian TV serials and Bollywood movies. For example, in the series *Crime Patrol* conceived to be reality-based, aired in Sony Entertainment Television, the police, who are shown to be acting righteously, are often shown beating and kicking the suspects. The practice of beating and torture by police is generally acceptable to larger sections of people, and expected and mostly accepted, despite India having laws prohibiting custodial violence.

Lokaneeta's book argues that the liberal states constantly negotiate to accommodate *excess* violence while at the same time maintaining legitimacy. Lokaneeta shows that though Weber's formulation about monopoly of violence that the state personifies is generally accepted as a defining feature of the modern state, liberal theorists also believe that the liberal state exhibits an attempt to constrain violence. While acknowledging coercion or violence as a necessary evil, coercion, violence, pain, and suffering inflicted by the state to maintain order among free peoples are subjected to scrutiny and kept to a minimum. Such an understanding apparently makes the prevalence of torture, an excessive form of violence, a particularly paradoxical proposition for liberal states. But, as Lokaneeta says, this paradoxical situation does not stop liberal states from using torture, or what she terms 'excess violence' (as conceptually distinct from coercion inherent in state action and the 'necessary pain' authorized by the state in its very functioning). What actually happens is a constant process of negotiation with violence, to accommodate excess violence by the modern state. Since the 'excess violence' is a constantly negotiated category, the attempt is always to define it within the law. However, it is always a constant negotiation because the state can afford to be seen as using only the necessary minimum of force, so that their legitimacy is maintained. The nature of the violence has to be such that it does not appear to supersede the acceptable levels of violence in society. She illustrates her point through the torture debates in post-9/11 United States. She shows that the specific techniques that came to light at this time existed prior to 9/11 and continued after the revelation of the torture memos. This implies that it was not an exceptional moment, rather a constant process. Further, from the fact that the use of torture was not through violation or suspension of laws, but through a 'hyper-legality'—an aggressive use of pre-existing gaps within laws; and that when the Bybee memo which authorized torture came into the open, the state withdrew it, despite bringing its contents substantively through another memo, show the liberal state's constant negotiation to accommodate excess violence while at the same time maintaining legitimacy. So even within an 'art of government' of Foucauldian sense, there is a continued centrality of violence in liberal governance (Lokaneeta 2010: 1–24).

In this argument advanced by Lokaneeta, we can find an understanding of a denial by the liberal state of its practice of torture: the state tries to stretch the bounds of legality to include acts of torture as legal use of force, that is, by denying that such acts constitute torture. Failing this they attempt to hide that torture is practised; if nothing works then they have to penalize a few 'wrongdoing', 'aberrant', and 'sadist' officers, in an attempt to maintain its legitimacy. In India, in the context of public debates around extra-ordinary laws such as the Terrorist and Disruptive Activities (Prevention) Act (TADA) and Prevention of Terrorist Activities Act (POTA), we see a similar attempt on the part of the state to repeal these laws but retention of the extraordinary provisions of such laws through amendments of regular laws.

When we look at the everyday enactments of the state, however, such everyday practices of illegal violence, do not *necessarily* be carried out by hiding and renaming. In police stations of Delhi, torture is not merely seen as a necessary evil but is often glorified as a way of delivering 'justice' beyond the liberal-constitutional model. It is talked of often and casually. Running through such narratives of torture practices by police officials, we find three readily available broad themes: one is that of a 'sad policeman' doing the dirty job of society. A theme of work related frustration and unbearable hierarchy making sadists out of policemen interact with this line of 'sad' job thought. The second theme is that of the 'enthusiast hero' who has taken on true paths of justice beyond 'petty legal restrictions' and are the 'tragic heroes' at the moment.[1] The third theme is that of torture as an enactment,

[1] Jauregui, in her study of 'police vigilantism' in Uttar Pradesh, discusses a very similar self-portrayal of police officers involved in encounter killings. She argues that the figure of the police vigilante is represented as a just warrior through the medium of three interdependent conceptual means, namely, ritual purification, social defence, and self-sacrifice. See Jauregui (2015).

as a spectator sport, where the performance of the torturer and the produced subordination/subjugation of the tortured, a mode of entertainment for the torturer and spectators at one level, also tells us about operation and production of power relations and identities.

## The Unhappy Policemen (sic)[2]: 'Dirty Work' in Poor Working Conditions and Unbearable Hierarchies

My initial encounters in police stations of Delhi yielded numerous stories about the 'sad' policemen. On such encounters, most of the officers from the ASI rank upwards to Inspectors seemed to be very happy to talk, and the one thing they were most interested to talk about was how bad the job of a policeman is. Some of them expressed how saddened they are by the accepted norms of society and the role they need to play in it. Once I had a chat with the ATO of the Uday Nagar thana, Ramesh Kumar Singh, while two minor boys were being interrogated outside his room. He talked about the inequalities in society, and why the boys sitting outside were 'thieves' and there were other children of their age who would go to fancy schools like VSKV International Public School (a name registered in anyone's mind who travels on the ring road to the north-west from the North campus of Delhi University, owing to its huge and frequent hoardings). He said,

> … the police has always worked for the rich. They have worked for the sovereign, the *rajas*, then the British and now the Indian politicians. So police catches only the small fishes. If there is so much inequality then thefts are bound to happen. As the rich need to save themselves they have created police, gave them uniform and sovereign power to repress the poor. (2012, pers.com, 7 March)

Some others were ashamed of being in the police force, due to the bad name it has got. A constable from the outer district said that he had

[2] Instead of police personnel which is gender neutral, I have used the word policemen, as for all practical purposes women are marginalized in policing work, and are thus rendered 'nobodies'. Most instances where violence is seen as required, is also marked as an arena of 'real' policing, and thus not suitable for women personnel. See Khanikar 2016 for a discussion of the dilemmas that women personnel face in the profession.

joined the police only because he had no other option. 'It is a bad job,' he said, 'I was weak in studies—that is why I had to join as a policeman. Otherwise I wouldn't have.' He was on record-room duty, which he said was not easy, as 'you have to tolerate a lot of scolding from superiors for every little thing'. However, outside work is even bad. 'There is such a bad image of policeman that you think twice even before eating anything outside, because people would invariably think that we have not paid'.[3]

There were other men who were tired of the working conditions. SI K.P. Singh is the division officer of Rasheela Bagh beat, known as the 'crime pot', of Uday Nagar police station area. K.P. Singh talked about violation of the 'human rights of policemen', as they are forced to work very long hours without proper facilities. He also talked about the constricting hierarchies in the system which stops them from bringing such work condition-related issues to the notice of the superior officers.

Bravo Anil Kumar Singh was angry too. He was angered by the inner power structures and how things work:

> In the whole year of 2011 I had not taken a single day's leave, all fifteen of my casual leaves remained unused. I did night patrol last night, till 6 in the morning today, and now I'm still sitting in the *thana* … there are no fixed duty hours … after night duty if something happens in my area at 7 in the morning then I still have to be working … there is no bifurcation of work. In theory there is … but in practice there is no bifurcation. Ideally I should not be doing patrol duty, that's not part of investigation, but I'm doing it … there is too much hierarchy in the profession. (2012, pers.com, 20 January)

He continued:

> The seniors want only numbers. The DCP will pressurize the SHO that case should be solved within 24 hours. SHO will be 'tight' with me. And in such a situation if I stretch too far, and solve the case, the SHO would think, '*tight kiya to kaam kiya na*' (he has worked as I became strict). So he would be 'tight' next time too. But nobody would consider to what extent we have gone, and what had happened to laws when we were solving the cases. Because everyone just wants results. (2012, pers.com, 20 January)

[3] Personal interaction, 18 January 2012.

He talked about how such work practices have affected his professional relationships:

> Here nobody complains. Everyone is afraid that somebody will take offence ... there is too much hierarchy. Everyone has the habit of speaking rudely to their juniors. I would shout at my junior officers, they might even shout back at me. The SHO would shout at me, I would just listen silently. Even SHOs, and ACPs and DCPs are not saved. Just the language used at different levels may be different ... now I'm back from night patrol ... if I have to again go for another case in the morning, without eating, without going home, and then a message comes in saying that I have been assigned night duty again for tonight, then I would be irritated ... will get angry. I'll not behave well if somebody comes with a complaint. Everyone needs to release their frustration somewhere, and where do you release it? You release it upon someone, on whom you *can* release it (*aap gussa wahi nikaloge jaha aap nikal sakte ho*). (2012, pers.com, 20 January)

The most stressful part is that such work pressure takes a toll not only on his professional life, but also affects his personal life: 'For nights at a stretch I cannot go home, and my four-year-old daughter would demand that I reach to put her to sleep. After reaching home tired and irritated I can only slap her to sleep' (2012, pers.com, 20 January).

The fact of police being an institution based on a rigid hierarchy along with the constant pressure to produce high statistics often leads its individual members to frustration. This coupled with the fact that it is an institution which wields coercion and violence as a tool, often leads the individual policeman (*sic*) under pressure to crack a case to dehumanize himself while dehumanizing the other, in a way which could be compared to the Fanonian torturer.[4] It may not always be the

[4] Frantz Fanon in his book *The Wretched of the Earth* shows that torture dehumanizes not only the one who is tortured, but it dehumanizes the torturer too. In his capacity as a psychiatrist he came across a couple of French police personnel working in colonial Algeria who were suffering from acute symptoms of mental disorders of a reactionary type. He narrates the story of a police Inspector, who, burdened by the requirement to solve cases and the pressure to compete with his colleagues in the process, showed reactionary symptoms. He got agitated in every little thing and even tortured his wife and

case that he is happy doing what he is doing. But he is even less happy when he does not do what he is doing. While he carries his frustration back home, as the above quoted policeman who slaps his four-year-old daughter to sleep, he still cannot stop the practice of torture. While sensing guilt or frustration from what one is doing, still the structures weigh so heavy on individuals that they do not reach out to employ their agency as emanating from their own sense of guilt. Every time it is not about cracking a case. It may just be that everyone needs to pass off the load of anger and humiliation to somebody lower than himself in the hierarchy, by showing it to someone they *can*. An accused from a marginal group within the bounds of a police station would be the last one in the ladder to bear the blows. Such acts assume a life of its own when one derives one's identity—as strong and respectable—from being rude and violent to others. Violence on the body of the victim is conceived as something which *confirms* the identity of the perpetrators. In such a sense, these acts could be seen as assuming a sacrificial character, as acts of violence are not practised only in some mechanical, emotionless manner, for purposes of information gathering, or for solving a crime. Rather, the torture on the body of the victim is often seemed to be perceived as a 'productive fuel for state power'.[5] Violence on the body of the victim is conceived as something which enhanced the perpetrator's masculinity, their strength; it is something which *confirmed* their identity.

While this was a narrative that was most easily accessible—almost every policeman talked on these lines in my first one-to-one interactions with them—another narrative of why policemen resort to violence came out to be a self-understanding of a pursuer of 'true' justice, who *unfortunately* needs to go beyond laws at times to serve society better. In such cases, the policeman is seen acting as the tragic hero,

---

little children at home, something that never happened before he had faced such kind of work pressure. The Inspector, however, did not see any way out of his regular job of torturing people, and asked psychiatric help only so that he could go on torturing people without showing any behavioural problems (Fanon 1963 [1991]: 263–9).

[5] I borrow this expression from Linke 2006: 213–14.

the Walzerian[6] moral politician, who violates a law in the interest of a greater good.

## Pursuers of 'True' Justice

Once, while I was sitting at the DO desk of Uday Nagar, a young SI was casually chatting with me. He was asking how much I had learnt about policing. I told him that I was very surprised to see how unhappy everyone there was, and then it was his turn to be surprised. He asked me, 'Who is unhappy? Why?' I asked him back, 'Are you not unhappy, then?' He said that he was very happy about his job, and wanted to know why I think he should be unhappy. This conversation led me to have many more chats with him and others, and to a different dimension of the acts of policing altogether.

SI Sushil Kumar is a young chap. He is lean, of medium height and with a light complexion and a thin moustache. He hails from Rohtak in Haryana and speaks Hindi with a Haryanvi accent. Sushil joined Delhi Police six years back, first as a constable. He wanted to join the armed forces, but could not clear the entry examination. However, he passed through the selection process for constables into the Delhi Police. He joined, and once the 14-month long training was over, he was sent to the police lines on his first posting, where new recruits are supposed to learn real policing. There he kept studying whenever he could manage time. Then he was posted into the traffic police. In the traffic police, if one takes up signal duties, then they earn a lot of 'extra' money. However, he opted for the 5B section, the summon branch, where it is a bit quiet, though there is no money flowing in. He kept on studying. Then came

[6] Michael Walzer (1974), dealing with the issue of morality in politics, arguing within a Machiavellian tradition, says that a good politician needs to know 'how to be good'. The politician acting in public interest, at times would be required to act in ways which are immoral. Politicians would no longer remain moral politicians if they hesitate from doing what is required by their commitment to public service. On the other hand, after committing an immoral act, to clean up one's dirty hands, the politician will have to go through a process of repentance and willing acceptance of punishment for the immoral deed that s/he had done. Thus, the politician acting on public interest will have to accept personal responsibility for the acts they had done. This moral politician of Walzer is thus a tragic hero.

the Commonwealth Games and the Delhi Police announced recruitment of SIs. Sushil appeared, and 'thanks to Delhi Police and CWG', he was selected. Therefore, he completed a journey from constable to SI in about two–three years, whereas to complete the same journey through the regular process of promotions it takes 30–32 years. After he was selected, he again spent 14 months in training. Then he had a year of probation. His probation was in Uday Nagar thana itself, where he is posted now. The computer printout pasted on the door of his room still reads PSI (Probationary SI) Sushil Kumar. It was pasted when the DCP inspected the thana last time, Sushil said.

To my impression of policemen and policewomen being unhappy, he partly agreed and said that there definitely are problems, like that of too much hierarchy, and thus there are reasons to be unhappy. People work under orders from superior officers only, but when something untoward happens, all responsibility is put on the subordinates. He talked about the Ramdev eviction saga[7] from the Ramleela maidan:

> Look at the Ramdev incident. No *sipahi* (constable) has the guts to beat up people without orders from superiors, when the CP himself is standing there ... they were given orders to *lathi*-charge. Now that court has given directives for inquiry, those who were caught in video camera while raising their *lathis* are gone. If somebody was in civil clothes then he would be saved, but all others are gone. The officers gave all the orders and then pushed the responsibility to the subordinates. (2012, pers.com, 14 March)

The departmental inquires generally exonerate the accused policemen, he said, as seen from precedents. However, the harassment of the people concerned during the period is unfortunate and frustrating:

> You will be asked to reach an officer's *daftar* (office) at 10 o'clock. You will keep waiting to meet him. Ten things will keep coming to your

[7] Baba Ramdev, a yoga guru, took part in the anti-corruption movement started by Anna Hazare in the year 2011 and organized a huge rally in the Ram Leela grounds in central Delhi in the month of June 2011. In a midnight fling, Delhi Police evicted the protestors and lathi-charged them. The matter was highly condemned by all sections as the police acted upon peaceful protesters. See *The Times of India*, 5 June 2011.

mind, about how to speak to him, what to tell him. You'll keep waiting the whole day. Then at 5 o'clock you'll be told: come tomorrow. (2012, pers.com, 14 March)

However, despite such issues, Sushil thought that there is at least scope in their job to correct wrongs, which not many jobs offer. In this connection, unlike many others who told me that they unwillingly violate laws, either out of frustration or under pressure, Sushil was quite forthright in telling me that laws are 'the problems'.

… That is the problem with the constitution. It says if you get one criminal after torturing hundred, then it is better to let that criminal go, to let him free. That is the problem with police, we are not at all allowed to use third degree and beating. People also know this, so if they come to know (of torture) they'd immediately complain. The human rights people are after us. That is why crimes are increasing, common people are suffering … (2012, pers.com, 14 March)

But Sushil was 'optimistic' about the future. 'This will not work for long,' Sushil said, 'How long will you let criminals go scot free? Things are bound to change. *Torture will have to be made legal again*' (emphasis added). Though they have their own techniques in the meanwhile, 'they are not enough'. Because these beatings are illegal, thus 'people cannot be made to fear police. We are the ones who have to work under fear; if we have to beat people, we have to find out a way to do that.' He lamented their situation: 'But for whom are we doing all these? We are not doing for our own sake, we are doing it for the society.' The situation was better earlier, Sushil carried on. He went on to tell the story of ACP Rajbir Singh:[8]

Criminals were dead afraid of Rajbir. He would keep his pistol on table and talk to people. The deals were in *khoka*. You know what is *khoka*

[8] Rajbir Singh was an Assistant Commissioner in Delhi Police (ACP) at the time of his murder by a property dealer in the outskirts of the city in March 2008, over a dispute regarding some shady deals. He was known as the 'encounter specialist' of Delhi Police, and was given out-of-turn promotions. He was the only officer in the Delhi Police history to be promoted to the rank of ACP in only 13 years. He was known as the 'face of counter-terror' in the capital and had over 50 'kills' to his credit. He, however, was a hugely controversial figure, and his 'notorious' 'fake encounters' were pointed out by various civil rights

> right? A crore. A *peti* is a lakh. Give *khoka*, and do whatever you want to do outside Delhi, but don't do anything in Delhi. If they'd done anything in Delhi, then *bas khatam kar* do (just finish them off). That time there was a fear of police in the minds of people. Now everything is over … (2012, pers.com, 14 March)

Rajbir had the support of the BJP government, Sushil said, 'We need such political support, otherwise police cannot work well.' But Rajbir was murdered, and his family is now in the same condition as where they started from, Sushil gave the 'sad end' of the story of Rajbir. I asked him, 'But Rajbir did wrong things, he took money from people and that too in crores?' 'So what?' Sushil retorted, 'He took money from criminals only.' (2012, pers.com, 14 March).

Such need of practices of torture going beyond laws was highlighted by focusing on the habits of people as well. An officer of Inspector rank who had been to Yugoslavia as part of a UN mission related his experiences in Yugoslavia to that of Delhi:

> There, even in the situation of civil war people do not lie. They have faith in the system … now here in India people lie all the time. So you cannot believe them … that is why Indian police has the history of third degree, because it is really difficult out here ... people cooperate with police only out of fear—of physical assault, or illegal detention.[9]

He however, added that use of third degree is 'out-of-practice' now, that these things have not happened in Delhi for the last 10–15 years. Now police can work only when there is direct evidence, or when they have high scientific tests to help the investigation. 'But,' he said,

> … such scientific tests are ridden with court directions; they can be used only in very urgent cases. Solving of everyday crimes has thus become very difficult. Now the situation is that, if police has no evidence then

---

activists. In the year prior to his murder, he was transferred from the Crime Branch to the Delhi Armed Police Unit after allegations of his involvement in an illegal land deal. He, however, was cleared of the charges and came back to head the Special Operations Squad of Delhi Police about five months prior to the murder. See *Hindustan Times*, 25 March 2008, and Sethi 2012.

[9] Personal interaction with a Delhi Police Inspector, on 24 February 2012, in a north-west district police station.

> they have to set the man free. This is giving advantage to criminals, it is an *imbalance* now, and will go on for some time. But things are bound to change. (emphasis added)

There were many others like SI Sushil Kumar who boasted of torturing people, because they thought that while torture is illegal, it is not immoral. Rather they held a belief in the high moral ground that they hold vis-à-vis some laws and the constitution itself, in the process of maintaining law and order. Constable Sonpal once narrated a story from an old Bollywood movie where actor Nana Patekar played a cop. In the movie, when Nana Patekar was dealing softly with 'criminals', they were not forthcoming and were rather 'taking advantage of him'. They could be handled only when they were beaten up. He then went on to say,

> ... our constitution is very bad. It is taught to us that the constitution is both rigid and flexible ... the flexibilities are too much. Here a goat is more valuable than the honour of a woman ... How? Simple, see the laws. The offence of stealing a goat is non-bailable, but section 363 (kidnapping) is bailable. So leaving out rape, any other offence where women's honour is violated is bailable. When the constitution is like this, then police needs to beat up people. (2012, pers.com, 14 March)

Thus, these officers talking of torture as a positive, made the point that torture is practiced because in this way they can make up for the loopholes of the laws and the constitution. Some others who talked of torture as a requirement for good policing lamented that it is no longer possible to use such methods due to restrictions put by laws. Despite not openly admitting its use, they glorified torture as a method to someone who is from beyond the community of police. The step from the glorification of torture to its practice behind closed doors beyond the view of the outsider did not seem to be very far or drastic.

## The Enactments and the Entertainments

Apart from these two ways of relating to torture, namely that of the frustrated policeman flushing out his anger in the form of torturing others and the pursuer of 'true' justice, there, occasionally appeared another perspective on torture: the feeling of enjoyment from the act.

Head Constable Surinder at Uday Nagar thana took pride in being a 'tough' and 'stylish' cop. He would never wear the official uniform. He told me that he is in the special staff and thus does not need to wear the official dress. Being in the special staff, he said, fulfilled the two desires that he had in life: one, not to wear uniform, and the second, to crack heinous cases. Once while I was sitting near the DO, he came and had to write something in the DD register. While he asked his colleagues for a pen, he smiled at me and said, 'My shirt and pants are so tightly fitted that I cannot keep a pen.' When I told him during one of our conversations that I did not see him doing anything, he perhaps felt challenged, and gave me a long list of murder and vehicle theft cases that he had solved and also talked about two awards from Deputy Commissioner and Commissioner of Police respectively. Then he boastfully said, '... *main maarta bahut hoon lekin ... aisa technique se maarta hoon ki nisaan nahi parta*' (but I beat up people a lot ... beat up in such a way that there are no marks) (2012, pers.com, 13 March). He went on to say that he earlier had two 'commandoes' especially to beat up people on his orders. Then he said, 'It's not nice to talk highly of oneself', and asked me to find out from Narender, the bearer to the Inspectors in the thana, about his work techniques and records.

'Entertainment' from custodial torture was visible in Uday Nagar, even in contexts more routine and nonchalant than that of investigating special staff cases. It often played out also as a spectator sport or a theatrical performance. Many of such cases involved young children from slums who were brought to the police stations on charges of theft.

On a relatively calm day at Uday Nagar, one of the calls received by the DO was about two thieves being held by someone. When emergency officer SI Rahul called up the number from where the complainant called, he was told that the thieves were being brought to the station in a PCR van.

After a while, the 'thieves' reached: one looked about 5–6 years old, the other was slightly older, perhaps about 7–8 years old. Each of them had a small polythene bag in his hand, and both were wearing tattered and dirty clothes. They appeared to be rag pickers. The complainant was a well-dressed man who looked to be in his mid-thirties. The complaint was that the 'thieves' had come several times to his house and had picked up little things. Today they were on the terrace when he heard some noise and gave a chase, but by the time he reached they already fled. Somebody in the house, however, saw the face of the younger boy through a window, and then they caught them when they reached the road in front of the house.

The case was allotted to SI Rahul. Rahul is a young officer. He is not very tall, slightly built, and fair-skinned. He is also a man of fashion. Whether it is his uniform or civilian clothes, he always dresses up carefully. He wears a watch with a big dial showing both time and directions.

Rahul took the boys aside to the bench outside the SHO's room and next to the DO's desk, and started interrogation while a crowd of policemen and policewomen gathered around. He asked the boys their names. The younger one was Saleem, the other one was Mohd. Shafiq. They denied having stolen anything, and said they were just passing by on the road, when the 'uncle' caught them saying they are thieves. Rahul calmly said, 'Why will he catch you without any reason?' '*Pata nahi*,' (I do not know), Shafiq replied. Shafiq was smart, he was answering questions without getting frightened. Saleem looked frightened. Rahul asked Saleem his father's name, while he was writing down the facts of the case. Saleem did not say anything the first two times, the third time he said, '*Mar gaya*' (he is dead). Shafiq supported him, '*Iska baap mar gaya*' (his father is dead). Rahul said, 'Still, there is a name'. Saleem did not know, Shafiq gave the name: Taufiq. Shafiq also gave both the addresses. They are from Jahangirpuri. While giving the jhuggi (slum dwelling usually made of mud and corrugated iron) numbers Shafiq said that he lives in his own jhuggi while Saleem lives as a tenant, a few houses apart.

Rahul then went back to the original question: 'What have you stolen from the house?' While Saleem kept mum, Shafiq was denying the charge of stealing. Rahul took the polythene packets from their hands, and checked the things inside: a small tin stand used to hold up mosquito repellent coils, a small broken part of a bicycle chain, a small screw, some iron nails. He sniffed the packets too. It seemed he could not sense anything there. Then he checked the pockets of the boys one by one. Then raised their pants till the knees, unbuttoned the shirts to see the chests, and then checked the arms too. While Shafiq helped him in examining his body by raising his clothes, Saleem was too young for that, and Rahul had to do everything on his own.

Once this physical check was done, SI Rahul went back to the questioning: 'What happened since morning?' He started with Saleem. Saleem was visibly frightened, he said he went to the house as Shafiq took him. Most of the time he just answered yes or no by gesturing with his head. Shafiq said in between, that Saleem was lying, that his whole family were thieves, that his sister had taken a *patila* (Indian sauce pot) from the place where she goes to work and have used it at home. Rahul scolded him, asking him to be silent. Then he asked the boys to change sides and started interrogating Shafiq. Shafiq started giving details from where he started, which side he was going/coming, etc. Rahul kept asking questions in between. But Shafiq was not giving any mismatched answers. So Rahul asked him directly, 'Tell me what you have lifted.' Shafiq started to say something in the negative, and Rahul snatched a rifle from woman constable Meena who was on lock-up duty, but was standing amongst others who were enjoying the 'interrogation' tamasha (a grand show). Shafiq this time appeared to be a little frightened, but he kept insisting that he had not stolen anything, that he had never been to the house of this 'uncle' and had only seen him on the road. Rahul asked him to sit at the corner, and took Saleem to the ATO's room nearby, where nobody was sitting. He told me, 'Madam I'll come in a while', perhaps to indicate that he did not want me to follow. I stayed back outside with the rest of the crowd.

After about 5–7 minutes he came out with Saleem, and told Shafiq, '*Isne sab kuch bata diya hain. Ab tujhe jail nahi jana hain to bata kya hua tha* (He has confessed everything. Now if you don't want to go to jail then tell what happened).' Shafiq had determination; he kept insisting that he had not stolen anything. Rahul asked a constable to bring the lathi from his desk. It was brought. It was a hollow iron rod painted green with three words on it written in Hindi in black letters, and was as thick as a broom's handle. He showed it to Shafiq and asked, 'You know how to read?' Shafiq nodded, Rahul said, 'Read it out'. Shafiq complied: '*Aan milo Sajna*' (Come, meet me my beloved). The spectators laughed loudly. Then Rahul asked Shafiq, 'Will you tell me now what happened?' Shafiq did not say anything, and looked around. He seemed to be a bit more nervous and frightened. Then he was made to go to a corner where there was a wooden board at a height with some court directives on rights of detainees written on it. Shafiq was about three feet tall. The board was at a height of five feet and covered till the roof. Shafiq was asked to raise his hands to touch a line in the board which was beyond his reach. He had to stand on his toes to reach it. He was asked to reach it by both hands without moving. There was a fire extinguisher next to where he was made to stand. Rahul then took the pipe of the extinguisher and pointing it at Shafiq said, '*To khara rah ab main tujhe current de raha hoon* (you keep standing and I'm going to give you electric shock).' Shafiq broke down finally: he started weeping and then crying aloud.

Rahul turned back towards me and smiled; a smile of victory. Then he asked Shafiq to sit: '*Baith ja baith ja*' (sit down, sit down). The *chai wala* (tea vendor) was getting tea for somebody; he asked him to give tea to the boys too. Then he left to attend to another case, asking the boys to sit. It was about 12 o'clock. The spectator crowd also dispersed. The boys were then kept seated on those benches unattended till evening.

This interrogation by Rahul, which was apparently believed to be an innocent enough one to be conducted in front of me, and which was thoroughly enjoyed and supported by his colleagues with laughs and supportive interventions, strictly speaking, was also illegal in nature. As per section 10 (1) the Juvenile Justice (Care and Protection of Children) Act 2000 (operative at the time of field work) a juvenile in conflict with law, as soon as apprehended by police, should be 'placed under the charge of the special juvenile police unit or the designated police officer who shall immediately report the matter to a member of the Board'. The juvenile justice system being a reformative and rehabilitative programme, investigation of crimes should not use threat to violence, and should be conducted only by special personnel earmarked for the purpose. The psychological pressure and humiliation put on the boys of barely school-going age while being enjoyed by the spectators, would not comply to a law of protective care and correction of offenders, even after their criminality is proved. The irony of the scene was that Shafiq was tortured by using a public notice board which was meant to remind people in the thana of the rights of arrested people.

## Petty Sovereigns at the Locales

Mbembe, talking of the postcolonial situation, argued that to exercise authority is above all to tire out the bodies of those under it. This is done to disempower them, the aim of which is not so much to increase the productivity of the subjected bodies, but to ensure their maximum docility (Mbembe 2001: 110, 113). What we see in the torture practices prevalent in the context of Delhi, also seem to follow such a rationale. Often excess violence and pressure is used not because it yields a result which other methods would not yield, but also because it has the effect of disempowering and humiliating the target, which work out as entertainment for those who witness it, and as a symbol of power and capacity on the part of the torturer. This leads us to see that despite being operative within a modern liberal democracy, within what is known as the governmental practices of enumerating, classifying, and governing, the principle of efficiency is not the only one operative in how the state works, but unique local versions of exercise of sovereign power, often wasteful, or ineffective, act to confirm and consolidate the authority of the state institutions.

The traditional understanding of sovereignty is that of a unified locus for state power; sovereignty as providing a legitimating function for the state. However, Butler in her work on the post-9/11 detention and torture of detainees in Guantanamo Bay (Butler 2004) shows that in the present the sovereign functions are re-emerging in a different form. In the present form sovereignty is reserved, Butler argues, either for the executive branch of government or to managerial officials, when they suspend rule of law on the basis of 'exceptions' *deemed* by them. Sovereignty is exercised here in the act of suspension of rule of law. Her argument is close to Agamben's theorization of 'bare lives' produced under a 'state of exception' by the invocation of sovereign power (Agamben 1998) and the Schmittian notion of sovereignty: 'Sovereign is he who decides on the exception' (Schmitt 2005: 1).

The practices of police violence in Delhi in a routine context, however, further complicate this question about sovereignty. The question arises whether such resurgence of sovereignty operates only within 'exceptional' conditions or whether it is again routinely enacted in the life of the state. Alternatively, the question may be raised as to if we can think of *two layers of extraordinarity*? The first layer is the one pointed out by both Butler and Agamben, of a situation when the rule of law is suspended and extraordinary laws operate, such as the imposition of a President's rule under Article 356 of the Indian constitution, or contexts in which extraordinary laws such as AFSPA operate, which is the legal-political context of the second field site of this work.

The second layer of extraordinarity, if we can think of it, is where laws (either ordinary or extraordinary) are violated/executed in an extraordinary manner, by the petty sovereigns operating at the locales, that is, at the level of execution. For example the Investigating Officer in a police station in a case of custodial torture, or a group of Indian soldiers forcing ethnic Assamese men of Lakhipathar to run in a formation making sounds like a train and beating them at the same time to speed up. The extraordinarity of the situation here is reinforced/maintained by the fact that the whole mechanism of the state in the form of its different organs allows such extraordinarities go without being tried or punished within the limits of law. How the entire juridico-legal-medical complex of the state allows such acts to be condoned or overlooked is visible from the operation of various nexuses between the institutions of army and police, the civilian administration, state doctors in charge of medico-legal cases, and judicial magistrates. In a case of custodial death investigated by a Peoples Union for Democratic Rights (PUDR) fact-finding team of which I was a member, the pack-up between the medical doctor in charge of conducting the post-mortem and the police officers concerned was clearly visible. How the judiciary too overlooks such cases could be gauged from a statement that the Metropolitan Magistrate concerned made to the investigating team, that he had more important cases dealing with the living to concentrate upon, and that a case dealing with the dead does not fall in his priorities (PUDR 2011).

As we see, the violations of rule of law take place on an everyday basis in the context of policing in Delhi. Petty sovereigns in the form of police officials use corporal power upon those whom they deem to be 'dangerous' or 'criminal', and at times for the sheer pleasure derived from it. They, working on the ground levels, also decide what a 'criminal' act is, and attempt to bring upon such 'justice' that the laws and the constitution are purportedly unable to deliver, through means and methods decided by themselves. This is the logic of sovereignty in its lawless[10] 'rogue' form as termed by Butler, but operating beyond the first level of extraordinarity of Butler.

[10] The use of the term 'lawless' here is not meant to necessarily indicate a negative sense, as the police officials themselves acknowledge that their acts many times violate the laws of the land, but express a very positive

They wield a sovereign power in that they decide to torture and even kill somebody that they deem to have deserved such a fate. In the context of what Butler is discussing, this is done through a formal suspension of rule of law in 'exceptional situations'. In the routine context of custodial torture, this formal suspension does not take place. And here the operations of governmentality also cut across the operations of sovereignty, as many a time the perpetrators of custodial crimes are charged under the laws, and are identified as *aberrant*. Meanwhile the practices of sovereignty do not end too, as the victims continue to get judged on their 'criminality' or 'dangerousness' by other petty sovereigns who are in office.

Such extraordinarity is another facet of the observed routineness of the acts. The act of torture is extraordinary as it requires an accommodation of the *illegal*, in an institutionalized fashion. It is routine because this extraordinarity has become a commonsense, a routine practiced in an institutionalized fashion and perceived as a part of the practice of policing.

## Torture, but do not Give it 'a Home in the Body'

Whether by the officer reluctantly torturing people and violating laws because that is the only option left, or the righteous officer who violates 'bad' laws to uphold justice, or the enthusiast torturer, the practices of custodial violence go on. It is so routine that it is not even hidden from an outsider. Neither were people uncomfortable with the word 'torture'—they did not think of using another word and quite often talked of how 'torture' is useful. However, despite such openness at one level, these practices of torture are hidden too, in another sense. The hiddenness or the stealth of the practices is to be apprehended in terms of an escape from legally verifiable evidence, while for all other purposes, torture is visible. To add a quick contrasting reference here, such need for hiding legally verifiable evidence did not emerge in conditions of Lakhipathar, where under the Armed Forces Special Powers

---

feeling about it by saying that these violations are at par with some higher moral principles. Thus for them, they can be 'lawless' but at the same time could be 'just'.

Act (AFSPA), the army regularly tortured and shot at people and the physical injuries did not need any hiding.

Elaine Scarry's important account on pain and torture describes pain of the body in torture as inexpressible. She emphasizes the incommunicable nature of physical pain, as there is an absolute split between 'one's sense of one's own reality and the reality of other persons'. While the person whose pain it is effortlessly grasps it, for another person, even with efforts to grasp, s/he may remain in doubt about its existence. In addition, even if with one's best effort of sustained attention one succeeds in apprehending the reality of the pain of another, the aversiveness of this 'pain' as comprehended by this other would be merely a shadowy fraction of the actual 'pain' as grasped by the sufferer (Scarry 1985: 4).

Scarry calls such pain of torture to be 'world destroying'. In serious pain, the body claims so much attention that it nullifies the claims of the world. It emphasizes the body so much that all contents of the world, all psychological contents—painful, pleasurable, and neutral—are obliterated. As an outcome, the questions, answers to which are sought by the torturer through interrogation would matter to the victim so little that he will give the answers. 'For the prisoner, the sheer, simple, overwhelming fact of his agony will make neutral and invisible the significance of any question as well as the significance of the world to which the question refers.' The person's basis in the world is destroyed. In the same process on the other hand, the world of the torturer expands. His world is reinforced in the questions he asks and insists upon, in the feigned urgency of these questions for a world, in the name of which they magnify and justify their acts. The space of the torturer's world is further enlarged by the shrinking of the prisoner's space: by the fact that the prisoner *answers* to questions showing their disintegration to all objects to which they might have been bonded in loyalty or love (Scarry 1985: 33–8).

In such a situation, the world of the tortured person is even completely destroyed if his or her pain is not recognized by others. The only thing that can reconstruct the lost world of a person in such a situation is compassion from others. However, this demands at least some marks of torture in the body. In the words of Veena Das, '(I)n the register of the imaginary, the pain of the other asks for a home in language, but also seeks a home in the body, tangling the victims and their communities in doubts, uncertainties and illusions' (V. Das 1997: 88).

The processes of investigation and interrogation by police in Delhi, and in India more generally, often involves such violence that could destroy the life-world of a person,[11] and the torturers also precisely take care not to leave a 'home in the body' for pain, that is, not to leave marks of torture in the body of the accused. The acts of torture, however, are so routine, commonplace and expected that the effect of 'not leaving a mark' is produced more for the consumption of the upholders of law, that is, the judiciary, rather than the world or community of the tortured person.

In the given circumstances, the world or community of a victim of custodial torture already knows and expects such a fate for a member of their community. We however, need to note, that the civic space to which a victim of custodial torture belongs is often a space demarcated from the civic and social space of many other citizens, or 'solid' citizens, to borrow a term from Rejali (2007). Thus, while the effect of invisibility is produced for the consumption of the state organ of judiciary, it is not rare that visibility of torture is at times asked for by a social world different from that of the torture victim. The common disgust shown by people as can be understood from gestures of daily life and other sources like comments on social media, etc., towards people who beg, or who live in slums engaged in irregular menial work, and the stated desire to see the state and the police to act more strictly against them leaves one with such an image. Also, the fact that a large section of people believe in and want to see use of illegal and brutal forms of violence as an exemplary form of punishment indicates that the state from time to time feeds such desires, if not legally, then in de facto ways through its manifestations in the form of police officials. While this work does not explore in detail such anxieties of middle class citizens in a metropolitan centre like Delhi, it attempts to look into various ways in which specific images of 'criminals' and 'victims' are produced by police for consumption of a specific section.

[11] In the book *Behind the Beautiful Forevers*, Katherin Boo heartrendingly depicts the destruction of life worlds of people under torture in the context of contemporary Mumbai slum dwellers, specifically through the character of Abdul (Boo 2012).

While visiting numerous police stations in Delhi, I came across officers who said that they generally take care not to leave marks on the body of the suspects, so that they can bypass laws related to custody which prohibit interrogational and other forms of custodial violence. Time spent in Uday Nagar thana, however, opened up a whole new materiality of 'stealth torture'[12] to my eyes.

One afternoon, it was comparatively less busy and nothing much was happening at the DO desk. The SHO was sleeping and thus there were no visitors. However, in the upper floor something was happening: some people were allowed to go upstairs by the DO, and then a call came from first floor asking why people were allowed to come up. The two women and a few men who went upstairs were sent back. To have a closer look and figure out what was happening, I went upstairs and saw that only two rooms were open, one of them being IO ASI Uday Singh's room. The door to Uday Singh's room was half open. The body of a pot-bellied man lying on the bed was visible. When I went in, the pot-bellied man Uday Singh got up from the bed, though he did not appear to be very happy to have me there. There were four adolescent boys[13] seated in the room, squeezed in a small space on the floor between the table and the wall. One of them was eating a *kachori* and *sabzi* (crisp deep fried Indian pastry served with potato gravy), something that his parents brought for him, who came and were sent back a while ago. There was a table in the middle of the room. While I passed the table to

[12] In the history of torture, various methods are used depending on the context. In the present times, when liberal democracies are committed to human rights as a core value, and when there are various public monitoring systems, there still continue practices of torture in ways which Rejali (2007) calls clean torture or stealth torture. Clean/stealth torture are methods of torture where pain is inflicted on the body of the tortured without any major mark of it. What makes such torture valuable is that allegations of torture are simply less credible when there is nothing to show for it. In the absence of visible wounds, stealth torture breaks down the ability of the sufferer to communicate to others (Rejali 2007: 8).

[13] The interrogations in cases involving adult males were perhaps kept for the night hours, as despite having seen many detainees in the thana, I never witnessed them being interrogated. On days there used to be people kept in custody though not in the formal lock-up. The room 5B, that is, the summon branch room, often acted as a de facto lock up room.

go across the room and sit on the bed, my body hit something kept on the lower shelf of the table and it fell off.

While picking it up to keep it back, I noticed it was a black rubber strip, smooth, thick, and heavy. Constable Rajat, who was sitting in the room too, was an enthusiastic chap. He immediately explained the tyre strap to me: *Ye hain Aan Milo Sajna. Iss se bahut tej dard hota hain lekin nisaan nahi parta. Par iss se kafi awaaz hota hain* (This is Aan milo sajna. It is very painful, and it leaves minimal marks. But it makes a loud thud). Rajat was even ready to give a demo on me, but I refused to volunteer and thus he instead slammed it on the table. It made a loud sound. ASI Uday Singh, who seemed to be already annoyed, at that point shouted at Rajat and asked him to keep the tyre whip in a lower shelf of the table. The beatings on the bodies of the teenage boys were already invisible.

## Invisible Pains of 'Justified' Beatings to Visible Acceptance of Police Violence

The techniques of torture that are used in the thanas hide the pains of torture. It becomes unprovable in the court of law, and often illegible to those who have not gone through the same. This, however, comes with a contradiction. The fact that some beatings/torture are seen as 'justified' by the policemen, is a discursive belief that has a wider support base. Thus, torture also often need to be visible, though to a different audience than the courts of law, in a context where people from the margins end up being the targets of violence by police, not only when actual crimes are committed, but also for various assumptions that are attached to poor and marginal people through a discursive intersectional meaning production. I would delve into this aspect of crime, policing and torture in the context of meanings produced through dominant communal, geographical, and economical norms of society in the next chapter.

3

# Spaces of Abjection and a 'Civic-Disciplining' Model of Policing

The meanings attached to geographical spaces make them places. Places are, within the contemporary organizations of political space, also territories, in the sense that they are not merely habitats of people, culture, and things, but are also bound to specific nation-states with the relation of territorial control. This control not only implies claim of ownership over the land, but also the claims of regulating life in these spaces. What shape such claims of ownership and rights to regulate manifests in is what we see as the practices of state. In this context, in this chapter I would turn to discursive production of some spaces as 'filthy' and 'criminal' places requiring a specific form of policing, in a bid to protect normative civic-cultural 'clean' places that are also part of the same territory. A related theme of discursive production of some spaces as exceptions to the national-space—an outside within the national territory—and hence requiring use of exceptional violence generally reserved for enemies beyond the territorial bounds of the community of nation-state, is found in the second field site which is dealt with in later chapters. While in these two contexts the 'other's are produced on slightly different terms—one outside the bounds of the ethos of civic community and the other outside the bounds of the ethos of the political community—where these two instances have a common ground is the fact of a specific violent relation of the state with these spaces, based on their discursive production.

In a way, the narratives of producing an 'other' that we discuss in this chapter, tells us the sources of legitimacy of a state that is violent. I draw on texts of laws and court judgments, reports of state bodies and rights advocacy organizations, and personal interactions and ethnographic observations in the field, apart from existing scholarly works.

## The Citizen and the 'Other'

The *Annual Report* of Delhi Police for the year 2010 portrays the self-understanding of the force as that of a 'service organization'. The police accords top priority to maintenance of public order and peace, keeping people safe, and keeping property safe (India, Delhi Police 2010: 1). These priorities remind us of what Hobbes said about sovereignty. While making a distinction between 'acquired' and 'instituted' sovereignties, Hobbes says that in the case of acquired (that is, colonial) sovereignty the sense of fear of the sovereign leads people to accept the authority of the ruler. Instituted sovereignty is established on the other hand, when people afraid of each other in a 'nasty' and 'brutish' state of nature, agrees to have a sovereign (by everyone ceding some of their rights) to maintain law and order. In this situation, the basis or legitimate ground for existence of the state could be seen in people's sense of insecurity in society.[1] We know that the Hobbesian state of nature was an extrapolation that he made, based on the understanding of his contemporary society, about what it would be like in the absence of a state. This was a kind of thought experiment, to justify absolute monarchy to his contemporary British society. If we attempt to stretch this thought-experiment a little further, and say that a situation comes where people are no longer afraid of each other, then the question whether the state would still retain its legitimate existence arises. One wonders if the state can survive without a figure of the enemy in the minds of the people it governs.

The Hobbesian idea of the state and its sovereignty is based on a protectionist principle. Iris Marion Young (2005), analysing the authoritarian nature of the state in the US after the 9/11 attacks, in the context of external wars and internal surveillance, argues that this state acts

[1] Discussed by Chakrabarty 2007.

like a 'protection racket' by promising to protect the servile citizens from threats from 'outside', by placing them in a subordinate position. Studying policing in the context of Delhi through the lenses offered by this conceptualization, one sees that the 'outside' from which the obedient citizens need to be protected is produced *within* the conceptual realm of a national citizen-body—which claims to recognise equality of every individual citizen's worth—but in practice creates second-grade citizens who are posed as threats to the lives and property of some more privileged sections of the citizenry.

The production of these second-grade citizens is effected by various discourses, practices and rhetoric. Writing about colonial north India, Nandini Gooptu (2001) shows how stereotypical images of the poor were created, portraying them as 'a menace to the peace, health and prosperity of the city' (p. 66), as 'prone to the lure of crime' (p. 67), and thereby projecting the relation between poverty and urban decay as self-evident and axiomatic. Such a projection, she elaborates, led to measures such as attempt to reform their religious and social practices, intensive policing, and 'cleansing' and 'sanitising' their habitats (p. 68). In fact, policing strategies for disciplining the poor—the 'prime culprits' in violence—and the middle-class preoccupation with improvement or reform, reinforced each other, and pushed the poor into a negative categorization (pp. 136–8).

The conflation of poverty with criminality, however, is not merely a colonial practice, and even the judiciary of independent India was not saved of such attitudes. In the Almitra H. Patel judgement of 2000, the Supreme Court likened the resettlement of slum dwellers in public land to rewarding of pickpockets, while commenting on the need to evict and limit slums for environmental protection of the city of Delhi, as 'domestic waste (being) strewn on open land in and around the slums'.[2]

The institution of the police, which is supposedly needed to maintain law and order, lays out its functions of policing by dividing geographic spaces and people into categories of 'good' and 'bad', of 'civilised' and 'criminal', 'clean' and 'dirty', legal and illegal: precisely, of those requiring 'protection' and those calling for 'regulation' and 'surveillance'. Stephen Legg (2008), writing in the context of policing in colonial India again, has

[2] See *Almitra H. Patel and Anr. v. Union of India and Ors* (2000).

examined such practices through a study of deployment patterns (p. 82). He noted that the ethos of protecting the new capital, that is, New Delhi, was that, crimes have to be prevented in the core by preventing invasion from the periphery. Thus, while the elite New Delhi was guarded routinely by disproportionately larger numbers of policemen, the city of Old Delhi, on the other hand, experienced policing for 'disciplining' only, in times of disturbances.[3] This chapter focuses on contemporary everyday policing practices in Delhi, and conceptualizes some of such categorizations and practices, and how they figure in the acceptance of the state in society.

## Civic-Disciplining in a Postcolonial City

If we attempt to place the investigation and interrogation practices of Delhi Police in the larger framework of the debates on use of torture, such practices seem to be shaped by a civic-disciplining model of governance as well as the trappings of a postcolonial situation specific to a city like Delhi. Most of the available theoretical literature on the use of torture is about the morality of the act and a few others discuss why and how the acts of torture are incorporated into the lives of states.[4]

[3] Such as riots or an anti-colonial uprising, in forms of flag-marches with armoured tanks unfamiliar to the Indian eye, or by promulgating preventive legal measures such as detention without trial, to produce a 'moral effect' (Legg 2008: 103–11).

[4] Theorists and philosophers like Mark Bowden (2003), Alan Dershowitz (2002), Oren Gross (2004), and McCarthy (2005), Henry Shue (1978, 2006), Michael Walzer (1974), and Slavoj Zizek (2002) recognize the need of use of torture in certain extraordinary circumstances, that is, the situation of the standard philosophers' example of the ticking bomb. All of them, however, differ in the intricacies of the process involved, or in terms of emphasis points. While Shue argues that such a situation where all the requirements of a ticking-bomb case are fulfilled is extremely rare, and thus relaxing rules for such situations would weaken inhibitions against more general use of torture, Oren Gross talks of 'pragmatic absolutism', 'official disobedience', and 'ex-post excuse', as he sees such cases of ticking-bomb magnitude as extremely rare but nevertheless very much real, thus needing an absolute ban on torture, though unrealistic, only as a practical matter required to uphold the symbolism, myth, and education about human dignity. Both of them argue for a need for public trial

The Indian constitution which promises civil, political, and human rights to its people, legally provides constitutional and procedural safeguards against torture. Article 20(3) of the Constitution gives the right against self-incrimination, which, ideally, should deter torture in

---

after the act is committed. Zizek on the other hand, while allowing torture as a desperate choice, also points out the need to retain the sense of guilt, and the awareness of the inadmissibility of what one has done, and thus refuses to discuss it in terms of justification, lest torture gets elevated to a universal principle. In Walzer's theorization, a moral politician would not refuse to torture when needed, but would admit his/her guilt, and would not just pretend that their 'hands were clean'. Bowden's argument is more or less in line with Oren Gross's arguments, in saying that torture should be banned formally in order to create a useful climate of fear, a fear that violation of laws would be punished, but it should be practiced quietly, even with a touch of hypocrisy. After the act, the torturer must be ready to stand up in court and defend his/her case, and if they can justify their acts then they must not be punished for violating laws. Alan Dershowitz, on the other hand, advocates more transparency in the matter of institutionalized torture, and argues for a certain kind of legalization of torture needed to handle extraordinary cases. He draws out a systematic institutional set-up involving torture warrants to be issued by federal courts and the procedure to be conducted under scrupulous judicial monitoring. Andrew McCarthy, slightly differs from Dershowitz while asking for a legalization of torture, as he proposes establishment of a national security court for the purpose of dealing with national security cases where torture would be allowed, and thus making the procedure more efficient.

Others like David Luban (2005) and Wantchekon and Healy (1999) advance a moral critique of torture and the 'ticking bomb' scenario argument.

The issue of torture and its prevalence in various forms of states have been looked at from two other aspects. One prominent way of looking at the issue theoretically and historically and arguing that torture is widely prevalent and is an unavoidable element in the practices of the modern state is advanced in arguments of philosophers like John T. Parry (2005, 2008) and Sarat and Kearns (1995) and such arguments have foundations in thoughts of philosophers like Walter Benjamin and Thomas Mann. Jinee Lokaneeta (2011), in her recent work on torture practices in the US and India, has developed the argument that torture is very much a part of liberal democracies, and the liberal states constantly struggle to accommodate violence that is 'excess' or beyond permissible limits, either by hiding it, or by redefining it to justify it.

custody. Article 21 ensures that there is no deprivation of life and liberty without a procedure established by law.

Apart from these provisions, the laws that are in place for regulating detention, trial and prosecution of guilty also looks at issues of rights of people in custody. For example in the *Evidence Act of 1872*, Section 25 says that confession to police is not valid, making use of torture to extort confession useless. Section 330 of the Indian Penal Code (IPC) says that if a police officer voluntarily causes hurt to a person for the purpose of extorting confession or any information which may lead to detection of an offence or misconduct, then that police officer has to be punished with imprisonment up to seven years and shall also be fined. Similarly section 331 of IPC talks about causing

---

Very few people ask the question as to why torture is used in existing and historical states. David Hope lists that throughout history, torture is used for various purposes: it may be used as an end in itself, just to satisfy the desires of the torturer; or as an instrument of coercion, to intimidate on a large scale, or as a part of the juridical process either to obtain confession or to extract information (Hope 2004: 808).

Darius Rejali (2007) shows that torture happens in three ways in the democracies: first, within a national security model, where officers practice torture as part of a proactive strategy to combat an enemy in an emergency, which generally takes place far away from the metropole in war zones or colonies; second, within a juridical model, when torture happens at home/in the metropole, through a legal system that highly values the confession of the accused. The accused are here ordinary criminals in contrast to the 'enemies of the state' in the national security model. Third, Rejali talks of a civic discipline model where torture is based on the insecurities so characteristic of modern democracies. Within this model, those who are tortured are not necessarily criminals, but labourers, street children, vagrants, loiterers, and illegal immigrants (we can add on to this list given by Rejali). These are marginal people about whom the 'solid citizens' are deeply anxious. Torture in these cases is both about intimidation and forced confession (Rejali 2007: 46–60).

According to Rejali, torture persists in interrogational contexts, that is, within the national security model, mostly due to a *myth* of its effectiveness. Once the state comprehends the futility of torture for interrogational purposes, the use of torture for this purpose would automatically go down. However, for this to happen we need good documentation of cases of torture so that effectiveness of torture in each case can be analysed.

of grievous hurt by a police officer in similar circumstances where the punishment is up to ten years of imprisonment and fine. Section 57 of CrPC prohibits detention beyond 24 hours from the time of arrest without producing before a magistrate. Section 346 of the IPC prohibits wrongful confinement in secret and gives a punishment of imprisonment up to two years in addition to any other punishment to which s/he may be liable. Further, the Government of India is also a signatory of the United Nations Convention against torture and other cruel, inhuman or degrading treatment or Punishment (UNCAT).[5]

Despite such provisions, however, the practices of custodial torture continue. Some of these are possible due to presence of contravening provisions, at other times it is the operation of extraordinary laws which are exempted from such provisions. For example, while Section 25 of the Evidence Act makes confession in custody inadmissible, Section 27 of the same act says that confession is admissible if any object could be recovered on the basis of information from custodial confession. So torture in custody would continue in the hope that it would help in recovering some useful information, whether it does or not finally is a different matter. Again, section 167 of CrPC allows extension of police custody beyond the 24 hours prescribed by section 57 of the same Act, up to 15 days. Again, although the Government of India has signed the UNCAT in 1997 itself, it has failed to ratify it till date. And as a result of pressure from international community, it has recently brought the Prevention of Torture Bill 2010. However, this bill has faced severe criticism on account of being a climb-down from the UNCAT, and as a dilution even of the already existing provisions of the Indian legal system, and has not been passed till date.[6]

While there is a perception that Indian police is repressive, inefficient, and ill-trained, the Supreme Court is commonly heralded as a beacon of rights against torture. The Supreme Court, since the 1990s, as Lokaneeta (2011: 148–62) has classified, has come up with two

[5] Though the government of India has signed the UNCAT on 14 October 1997, it has not ratified it yet. For a critique of the Indian governments legal stand on the issue of torture, see Fereira 2010.

[6] For a critique of the Prevention of Torture Bill 2010, see Burman (2010). Also, see Commonwealth Human Rights Initiative (2010) and Ferreira (2010).

innovative ways of dealing with custodial torture and custodial death cases. One, is the right to compensation for custodial death and torture, and the second is, the formulation of a custody jurisprudence.

These responses of the Court came out most clearly in three landmark judgments in the 1990s. In the *Nilabati Behera vs. State of Orissa* (1993), the Supreme Court said that the police is responsible to explain the fate (that is, injury marks, etc.) of a person once it is proved that the person had been in their custody. Further, it also significantly established the right to compensation for violation of Article 21 in custodial death cases.

Further, in 1996, through the *D.K. Basu vs. State of West Bengal*, and *Ashok Johri vs. State of Uttar Pradesh*, the Court suggested further mechanisms to deal with cases of custodial torture and death. In the D.K. Basu case, the Court emphasized the peculiar nature of custodial violence and the 'helplessness' of the victim in custody. The Court, recognizing the findings of several democratic and human rights groups such as PUDR and PUCL, explained the modus operandi of how custodial torture and deaths take place in the context of investigation by the police. The Basu judgement came up with specific ways to deal with the issue of custodial violence, such as reiterating the need to transfer the burden of proof to police, issuance of arrest memo/custody memo to be signed by the arrestee and a witness, medical examination of the arrestee if requested so, etc.

However, the Law Commission Report on Review of the Indian Evidence Act 1872 stated in 2003 that the D.K. Basu case has not been effective as the guidelines or precautions suggested by it have not been followed by the police (Law Commission of India 2003: 137). And, apart from the persistent issue of non-enforcement of Court decisions, there has also been a shift in the Court's response in the post-1990s, from a strong stance against custodial violence. The Court exhibits a tension between a complete rejection of torture and the inability to reinforce and follow its own directives regarding the issue, in the case of *Shakila Abdul Gafar Khan v. Vasant Raghunath Dhoble and Anr.* (2003), for example. The Court judgments reflect a newly expressed concern about avoiding any encouragement of false cases. The move away from putting the burden of proof on police and emphasis on 'totality of circumstance test' and 'unreliability of the witnesses', initiates a new trend in jurisprudence that dilutes the understanding that custodial torture and death cases are a separate category of offenses with specific problems of prosecution and evidence (Lokaneeta 2011: 148–62).

Thus, the long-term trend of the judiciary shows that attempts to theorize and come up with innovative ways of dealing with custodial violence are immediately contradicted by other measures. Even within a democracy, the judiciary is unable to refuse accommodation for certain forms of violence (Lokaneeta 2011: 162).

The context of such a legal and judicial scenario is the postcolonial realities of a developing country ridden with deep schisms on lines of class, caste, religion, and gender. This context seems to have been complemented by a Rejalian 'civic disciplining' model of custodial torture, which is intended to produce both intimidation and confession. Rejali, studying torture and democracy, talks of a civic disciplining model where torture is based on the insecurities characteristic of modern democracies. Within this model, those who are tortured are not necessarily criminals, but labourers, street children, vagrants, loiterers, and illegal immigrants. These are marginal people about whom the 'solid citizens' are deeply anxious. In such a context, torture generates different disciplinary orders, sharpening differences among people. Torture here is also something which makes the civic experiences of sections of people and accordingly shapes expectations and future behaviour. What is crucial about practice of torture within this framework is that onlookers may and do often look at such behaviour with understanding, suggesting the presence of an opinion where the sufferer of torture is seen as deserving it or asking for it (Rejali 2007: 55–60).

Rejali (2007: 55–6) discusses the way torture was practiced upon the bodies of slaves, the non-citizens, who were, being seen as lesser humans, were believed to be more likely to tell the truth under torture, in the ancient Athenian democracies. Torture or the lack of it were tied to presence or absence of citizenship, and thus constituted and reconstituted the bodies and identities of both citizens and non-citizens.

In postcolonial democracies like India, *formally/legally* everyone irrespective of their class, caste, religion, or sex is seen as an equal citizen. But deep under the formal niceties lie the indurated divisions based on caste, class, religion, or sex, most often several of these signifiers gelling together to give the (un)desired identity of a given person (like a Dalit Muslim, or a Muslim slum dweller, or a Dalit slum dweller). Based on such signifiers fixing identities, some people are de facto perceived as quasi-citizens, the marginals, the 'slum dweller' or the 'Bangladeshi'. A solid citizen who is again defined by the very signifiers, but is placed on the other end of the spectrum, nurtures deep anxieties about these quasi-citizens: about the (il)legalities of their actions, about their 'dangerousness', about who rightfully deserve legal protection and welfare benefits of the state and about how to safeguard oneself from such people. Police, being the keepers of 'law and order' in society, respond to such anxieties of the solid citizens through use of torture. At other times, other motives the 'law-keepers' might have had were disguised by appealing to this sense of insecurity so much a mark of the average middle class citizen of a city like Delhi. Most often, the people that the police thus act against are not even criminals or offenders. As noted in Chapter 1, reports of democratic rights organization Peoples Union for Democratic Rights (PUDR) over the years have shown that, during the period between 1980 and 1997, approximately 23 per cent of those who died in police custody in Delhi were without any alleged offence.

The ancient Greek belief that slaves are more likely to tell the truth under torture is reproduced, sometimes in subtle and at other times in not-so-subtle ways, in the belief that such underclass citizens, who are 'uneducated' and 'addicts' yield only under torture. As an SI from the New Delhi district, when asked how people respond to interrogation of police, put it:

> Actually a lot depends on who is the person (in custody). If they are good people, educated, then they understand that it is no use lying. They know that if there is evidence that there is no use. But those who are illiterate, who don't know laws, they only lie. Then we need to beat up such people.[7]

The category of 'uneducated' is another way of talking of people who are low-caste, poor, and marginalized, beggars, migrants, homeless, casual labourers, etc., as these identifiers coincide most often than not, in the context of the Indian society.

[7] Personal interview, 11 February 2012.

## Who are the Suspects?

The Annual Reports of Delhi Police systematically mention the presence of slums in proximity of high and middle class localities as a major reason for higher rates of crime in the city. For example, the *Annual Review 2012* mentions expansion of new colonies and thousands of unplanned colonies as an important crimogenic factor, and then goes on to list 'proximity in location of colonies of the affluent and the under-privileged', along with 'loosening of social structures and family control' among other factors responsible for crime in Delhi (India, Delhi Police, 2012: 26). 'Uneducated' people, areas with 'dense' population, 'Muhammedans' with practice of 'multiple marriages' and thus 'large number of children' along with poverty, are often cited as sources of crime in the city. An ASI in a police station in the North East district, one of the most 'notorious' and crime-prone areas of Delhi, said: '(I)n these areas the space available is very less, while population is very high ... Majority of the population is Muhammedan, and they marry three–four times. So they have twenty–thirty children. So when it comes to division of the scant resources that the father had, they end up fighting.'[8]

An Inspector from the Outer district, talking of the law and order situation in his area and the nature of the common crimes, said:

> The area of the *thana* is basically divided in two parts: the west side is a poor and middle class locality; the other side has the houses of business class people and senior bureaucrats etc.... There are a lot of crimes. Poverty is one of the reasons ... These happen because both husbands and wives go to work and there is no one to look after the children. So the children engage in criminal activities. We also have a lot of elopement cases. Girls and boys elope. This happens again due to the poor conditions. They have small houses; everyone sleeps in the same room. So children see when their parents copulate. So they also start doing such things ... Juvenile crimes happen because of poverty and inability of parents to look after their children ...[9]

Another Inspector in the North West district too attributed the petty crimes of the area to juveniles. He, however, added another

[8] Personal interview, 6 January 2012.

[9] Personal interview, 18 January 2012.

attribute to them, that these are 'Bangladeshis' with ration cards. Another officer from a posh locality in the South district said that earlier they had the problem of an illegal liquor den. However, the specific slum due to which problems occurred was near the Jawaharlal Nehru Stadium and before the Commonwealth Games of 2010, it was evicted. Since then the troubles are over. The officials from various police stations across the city explain the high or low rates of crimes in their respective areas, by the presence or absence of slums. Thus, the North East district of Delhi is given as the most crime-prone area of the city, as it has a lot of slums within its jurisdiction, and because criminals are 'people from slums, who are uneducated, where population is dense.'[10]

The troubles or challenges faced by almost every police station seem to have come from the presence of a slum. The slum is seen as an 'other': the 'other' to the educated, urban, middleclass, monogamous society. This 'other' is the underside of the sleek and disciplined world of planned colonies, steady jobs, steady marriages, 'disciplined' consumption (of food and other things) habits. This 'other', however, is a crucial presence, both for the middle-class citizen-self and the state that claims to protect it.

While targeting of slums as 'criminal areas' and questioning of adults and children from slums are regular practices, such practices are justified by the officials at several levels. A major ingredient of this discourse of justification is how they look at the slums, in both their sociality and spatiality. Slums, which are characteristic parts of most big cities in the world, have historically been seen as 'centres of crime'. This process of criminalization of the margins happens in the context of metropolitan Delhi as well.

## Slums, Vice, and Violence

Slums are urban locales marked by overcrowding, lack of proper housing, inadequate or no access to safe water, lack of sanitation facilities, and insecurity of tenor (Davis 2006). These are spaces where the poor of the city live. The Slum Areas (Improvement and

[10] Personal interaction with an SHO in the West district on 27 December 2011.

Clearance) Act, 1956 defines slums as those areas with buildings 'unfit for human habitation' or are 'detrimental to safety, health and morals' due a list of reasons. The Delhi Urban Shelter Improvement Board Act, 2010, retains this definition of slums, and defines *jhuggi–jhopri bastis* in exactly the same words, apart from adding a criterion of a minimum of 50 households.

Slums of south Asian cities like Delhi, as pointed out by Baviskar (2003), are often a 'Siamese twin' of a planned model city. While the Master Plans of Delhi (1962, 2001) envisaged a clean and orderly city through building of planned and gated apartment societies and roads, the labourers who came from various rural parts of the country for construction stayed back looking for more work. Ramanathan (2005) describes the slum dwellers as 'migrant workers who build up cities for those who can afford to buy what they build ... whose labour is recognised, but not their need for residence when a city is planned' (p. 3607). The Delhi Master Plans did not have any concrete plan for these people in the landscape of the city, and thus shantytowns were built by construction workers, small-scale vendors, and other working-class people, along railway tracks or in barren lands under the Delhi Development Authority (DDA) (Baviskar 2003). As a result, there developed a city of slums alongside the 'planned' parts of Delhi. As the slums did not find a place in the 'legal geography' (Sundar 2001) of the city, by their very presence they were turned into crime zones and people living in them to criminals. During the Emergency regime of Indira Gandhi, in the name of beautification and development, numerous people living in slums of central areas of Delhi were evicted, and were resettled in the then outskirts of the city, many times only after production of a certificate of sterilization for birth control (Tarlo 2003). With the expansion of the city, such resettled slums have again come to be part of the metropolitan Delhi, and with changing political rhetoric, the earlier policies of clearance of slums have increasingly been replaced by struggles for and policies of their regularization. The continued presence of the slums and its population in the urban geographies are facilitated by various mechanisms and logics of 'political society' (Chatterjee 2004) and governance.

Powerful structures of inequality and hierarchy, however, are produced and maintained simultaneously to leash, control, and curb these 'necessary evils' of modern city life who act as a source of cheap labour for the adjacent 'civil', 'modern', and 'respectable' colonies. But interestingly, beyond this 'necessary' role that these places and people play, the slums also appear to provide a portion of the much-needed fiction that every modern state requires to thrive on: the image of a vicious and violent 'other', the presence of whom provides legitimacy to the state's presence and functioning.

This fiction involves violence upon a slum dweller—structural and physical—at two related levels. The very idea of a slum dweller gets marked by violence, brought in by a mix of bourgeois notions of rights and justice, and the production of 'suspect communities'. Paddy Hillyard in the context of United Kingdom (Hillyard 1993), and Ujjwal Kumar Singh (2007) in the context of India writes about construction of 'suspect communities' within a discourse of legitimating extraordinary laws. The 'suspect community' is constructed as the 'other' of the 'normal' 'law-abiding' citizens, and this 'other' is linked to a specific religious/racial group, to mark it as the 'other'. We, however, see that such construction of 'suspect communities'—religious and caste-based as well as spatial—is not only a tool in the context of legitimating extraordinary laws, but is routinely used in the context of day-to-day policing.

The structural effects of such discourses could be seen in the everyday struggles for basic daily necessities like clean water to drink or space to defecate[11] next to lavish bungalows with private pools, which exist in luxurious peace next to clamour for basic rights. The production and generalization of those who lead precarious lives in poverty as 'criminals' *en masse* lead on the other hand to manifestation of such structural violence on private bodies of these citizens who are second grade in practice, as we can often see in the routine beatings and torture of people from slums, the 'BC's and the 'criminals'.

While people from the slums are routinely rounded up for interrogation and are tortured in violation of laws, the complicity of the 'respectable' sections of the society in such acts is remarkable too. The

[11] See Baviskar 2003, and PUDR August 1996 for a narrative of how 18-year-old Dilip, who came to visit his relatives living in a slum named Shaheed Sukhdev Nagar adjacent to the well-to-do colony Ashok Vihar, was beaten to death by house-owners of Ashok Vihar along with two police constables, because Dilip came to defecate in a public park located between Ashok Vihar and the slum cluster.

image of a neighbourhood 'other'—'criminal' or 'prone to crime' and 'dirty'—who needs to be policed, restrained, and punished is a common phenomenon prevalent among the middle- and high-class sections of Delhi. Such attitudes could be gauged from instances such as, cases of domestic helps who come from slums to work in middle class homes in gated societies, and are not allowed to use the elevator (Malabika 2011), or people beaten to death because of defecating in a public park.

## Filth, Geographies of Crime and Reasons of the State

Rasheela Bagh is known as the 'crime pot' of Uday Nagar area, with 20 out of its 28 BCs living in Rasheela Bagh. For the purposes of maintaining 'law and order', it is argued, that 'disciplining' and 'sanitizing' of spaces like Rasheela Bagh and its residents, are required.

To take a close look at the way such spaces—both geographical and human—are perceived as dirty and the way they are dealt with, I examine the terms 'dirt' and 'abject' as conceptual categories. Within post-structural theory, the term abject has been explored as that which inherently disturbs conventional identity and cultural concepts. Mary Douglas sees the notion of 'dirt' as prevalent in some societies as essentially that of disorder: '(I)n chasing dirt ... we are not governed by the anxiety to escape disease, but are positively reordering our environment, making it conform to an idea.' (Douglas 1966: 2). Kristeva develops the idea of the abject as that which is rejected by, or which disturbs social reason—the communal consensus that underpins a social order: 'It is ... what disturbs identity, system, order. What does not respect borders, positions, rules.' (Kristeva 1982: 4).

The 'abject', the 'dirt', or 'filth' are things that are seen as an outside or as a deviation from the organized or mainstream dominant way of life. Postcolonial thinkers like Dipesh Chakrabarty (1992) and Sudipta Kaviraj (1997) note that the notions of 'dirt', 'disease', and 'disorder' are products of a modernist 'bourgeois' notion of hygiene and order. Chakrabarty (1992: 543), re-reading Mary Douglas, notes that dirt is equated with what is 'outside' the purity of the ritually enclosed 'home': the bazaar, not bound by a single set of rules, and thus the malevolent.

In Gooptu's work we find how the poor were major targets of all kinds of reformist measures, as the source of such 'dirt'. The 'insalubrious living environs' of the poor were considered not only to be a threat to public health, but were also seen as the factor that 'lie[s] at the root of the characteristic inefficiency, slothfulness and other short-comings' of the poor (2001: 70).

In the context of contemporary Delhi slums, a similar logic of association, moving back and forth between filth and deviation, is made out. The association is seen as a given, and any exception thereof has to be explained. Once a woman from Rasheela Bagh area of Uday Nagar complained about three men that they had beaten her up; Duty Officer Jyotsna was surprised that the woman had not alleged other charges of sexual violation on the men. She expressed her surprise: 'She is from Rasheela Bagh only, but probably honest!'[12]

In a society marked by practices and beliefs of caste and religious purity and pollution, the notion of 'filth' that operates within the discourses of policing is often attached to a person's caste or religious background, in turn making certain communities and groups of people marked as 'filthy' and thus 'criminal'. While the idea of a 'criminal tribe' is widely prevalent, and to some extent even officially sanctioned, the way in which even those who live in slums try to prove their innocence by stating their 'high' caste status is a revealing fact here. Prem Lata and Dinesh Giri—neighbours living in Rasheela Bagh—had a fight and police intervention was sought. When police was trying to work out a solution, both of them were trying to prove their innocence by stating their 'high-caste' status. Dinesh Giri said: 'I am a *pandit* by caste, will I do such a thing?' Prem Lata, who too was attempting to present herself as a 'respectable' woman said: 'We are also *Brahmin*, due to misfortune we are living in Rasheela Bagh. We are not people of such a place. We have a lot of land in the village.'[13]

The construction in the popular imagination of slums as 'vicious' spaces where 'criminals' live is a phenomenon that has been observed across countries, as noted by Davis (2006). He identifies that establishing such an association is often for reasons of facilitating 'beautification' attempts of cities—democratic and authoritarian alike—so that the 'scum' and the 'dirt' of the cities could be got rid of easily.

[12] Personal observation, 10 March 2012.

[13] Field notes, 9 March 2012, Uday Nagar police station.

In the context of urban poor spaces in the city of Delhi, however, along with this logic of cleaning up the city, another more persistent factor seems to be operating. While slums have been evicted periodically, such as during the Emergency, or on occasions like Asian Games of 1982 or the Commonwealth Games of 2010, the rhetoric of criminality imposed on the slums, seem to be of a more continuous nature, employed in the case of any slum, whether or not its eviction is immediately sought.

The 'filthy criminality' of the slums seems to be evoked here to perform another crucial role in the enactments of the state. In a context of high rates of crime, the slums appear to act as fodder for the state. In a narrow sense, these people provide the state with fodder by doubling up as easy targets—as expendable lives—people who could be detained and tortured and even killed, without much hue and cry—so that the middle- and upper-class security seekers could be kept happy. In a more foundational sense, the capacity of the state to maintain a population which could be constructed as 'criminal' may act as a justifying factor to the whole idea of a state—as an organization which promises security and welfare and draws its powers on the basis of such a promise.

To grasp the interconnected nature of the constructions of 'crime' and 'filth' in such a context, we need to look at some pronouncements and practices a bit more carefully. The slum dwellers are often portrayed/categorized as deviant and thus needing reforms (in terms of their morality as well as levels of awareness), by focusing on their habits of doing drugs and consuming *desi*[14] liquor, which are seen as signs of both physical and moral debasement or ill-health. The signature of ultimate debasement is when both men and women are habituated to liquor. Rasheela Bagh is the most abject of the spaces that come under Uday Nagar. After the festival of Holi,[15] the story that ran in the thana was about how everyone from Rasheela Bagh, both men and women, and even 15–16-year-old girls were totally drunk and falling over each other. Even pregnancy does not deter the women of Rasheela Bagh, as an SI commented upon how a woman with a full belly was drinking. The conditions of living in the slums were often referred to

[14] Literally, local, here referring to liquor brewed locally without a license.

[15] An Indian—mostly Hindu—festival celebrated by playing with colours at the onset of the spring season.

as 'disgusting', where husbands and wives copulate in front of their children, requiring NGOs to come forth and 'counsel' the young. The slums 'need sanitization' programmes from time to time in order to restrain the young people from being criminals. The descriptive terminologies and the suggested remedies affirm the association between deviation and filth.

People are also seen as prone to crime due to incapability of thinking and lack of knowledge. Therefore, Delhi Police claims that it emphasizes on proper education, vocational training, and awareness campaigns. It officially portrays an initiative named the Yuva Foundation, whose stated objective is to 'wean away' young adults and underprivileged children who 'for want of proper education and sports facility may take to crime', through 'arranging art workshops and vocational studies'. The contention is that, such training would make these young adults and children 'responsible citizens'.[16]

Such attempts at cleaning up and sanitizing slums are, however, more to *restrain* them rather than to make them equal parts of the city. The reform measures are targeted at reducing crimes committed by people coming from these areas in neighbouring middle and upper class localities. The people living in slums are not seen as requiring any serious 'positive' policing services. The typical crime prevention measures that police generally talks of, such as foot and motorcycle patrolling, are not practised—neither are they seen as required—in Rasheela Bagh, despite frequent complaints coming from that area. A constable from Uday Nagar captured the point when he talked about patrolling in Rasheela Bagh: 'The lanes are narrow, what kind of patrolling will you do? Otherwise also, everyone living there are *such* people only. So we put four motorcycles on other sides, and keep one at Rasheela Bagh.'[17]

## 'State-talk' and Invisibility of Custodial Crimes

In the last chapter we discussed how a discourse of self-understandings and self-justifications operate within the force, rendering acts of

[16] Delhi Police Yuva Foundation, Objectives and Functions of the Foundation, p. 1 (available at http://delhipolice.nic.in/home/about/dpcharter.aspx; accessed on 12 December 2013).

[17] Pers.com, 12 March 2012.

custodial torture—despite being illegal—to be acts of a higher moral order beyond the present laws. How practices of custodial violence targeted at specific sections of people are justified to the wider public is, however, another matter of interest. A general acceptance of widespread inequalities and violence towards people, based on their caste and class, both nurtures and helps sanction these practices.

Joe Sim and Steve Tombs (2009: 88–9) use a concept of 'state-talk', to show how any physical violence used against those who maintain state power, such as police and prison officers, is shown as an affront to the state itself; and the discursive processes whereby state servants within the criminal justice system misrepresent the dangers in their jobs to legitimize their often-coercive interventions in the society. We can further take this notion of 'state-talk' to examine police rationalizations or denials of use of torture.

A look at some cases of death occurring as a result of torture in police custody in Delhi elaborates the point. Custodial deaths in Delhi over time have been talked of by the police, when inquired by the media or civil rights activists. However, while talking of these deaths, police invariably talks of some 'markers' of the person who dies: markers which construct and push someone into a 'suspect community'. Very often, such identifications have nothing to do with the reason why a victim was in police custody in the first place, but they are employed as post-facto justifications for custodial violence. Thus, when a person dies in custody, police says that the person was a 'known bad character' (PUDR March 1992), 'a drug addict' (PUDR April 1993), a 'known criminal' (PUDR February 1998), or a 'Bangladeshi' (PUDR February 2002).

Custodial deaths are extreme cases when people *come to know* of police torture. Numerous such talkings take place in relation to almost every case of 'alleged' custodial torture, which we never know for sure if happened or not. For example, the *Mail Today* of 3 August 2009 reported that one Sonu was captured and then tortured in custody by the Delhi Police while he was taking an injured man to the hospital. The police immediately came out with a rejoinder which mentioned Sonu as having a criminal record with two cases of robbery, one case of snatching, and one case under the Arms Act against him (India, Delhi Police Rejoinder, No. 271).

In all such cases, while attempting to reduce responsibility, or to justify their own actions, the victims are put on a 'trial'—with stories of their criminality, immoral character, etc., though these were not reasons for which the victims were in custody in the first place most of the time. Judith Butler, in a critique of the Rodney King trial, invokes Fanon's account of interpellation, and explains how the jury acts under a 'racial logic of probability', where 'the black body is circumscribed as dangerous, prior to any gesture' (Butler 1993: 18, discussed in Chappel 2006: 320). A similar logic seems to be operating here, where the body of those from the margins is seen as either dangerous, even before they get a chance to show their dangerousness, or as unimportant, social drags—a burden on society, family, and so on.

We can comprehend programmes of Delhi Police like Yuva, too, in the light of such an understanding, where special training programmes are organised for youths from slums, so that they could be stopped from being involved in crimes. There is an attempt, in the words of Delhi Police itself, to 'Catch Them Young' (India, Delhi Police 2012b: 164). A more blatant advertisement on street children which the force withdrew after getting notice from the Delhi Commission for Protection of Child Rights read: 'Help him learn how to chop an onion. Before someone teaches him how to chop a head', followed by an assertion that the 'only hope' for them is timely intervention (*India Today* 1 August 2013). What draws one's attention is, the way in which some young people—precisely those who are from slums—are seen as requiring special training to prevent their turn to crimes (which is seen as inevitable otherwise), while other young people who are not from slums are cleared of any such 'natural' proclivity to crime.

These practices of state-talk accomplish a two-fold task. First, such practices in totality sustain and perpetuate the idea of the 'dangerous other' lingering behind the 'rightful owner selves' developed through long histories of exclusion, exploitation, and inequality, thus stabilizing the 'need' for a powerful state. Next, they not only legitimize police use of torture and save the perpetrators/police from accepting any responsibility, but also colour these very perpetrators in the role of 'protectors'—those who protect the society from the dangerous elements, or those who help the society get rid of the 'disorderly' 'peace-breakers'. Thus, a division of spaces and people into distinct groups and posing one against another through rhetoric of filth and cleanliness, legality and illegality, right and intrusion, criminality and civility turns the basic assumption about our society into a space of constant fear, which needs to be seamlessly guarded. The same discourse also produces both a visibility and an invisibility of the acts of custodial torture by police. The visibility of the actual acts of violence to onlookers, often carried out in full public view, sustains the image of police as the protectors of civil life in society, and at the same time, the various 'talks' about the 'criminality' of the tortured person produces an invisibility of the violation of laws by the police.

The construction of such an image of a conflict-ridden terror-provoking society generates acceptance for the violence of the state institution of police. Such endeavours in their material forms often translate into everyday structural and direct physical violence on some people who were classified as the 'criminal other'. We observe that in such a context, the institution's claims to authority are granted by the fact that it can construct, sustain and reconstruct animosity and terror in society and can present themselves as capable of sorting out such situations, though never conclusively. In addition, systematic violence towards the 'criminal other' thus constructed comes to be sought after by the middle and upper class security seekers, thus highlighting the need of the institution of police. This said, however, it is intriguing to study how the people who are targeted for such violence relate to the institution. In the next chapter, we turn to that very question.

4

# (Mis)Use, Agency, and Acceptance

## Interactions with Police Violence

In the previous chapter, I discussed the discursive production of some spaces and some people as places of crime and criminals. In this chapter, an attempt is made to study to what extent such discursive meanings find place in the vocabularies of the marginalized: the people who are targets of police violence. Are those at the receiving end of police violence convinced of its usefulness? Are they mere subjects of police violence or do they, as active agents, interact with the violence of the state? What are the terms of the relationships these people form with the police? What do such relations tell us about the place of the state in the socio-political imaginations of people?

Probing into the nature of interactions of people from margins with the institution of police in Delhi, in this chapter, I analyse if such interactions explicate the reasons behind the acceptance or rejection of the authority of police. The inquiry thus opens up questions of trust, belief in efficiency, desert, and fairness. This is done, first, by looking into everyday interactions of people in the margins with the police, and then, going on to study the aftermath of two cases of custodial death, in terms of experiences and expectations of the people close to those who died. The chapter draws extensively on field-based narratives and observations, which are supported by primary documents such as First Information Reports, post-mortem reports, records of communications of National Human Rights Commission, and reports of PUDR.

After going through discussions of how police personnel themselves and the common people who are often onlookers of violence towards marginal sections comprehend the role and place of violence from the state, in this chapter, my attempt has been to answer the third part of the larger question of how state violence affects state's legitimacy, by examining impact of police violence on the suffering groups' perceptions of the state. As we proceed in this work with legitimacy as a sociological phenomenon, instead of looking into the universal normative definitions of how a power ought to be to qualify as legitimate, we attempt to uncover *people's ideas* about what a power ought to be, or what role it ought to play, for them to see it as legitimate.

The fact that the people in society are not a homogenous group, however, adds layers to this question. Invoking the presence of diverse sections of people in society, or what we may call 'multiple publics' (Kaviraj 1994; Singh 1998), Rodney Barker (1990) noted that a holder of power may be legitimate to some while being illegitimate to others. Ethnographic evidence suggests an addition to this assertion: that the same institution may be legitimate (or illegitimate) to different sections of people for very different reasons.

Legitimacy of an institution is a condition where people accept it as a valid authority while evaluating its actions and behaviour. The task in hand is to comprehend how the police, which performs diverse acts—some involving use or threat of violence while others being such that cannot readily be called violence—is evaluated by sections of people who often see its violent side. The purpose is to examine the link between the coercive functions of the police and the generation or erosion of its legitimacy.

## Probing the Relation between Police and the Marginal People

The police in Delhi, in general, do not enjoy a very favourable public opinion. A look at the mainstream media and social media gives a picture that the average middle class person is highly dissatisfied with the police. A news report in the aftermath of the brutal 16 December 2012 rape case[1] articulated the impression of police amongst people in Delhi thus: 'The city cop is an elusive creature. Either you don't see him at all. Or, if you happen to spot him, chances are high that he declines your request or puts you off by asking too many questions' (TNN 2012). The middle classes and upper classes are most vocal against the police talking of their inefficiency and corruption. A post in a page named 'Delhi Police' in the social networking site Facebook said: 'Dear Delhi police you have become incompetent actually you guys are the puppets of the corrupt politicians … if she was your daughter you would have done encounter' (Facebook 2013). While police is widely loathed, the armed forces and the *jawans* are seen in high esteem and are idealized for their 'bravery' and 'heroism'. A post in a social media platform suggested:

> Each Delhi Police constable ought to be made to serve for 1 year in Army on LOC in order to be eligible for promotion and if unwilling to do so, should be demoted to a posting in Bihar, or Easter UP. The only way to improve this force is to get rid of contended people!! (ashis2k 2013)

Such declared 'disheartening', however, is due to the fact that the people who 'men' the positions are not 'worthy'. Here, in judging efficiency and capability of the police force, policing is seen as personified in the police personnel. While the individual police personnel is seen to be either corrupt, or inefficient or ill trained, or with an evil mindset, the institutional structures and ideologies of the organization are not questioned.

Along with the lens of efficiency and capability, trust in intentions is another parameter of evaluating the police here. Evaluation on the basis of these two parameters, however, may lead to different judgements by different sections of people. While there are people who do not believe either in intentions or efficiency of police, as we can see in the above instances, for people from the marginal sections, I argue, the police often has an 'efficiency' value, though they too may not nurture a high trust of its intentions.

[1] On 16 December 2012, a 23-year-old woman was beaten and gang-raped in a moving bus near Munirka, in the southern part of New Delhi. The woman died 13 days later while undergoing emergency treatment in Singapore. Public protests followed the incident of rape and the death, and in many instances the protesters clashed with the police. The police was widely accused of brutally lathi-charging people, apart from shooting water cannons and tear gas shells.

The people from the marginal sections too, those who are widely believed by police officials as having no respect and trust for police, often publicly spell out their disaffection with the police. Many view the police in their vicinity as a troublesome but unavoidable part of their daily lives. Satish, a young man who works as a driver, living in a jhuggi cluster located in front of a North East district police station said: 'It is very difficult to live near police. They always trouble us. Something or the other keeps happening all the time.'[2]

Everyday instances of confrontational interactions with the police that one can observe in a police station also explicate such distrust. Once, while I was sitting with the Duty Officer (DO) at the Uday Nagar police station, a man came with a complaint that some policemen had beaten him up without any reason. He said that he came to the *thana* the previous night as well, and a *ladki*[3] sitting at the DO desk kept both copies of a complaint letter that he gave, without returning one copy to him. There was no record in the DD about this. The DO told him that he must not have really given any application, and had he really given one, he would have been returned a copy. The man replied: 'What do you think, do you think I am lying? You think I can't do anything?' Such interactions show that the people from the margins generally do not believe that the police work as a neutral arbiter. Rather, they are very much aware of how power and position influence the way the police would deal with them.

In another instance, an old woman and her son came to Uday Nagar police station, to complain about a threat that the woman and her husband had been receiving during nights, while the son stays away at work. The DO Chhaya asked them to come back later, as the beat officer who had duty in that area was not available in the thana at that time.

[2] Casual conversation in front of his hut put up on a sidewalk, 5 January 2012.

[3] *Ladki* in Hindi refers to a girl, and its use is notable in this context as it contrasts to the more respectable ways of referring to a woman police personnel as 'madam' or *didi* (elder sister).

The woman and the man were, however, suspicious that the police did not want to help them, and the woman kept asking, 'Wouldn't police help us?' The son showed a slip with a phone number written on it and said that he called up the police control room the previous night from that number. He asked why the police had not sent anyone until then. According to him, the number was that of a mobile phone belonging to his neighbour, but the DO after looking at the number said that it was the number of the landline phone of the police station. When he was told by DO Chaya that this was not the number of his neighbour's mobile phone, he openly showed his suspicion and retorted: 'Let us try this number from a PCO now, and we'll come to know whose number is this.'[4]

However, despite such widespread expressed mistrust of police and complaints about it, people from the margins still interact with the police on a very regular basis. It is not only when police summons them to the thana, detains them in relation to some case of crime, or visits them to collect regular *hafta* (weekly bribe) on various grounds that they come in contact with the police, but they themselves often call in the police to intervene in issues of diverse nature.

Such a phenomenon complicates the general observations of people's lack of trust in the police. It leads us to inquire why such people, who do not have much trust in the intentions of the police, would ask for police intervention in their lives, often in circumstances which are not so urgent. Does it imply the absence of any other forum for resolution of conflicts? Does it imply that the institutions of state, even when not fair and impartial, have become inescapable? In an attempt to answering these questions, it can be seen that efficiency of a different kind—which is perceived to be held by the police—is what makes it valuable. In such contexts, rather than trust, the fact that the institution wields a certain amount of exercisable power, to intervene in various situations, appears to have curved out acceptance of and support for the institution. While the individual members or the personnel of the institution may be loathed by people, the institution is allowed to operate and even invited into people's lives. The efficiency of police in these cases is derived from the marks of its power. This efficiency is not about

[4] I observed this episode sitting with the DO on a regular day at the police station.

swift delivery of prescribed functions of policing, but often about being 'effective' in a given situation in a certain manner. It is efficient by its presence, which is a derivative of the sanction behind its use of force. By dint of this 'efficiency', the material practices of the institution enter into a dialogue with every-day lives of people.

The question of why people from the margins often call in the police to intervene in their lives, also makes one probe critically the assumed role of police as 'protectors' of the 'haves'—protecting their life and property, and the disciplinarian of the 'have-nots'. If police simply acts for the powerful in society, why would people from the margins want to invite police into their lives? Why would they want the police to intervene even when the matters are not of desperate urgency or helplessness?

These questions may lead us in several directions. First, we may assume that the allegations of the police being partisan are false and police as a state institution acts as a neutral arbiter in society. However, any such assumption is quickly rendered invalid by observations of day-to-day practices in a police station that are discussed in preceding chapters. Various forms of hierarchies mediate the notions of fairness and morality inside a police station, and an observation of this quickly demystifies any notion of the police as a neutral arbiter.

Second, we may think of a situation, where the common masses are 'hegemonized' to think that the institution of police works as a neutral arbiter. However, any assumption of hegemonic control is dismissed by the fact that people, including those from the marginal sections, are widely convinced that the police is mostly on the side of those who have resources.

We may further think that the governmental practices of the state has penetrated so deep into the lives of people, that the condition of not having police in their personal lives, or living beyond police has become unimaginable for anyone. In this scenario, we would expect an active participation of people in being and getting policed. Another scenario may be that of active engagement of the people from the margins with the police—the institution which most often relates to them through its use of force—where the marginal sections may have some amount of agency to utilize the institutions of the state, on their own terms, to work for them. If we find evidence supporting this scenario, then this follows a reinforcing cycle of acceptance and further acceptance of the institution. This, one can argue, represents the ways in which the idea of the state as the only viable political community and upholder of authority has seeped so deep, that what seem to be creative engagements with a state institution of violence providing autonomous spaces to act to individuals and groups placed in margins, are also tools in further normalizing and legitimizing the state. These little acts of resistance that we may see in attempts to use police power for personal gains, however, may still rework their subject position to some extent.

In the following, we attempt to analyse through observation of some day-to-day interactions of people with the police, the last point that I explored above: whether the capacity for violence and the actual violence yielded by police could be used by the apparent 'target' populations to reorganize their agency not by bypassing the state but by a creative manipulation of its institutions and in the process making the violence of the institution and the institution itself more acceptable.

## 'Use'/'Misuse'

During my fieldwork, it was often reported by policemen of various ranks that people keep calling on the 100 number police helpline indiscriminately, without good enough reasons. They complained that such 'misuse' of facilities given by the *sarkar* (government) unnecessarily increases police's burden.

I saw several instances of such 'useless' calling in by 'nuisances' and 'lazy' people, as defined by police. But it was observed that such 'misuse' here has a double connotation: the 'misuse' which irritates the police personnel, when police assistance number is called frequently for matters that are not really 'concerns' of policing, and the knowing 'use' of police and law by people from marginal sections for their own concerns, whether individual or group. Three such instances discussed here would elaborate this process.

1. There was a call about a quarrel in a locality falling under Uday Nagar. When I reached the place along with constable Pradeep, two Police Control Room (PCR) van personnel were already there. A crowd of women were loudly reporting the incident. It was just before the festival of Holi, the festival where people play

with *gulal*[5] and water. The mother of a young boy who was beaten up by another woman called up police. It started with a young boy putting gulal on another boy. The first boy was beaten up by the mother of the second boy, who according to his mother, was very unwell. Then the mother of the first boy who was beaten up came over and beat up the mother of the second boy. The second boy's mother showed us bruises resulting from the beating, with traces of blood. The first mother, while liberally using abuses and curses, said that these days even teachers do not beat up children in school, '... how dare she beat up my son?' In every sentence, she was using abusive terms to refer to the second mother. All the three policemen stood silently witnessing the squabble. After a while, Pradeep got restless by her use of swear words and shouted at her: *'Kya behen ki laudi behen ki laudi bolte ja rahi hain, sun liya humne, bahut baar bol di'* (we have heard enough of *behen ki laudi*, now stop it). The woman stopped using the swear words for a while, but all of them kept shouting at each other. None of them asked the policemen present to take any specific action against anyone, and the policemen left the place after a while.

2. There was another case of quarrel between neighbours. Pradeep was the constable on call again, and SI Om Pal, who was the officer on call reached from some other place. Two PCR personnel were also there. It was a quarrel between a woman and a man. The woman complained that the man who was her neighbour and lived in the lower part of the house, had broken some part of the wall on her side, tried to throw a brick at her, and had also abused her verbally. The woman kept talking constantly, and did not let anyone else speak much, including her husband and the policemen. She, however, talked to the policemen with respect and also offered them tea and water, while at the same time hurling abuses at her opponent. As the issue could not be resolved, the accused man was taken to the police station in the PCR van and the woman and her husband were asked to follow.

   In the thana, at SI Om Pal's room, it was again only the woman who could speak. She was shouting so much that the policemen

[5] Gulal is a powder in vibrant colours, which is used to play, both in dry form and mixed with water, during the festival of Holi.

sent the neighbour out of the room in an attempt to calm her down. This, however, did not work. Her husband looked a little timid. He tried to calm her down, and told the policemen that he did not want a fight and wanted an amicable end. He softly said that his wife had made it bigger than necessary. However, this further infuriated his wife. When the wife started shouting even louder, he immediately corrected by saying that the man should not have done this to his wife. The police advised all of them to come into a compromise. They asked the man to apologize and the woman to pardon him. However, she kept insisting: 'Keep him inside for a few days. Then only will he learn.'

Finally, the police persuaded the woman to accept the apology of the man, who did it with folded hands. She, however, did not look fully satisfied.

3. Prem Lata and Dinesh Giri were next-door neighbours in Rasheela Bagh. When Dinesh and his wife went to work, Prem Lata looked after their children together with her own kids. Prem Lata had complained to the police that Dinesh had beaten her up, and police brought Dinesh to the thana. All other members of both the families also came to the thana, and gathered in and out of ASI) Uday Singh's room. Dinesh, his wife, and children, all of whom were interrogated by police, denied that Dinesh had beaten up Prem Lata. Dinesh added: 'I am a *pandit* by caste, will I do such a thing?' Prem Lata, who too was attempting to present herself as a 'respectable' woman said: 'We are also *Brahmins*, out of misfortune we are living in Rasheela Bagh. We are not people of such a place. We have a lot of land in the village.' While Dinesh and his family was denying all charges, his younger sister-in-law Pinki, who was dressed up in jeans and a T-shirt and looked slightly better off, was trying to wriggle them out of the matter by paying up. She was paying either a bribe to the police or the medical cost of treating the injury that Prem Lata showed on her hand, on behalf of her brother-in-law. She pleaded with the police that Dinesh had five young children to look after. While the police was satisfied with the arrangement, Prem Lata was not satisfied with Pinki's offer of taking her to the hospital and buying the required medicines and was asking for cash. If cash was not given, she rather wanted Dinesh to be arrested, and showed concerns

about her husband who was old and was unable to fight Dinesh back in case he came again to fight. Both parties wanted the police to make an arrangement convenient for them.

## Reworking of Subject Positions

In the instances discussed above, the intervention of the police was sought in relatively minor matters. The context of the incidents where intervention was sought was, however, interesting. In the first case, the woman who called in the police did not ask the police to take any action against the other woman that she had complained against. When the police reached, they neither needed nor allowed the police to do any kind of mediation. They had a verbal fight amongst themselves with the support of neighbours on each side. Still, the *presence* of the police was sought. They wanted the quarrel to take place in front of police eyes. Such an act indicates that the police are trusted as authorities to oversee a fight between two parties. It also perhaps kept them away from the risk of any one side going violent during the fight when a party with a superior force is present. Thus, the police in this scene acted as a check on each of the parties, as their very presence was a threat of violence. The capacity of the police to act violently—the role in which the police is efficient—was 'utilized' here by the group of women. As its image of being coercive is very effective, thus its very presence becomes an efficient way of ensuring the needs of safety and security. Interestingly, however, the intervention of the police is not sought here to arbitrate the fight and people choose to fight it out amongst themselves. This has implications for trust of the intentions of the police.

In the second incident too, the intervention of the police was sought, in what appears to be a minor matter. The woman seemed to be exaggerating facts in an attempt to influence the police to her side. In this case too, the police is clearly seen and accepted as an authority for the reasons of its ability to act violently, that is, due to its perceived efficiency in violence. The woman wanted the police to 'teach' the man a 'lesson'. She wanted him to be detained by police, and perhaps also to be beaten up. She knew that the police had the capacity to arrest and beat up a person. For this reason, she called in the police and tried to influence them, so that her personal goals of insulting an opponent and avenging could be fulfilled while she herself could not rightfully do that.

In the third instance too, Prem Lata wanted to force money out of the Giri family through the police route. What she asked for, to avenge the alleged beating up by Dinesh, was either cash from Dinesh or to get Dinesh into police custody. The violence that is understood/presumed on the body of a person in police custody, she seemed to have thought, would act as an encouragement for the Giri family to pay up. The possibility of violence in custody was known to the Giri family too, and thus Pinki wanted to avoid that by paying up the police. Both the families wanted to 'use' the police for their own purposes. Both the parties also attempted to play all possible resources they had in terms of social and economic standing of their castes and community, to influence the police to their versions of criminality and innocence.

In all these instances, the attempt was to turn the police itself into an instrument through a creative 'use'/'misuse' of laws, procedures, and institutional provisions that are operational. While the police had to intervene, its interventions were not self-guided or guided by the formal logic of rules, but by the requirements of the people in a certain situation. The specific role that the police had to play, or not play, was not definable for the police beforehand. Though the police is often called in such cases of petty quarrels, for requirements of preventing a situation from spiralling into violence, they are not necessarily called in to arbitrate or decide. Instead, this relationship to the police may be closer to the idea of *danda*[6] in the Indian tradition—defined as the capacity for punishment. The idea of danda suggests that violence can have, if not a moral agency, at least the capacity to safeguard order: at any rate violence as producing a certain authority. We observe from the discussed instances that the violence of the police and the fact that people can call them to intervene, has an empowering effect on the marginal sections, no matter in however minute a way, and this has larger implications about the place of the state.

If we already know that the police is not a neutral arbiter, and if divisions based on the class, caste, communal, religious, gendered, and other possible hierarchies prevalent in a society influence how police work, then the people from the margins having spaces for manoeuvring the work of police seem to mean some amount of reversal of the power

[6] In Kautilya's *Arthashastra*, *danda*, or the rod of punishment is defined as the indispensable requisite of social order (Troutman 1979: 86–102).

equations. It not only makes the coercive state more bearable to such people, but also makes coercion and violence themselves as signifying factors for the acceptance and recognition of the state institution of police by people. In a situation when the police is widely loathed as 'corrupt' and 'trouble-makers' for the people of the margins, their very capacity of trouble-making is transformed into a resource for the marginal people in such instances.

By 'misuse' of the state, the state is made to 'work' for the people. It does not appear to be an instance of the bargaining of the 'political society' *a la* Partha Chatterjee (2004) as the happenings here are not instances of attempts at securing welfare measures or semi-legal accommodation of their demands by the state. It is also different from Eckert's (2004) conceptualization of the 'homogenization of the legal sphere', as it is not about use of state rules and institutions for achieving an ethical normative. The awareness of 'misuse' of perfectly legal procedures is the point here, which in turn has an effect of reconfiguring power locations of subjects. The people who want to 'use' the procedures of a coercive body like police do not want to 'use' them for some high moral or ethical goal, nor do they want the police to act strictly in accordance with procedures defined by law, but for the purposes of their daily living and the politics of daily life.

While we can observe some amount of agency on the part of the marginal sections here, we perhaps cannot term this as an instance of complete absence of operations of governmentality, as governmentality cannot be restricted to formal tactics and tradeoffs, but also includes informal strategies of handling transactions of different sets of the population. What we have here may be an instance of the flexibility of modern governance strategies themselves. However, at the same time, we also get to see that governmental strategies do not necessarily produce subjects who are easily inserted into the plans of the state. Just as governmental strategies may seek to insert populations into the embrace of its power, correspondingly the objects of governance also try to produce their own rules of governance by deploying the institutions of the state itself, in turn producing an acceptance of these institutions, not on terms set by the state but on their own terms.

At the same time, we must also keep in mind that such acts may not always be progressive. In the next section, we deal with how the state has penetrated into the apparently non-statal sphere[7] of the family, and through various episodes of the entry of the institution of police into the family we deal in more detail about the liberatory/non-liberatory aspect of the perceived agency of people.

## The Police in the Home: The Strongman of the State

The sphere of the family is not beyond the laws within the ambit of the Indian state structure. Practices within the family like procedures related to birth and marriage are standardized and codified. There also are specific laws like the Protection of Women from Domestic Violence Act, 2005, the Dowry Prohibition Act, 1961, and various sections of the IPC dealing with protection of individuals within a relationship inside the family. What we look at in this section is, however, another dimension of the state's involvement in the family. Here we look at how an institution of the state is looked at as, and expected to be, merely a 'strongman' to keep things under control rather than expecting it to follow a specific incident through proper procedures.

While the proclaimed goal of various laws relating to the family is to maintain a normative standard in interpersonal and intra-familial relations, the happenings in which the police is sought in the affairs of the family do not necessarily toe the line of the formal state-drawn ideas of normativity.

Officers in most of the police stations having slum localities under their jurisdiction say that *mian-biwi jhagra*[8] is the most common matter requiring police involvement in their areas. Other kinds of family disputes such as amongst brothers, between father and son, between two wives, etc., also take place. Police at all such places project their role in such cases as counsellors and mediators.[9] Delhi Police has an

[7] While one is aware that the dichotomies like state–civil society and the public–private are debated ones, I suggest that we can still talk of a sphere which is statal and a sphere which is non-statal, in terms of an institutional view of the state, though in the present research itself the spheres are overlapping and influencing to each other.

[8] Literally, quarrel between husband and wife.

[9] Field observations, period: October 2011 to March 2012.

official initiative called the *Parivartan*, which, as mentioned in the official website of Delhi Police, is aimed at changing the 'patriarchal mindset of society towards women' (Delhi Police Website 2013). A booklet published by Delhi Police talks of the scheme thus: 'Parivartan has questioned the social acceptability and "taken for granted" attitude of people about VAW, thereby creating an atmosphere that will welcome a change towards gender equity' (India, Delhi Police n.d.).[10]

What the police in Delhi do under this scheme, as articulated by an SHO in the Outer district, is the following: 'We have community policing programmes, like the *Parivartan* scheme, in which lady officers go and talk to fighting husband–wives/couples, counsel them, and try to see that their family is maintained.' (2012, pers.com, 18 January).

While feminists may argue that this is not exactly what Delhi Police requires to do to change the 'patriarchal mindset of the society', and that such practices in turn, may rather fortify the patriarchal structures and practices, we would, through some examples, look at how people from marginal sections, who are most often the target of schemes like *Parivartan* also use the same institutions in matters of the family, in accordance with their own familial or communal normative standards. What makes such people to come to the police seeking intervention in a *mian-biwi jhagra*, or in a broader context, a matter strictly from the familial sphere?

There was a *jhagra* in Rasheela Bagh, the 'crime-pot' of Uday Nagar area, as the caller to PCR helpline number 100 reported. ASI Om Pal took a constable and me along, to attend to the call. Once inside the Rasheela Bagh area, the two policemen parked their bikes at an open space in the middle of makeshift huts.

After a while, a woman came out from one of the narrow lanes, with a baby in her arms. She was wearing a salwar suit, with a deep-necked design at the back and her head covered with a dupatta. Her name was Ruby. Ruby reported that her husband was beating her up, and showed the policemen marks of beating on her body. Om Pal asked what she expected from the police. He asked if she wanted her husband to be counselled. She replied: 'He always drinks and picks up fights. Keep him inside till Holi.' The policeman replied: 'How can we keep him inside?

[10] VAW stands for violence against women. The document uses this acronym at p. iii.

Both of you come to the thana.' But the woman replied that she would not come to the thana and left.

Ruby, it seemed, did not want to go through the formal procedures of filing a case, and lodging a case of domestic violence or anything of that sort against her husband. What she wanted was that police informally keep her husband in custody for a few days, which would have an effect of intimidating him for a while. While anyone else doing the same would be seen as an abductor, she believed the police could do it without trouble. The police was sought here as the 'strongman' who would teach the abusive husband a lesson. Such an attitude is reflective of the relative acceptance of the violence of the police, or the acceptance of the police for its ability to play the 'strongman', in contrast to the formally outlined legal procedures.

One has to note, however, that while bringing the state into the family in an informal manner to 'correct' an 'errant' husband may provide respite to women at times, in many other instances the state institution may thus be used to perpetuate authoritarian and undemocratic customs and practices.

One common instance of this is a certain type of 'kidnapping' case, in the context of inter-community, inter-caste, inter-class or intra-*gotra*[11] marriages. As a policeman serving at the New Delhi district had explained: 'Girl elopes with some guy, parents cannot accept the matter, and complain that their daughter has been kidnapped.' According to him, what the parents want in such situations is to get the boy arrested and take the girl back so that with time they can influence the girl over to their beliefs about a good marriage.

While the policeman talked only about what the parents think, he did not elaborate on what role police plays in such cases. It is observed in earlier chapters, however, that police actively indulge in maintaining caste- and religion-based orthodoxies. The role of the police, and how the police consent to work for the interests of undemocratic and unlawful moral assertions, in exchange for money at times, and at other times as 'moral custodians' of a society is visible in the case of custodial death of a young couple in the year 2000, in the Mangolpuri Police Station of the Outer district.

[11] Among patrilineal Hindu communities, a *gotra* refers to people who are descendents in a male line from a common male ancestor.

A third-year college student Reena and 25-year-old Bijender, who were neighbours in the S block of Mangolpuri had eloped in the month of October 2000, but Reena's family did not approve of it. Reena's family was from the Jadav community, while Bijender was a Labhana Sikh. As Reena's family lodged a complaint of abduction against Bijender, and the police was after them, on the advice of his family Bijender along with Reena came to Mangolpuri police station and surrendered in the morning of 11 October 2000. As both were consenting adults, the case should have been closed thereof. However, that did not happen. The police allowed Reena's family to meet Bijender while he was in their custody. After a few hours, Bijender died of poisoning. Once Bijender died, Reena also committed suicide in a lavatory of the police station by consuming poison, after expressing her intention of killing herself. Bijender's family members, who accepted the marriage of Reena and Bijender, later reported that they had bribed the investigating officer (IO) of the case for the safety of the family members, but that did not work and ultimately both Bijender and Reena were killed under pressure from the girl's family. Reena's family, on the other hand, exonerated the police completely and maintained that the boy's family pressurized Reena to commit suicide (PUDR 2000). Interestingly, while the police thus worked into the hands of communal logics of caste purity and patriarchy, the National Human Rights Commission (NHRC) also could not see through the episode to highlight the complicity of the police in maintaining undemocratic social hierarchies.[12]

[12] The NHRC even failed to raise issues of negligence on the part of the police regarding people kept in its custody, and closed the file by exonerating the accused policemen. In a letter from the Assistant Registrar (Law) of the NHRC to the DCP North-West district it was stated:

> The Commission has considered the matter. The material on record shows that a boy and girl, who were deeply in love, committed suicide by taking poison. The death took place in a police station as the girl's parents had lodged a F.I.R. under section 366 IPC wherein the boy was arrested … It is an unfortunate case but no negligence or fault can be found on the police personnel. Probably the lodging of the F.I.R. prompted the boy to take poison (cynamide) and after hearing the said news, the girl also took poison.

The irony of this remark was that while the NHRC took note of the fact that the boy and the girl consumed poison while in custody of police, it failed to

PUDR, in its publication *Courting Disaster: A Report on Inter-caste Marriages, Society and State* (2003) notices that antagonism of the state, its institutions and their functionaries to love marriages is not based on the whims of an official in power, but exhibits a pattern and intention.

Democratic or not, such acts of inviting the police into one's family raises questions about the role in which the police is accepted by the people. The people of the slums are not policed in the way the upper and middle class colonies are policed. They are seen more as storehouses of criminals rather than requiring positive policing to save these people from any possible threat to their life and property. Despite such an attitude of the police, the people living in such spaces still call in the police, and specifically call in that face of police which is directed towards them in general, that is, the violent side of police, for the purposes of upholding their ideas of social organization and behaviour. The police is here accepted more as a 'strongman' and this form of the state becomes a close ally of the people.

## Narrating Deaths and Lives: 'Criminality', Justice, and Resignation

This section looks into narratives around two deaths in the custody of police in Delhi to understand how such deaths have affected lives and attitude of people who had lived in close affinity with the deceased. The first one is from the year 1987 and the second one is from 2005. Tracing the police narratives and the versions of relatives and neighbours, I examine if the apparently opposed narratives have discursive commonalities producing overlapping images of criminality, desert, and justice.

Kleinman and Kleinman (2009) in their anthropological exploration on suffering argue that, when suffering is experienced as a collective,

---

see negligence on the part of policemen regarding those in custody. The questions like how one got access to poison while in custody and why necessary steps to prevent a suicide were not taken even after the girl expressed her wish to commit suicide were never asked.

the collective modes of experience shape individual perceptions and expressions. In such contexts, how to undergo troubles are taught and learnt in the community sometimes openly, often indirectly. In the context of people living in the margins of a metropolitan city like Delhi too, for whom violence upon the body and suffering is a most ordinary and most expected fate, suffering assumes a social nature. While people from these sections get socialized into tackling real and possible experiences of suffering, here we make an attempt to look beyond this, and see, if everyday violence, and even severe forms of torture, often come to be accepted as normal and acceptable. Is acceptance of violence seen as another of several adjustments and accommodations that one has to make for living in the city? Does the 'talk' of the 'state' (Corrigan and Sayer 1985)[13] seep deep enough into the very sections that are coercively policed, to make them believe the death of a fellow man/woman as forgettable and inconsequential?

## The Death of Mahir: 'A Useless Reality'

Mahir, an auto driver who lived in Janta Colony near the present-day Welcome metro station died on 23 August 1987 at the age of 26. He was brought to Shahdara Police Station a day prior to that according to the FIR filed.[14] According to the Delhi based organization PUDR, Mahir was brought to the thana on account of investigating a case of petty theft. The cause of death as reported to PUDR by police was suicide.[15] Mahir's mother, Smt. Jamshadi on the other hand, accused and specifically named several policemen of beating up Mahir, and reported in the FIR filed on 31/08/1987 that Mahir had died as a result of injuries sustained during his custody in Shahadara thana. She stated in the FIR: 'I was at my place today, Jagannath Pradhan came and told that Mahir's condition is very bad, lying on the terrace of our house. This was at about 11 in the night' (FIR 373/87).

[13] See the second chapter for a discussion of the notion of 'state-talk'.

[14] FIR no. 373/87 at Shahdara police station, East District. Copy of the FIR was received through an application under the RTI Act 2005. All translations to English are mine.

[15] PUDR reported this in two of its reports: PUDR October 1989 at p. 4, and PUDR March 1998 at p. 15.

The FIR further read: 'When she came to Jagannath Prasad's house she saw that Mahir was lying on the terrace, and was bleeding from his nose and mouth, and was also puking' (FIR 373/87). Mahir's mother was quoted further:

> My son was taken to the police station at 11 am on 22-08-87 ... In the police station ASI Kishan Chand, Chowki incharge ... (illegible), constable Ali Kabar and HC Chandar Singh had beaten him mercilessly. This fact was told to me and everyone else by Mahir once he was back at home. His body had a lot of internal injuries because of which he was groaning. He had injuries in his ... (illegible), on his kidneys, on his chest and on the heels of his feet. (FIR 373/87)

The FIR mentioned a post-mortem report which gave the cause of death as 'death due to cameou cerebral injury' (FIR 373/87). Despite allegations of custodial torture and death as a result of that, there was no magisterial level inquiry into the case. Departmental action was taken against three policemen in the form of transfers. There was no other prosecution and neither was there any compensation to the family. There was no public response to the death either, despite the fact that it was well known in the locality that Mahir died after he was beaten up in police custody (PUDR October 1989; PUDR March 1998).

Twenty-five years have passed since, and Janta Colony has changed a lot. The erstwhile unauthorized Janta Colony is now a regularized slum under the Slum department of the MCD, divided into several blocks. Following the address—17, Janta Colony recovered from the yellowed pages of the FIR, led to the discovery that now there are number 17 houses in every block. These days the area is predominantly populated by Muslims, with a small percentage of Hindus alongside.[16] A wrong address with a story of death, however, still led to the right places.

The *mukhias* (headman) of the urban slum clusters of Delhi are supposed to know all the people who ever lived in their colonies. The mukhia of Janta Colony is the owner of a tea stall under a tattered shed. It was not very well lit inside his shop and the shop looked more like a storehouse of old things with iron scrap and other junk stacked inside. An elderly man with a long beard, wearing kurta-pyjama and a skullcap

[16] According to an estimate given by a man from the slum there are about 80,000 people in the area out of which about 7,000 are Hindus and the rest are Muslims.

was the mukhia. There were several other men sipping tea and talking. The mukhia remembered Mahir. He said: 'He did not die in the hands of police. After police left him, he died at the terrace of somebody's house.' Then he looked at the others sitting there and said: '*Are wo Tahir ka bhai tha*' (He was Tahir's brother). Mahir's brother's family and his mother still live in Janta Colony. However, the mukhia advised me not to meet them: 'It is better if you don't meet … he is a BC, what will you do meeting him. He is not a good man.' He, however, told me that I could get all the information I needed from another man.

Master Abdul's[17] tea stall was a bit away from the mukhia's stall, at the end of a dark narrow lane littered and dampened with drain water. He is a man in his late sixties. My conversations with him were full of stories enthusiastically narrated by Abdul *bhai* (one who is like an elder brother). He had been a leader in the long struggle for the regularization of Janta Colony. In an old tin suitcase, he has kept each and every paper related to the slum since then. He has even kept copies of identity documents of all the family heads living in the slum. He explained to me that these documents are crucial to their living in the slum, which he still views as precarious. 'All these are our resources', he said, '… may need them any day. I might not need them today, but my sons might require them in future.' He took out all the papers from his suitcase and handed me some to read aloud.

Nothing of this enthusiasm remained whenever I asked him about Mahir. He wearily used to talk about Mahir as a small-time thief: 'He was involved in petty thefts … he would pick up something one day, another day he would pick up something else.' He, however, also said at another time that Mahir was a known bad character (BC). Before his death he was caught by the police for some theft. However, he did not die in the station. He died at Jagannath *pradhan*'s (the headman of the area of that time) house as he was feeling unwell after the police left him there.

Most of the time Abdul bhai redirected the conversation to the slum people's struggle for regularization, showing complete disinterest in Mahir's story. When I interrupted asking about Mahir while Abdul bhai was talking of another of the various episodes of the struggle, he said

[17] Name changed, as this person did not want to be identified by his real name in fear of possible repercussions from the police.

'We were engaged in the work for the colony, but he was—now you are going he would be thinking of snatching your mobile, or your purse—what work will he do for the colony. Neither did his family members.'

Another time he advised me: 'You don't write much about that story.' Then he went on to say that according to old records, his father had pushed a woman into a pit, and that he was in jail for this. *'To kuch khaas log nahi the'* (So they were not very special people), he said.

He also told me that he is concerned if whatever he had told me would come into public. He talked about how the police uses *mukhvarees*[18] and victimizes innocent people in collaboration with them. He went on to say:

> If I tell you everything clearly and if it comes in written, then there is life-threat to my children. So the reality is useless. And those people who were there during that time, they have passed away.

For Abdul bhai, the knowledge of the intricacies of the death of Mahir is something that does not help him in the present. Thus, this knowledge is *bekaar*, it is useless. On the other hand, the knowledge and remembrance of the events of a struggle for regularization is something, which he believes, they might need 'any day', that even his son may require them in the future. Two sets of events from the same time period have been neatly organized into 'bekaar', useless truths, and crucially useful knowledge.

Other people in the locality refused to talk about Tahir, the brother of Mahir, and others in the family. A young man who pulls a rickshaw divulged to me the reason why everyone says they do not know anything: 'He is a BC, why would anyone talk about him? Mahir, who died more than two decades back, was remembered as a "BC". He was referred to as "Tahir, the BC's brother".' When asked about Mahir's death, everyone emphasized more on his antecedents as a BC. One can trace the play of several factors here. The police terminology of 'BC' has been completely internalized by people who are from the same socio-economic category as Mahir and Tahir are. A BC, according to police definitions, is a person who is accused of being involved in three or more cases of criminal activity. A BC is not necessarily a convicted criminal, but could be merely an accused, a suspect. However, when

[18] Informers.

police talks of a BC they talk of one as a criminal, and the people follow suit. His neighbours would talk of him as a BC, that is, a criminal. Thus, accusing a person of a few offences and officially terming him a BC not only marks the person in the registers of police for the purposes of surveillance, but also marks the person in a social register where the person is alienated from his own society. The 'talk' of the state is incorporated into the popular 'talk' here.

Second, no one seemed to be concerned about the fact that a person's being a known 'bad character' or being involved in any crime does not legally entitle the police to kill him. Whereas the fear of people like Abdul bhai from the police was palpable and it is a strong possibility that fear of repercussions is one reason why people do not talk about a custodial death, it is also crucial to note that the narratives of criminality of the victim and his family are not withdrawn from the popular discourse. The narratives about the struggle of the people for regularization of the slum colony, and futility of lives like that of Mahir for the civic life of the locality immediately draws out lines separating the 'good'/contributive members of a community and 'degenerative' elements thereof. While they might not celebrate the death, they would let it pass as an inconsequential event for the community, which has many other things to take care of.

## The Present Requires that the Past is Forgotten

Kishen Singh was about 52 years old when he died in the premises of Shahdara police station, on the 17 March 2005. He was arrested the previous day on charges of having robbed a mini-truck. The accused policemen were arrested and were tried in court. In late 2005, there were reports in the media that the sons of the dead Kishen Singh, who were crucial witnesses in the case, turned hostile and thus all the accused policemen were acquitted by the court. Seven years later when I traced the address found from the FIR,[19] the sons of Kishen Singh were not living there. A close relative, a part of whose house they took on rent at that time, and who too was a crucial witness in the case, was present.

Balbir Singh lives in Sarai Basti in the Sarai Rohilla area of North Delhi. The neighbourhood is a recognized and authorized slum under

[19] Received through an RTI application (FIR 89/05).

the Slum department of the MCD. He is a property dealer in the slum. Kishen Sigh was Balbir Singh's *sadhu*, the husband of Balbir Singh's wife's elder sister.

Balbir Singh narrated the following story of Kishen Singh's death. Kishen Singh owned a mini-truck which he used to ply commercially from the Shahdara stand. On 15 March 2005, he had a drink with a fellow mini-truck driver and agreed to accompany him to Manesar to deliver goods. On the way, however, he felt like going back home, and thus asked the other driver to drop him at a place from where he took a bus home. The next morning he was sitting in his mini-truck at Shahdara stand reading a newspaper, when at about 8 o'clock, policemen from Shahdara thana came looking for him. He was not aware of the reason, and he took the papers of his vehicle along when he was taken to Shahdara thana. The sons of Kishen Singh and Balbir Singh went to the thana after they got the information of his arrest.

What happened the previous night after Kishen Singh took a bus home was thus: the driver of the mini-truck was heavily drunk and he left the truck on the road and came back home. When the owner of the truck asked where the vehicle was, he replied that it was taken away by "Dimple *ke* papa", that is, Kishen Singh. The owner lodged a complaint of robbery naming Kishen Singh as the accused.

The police arrested Kishen Singh in the morning. The IO had sent messages to all the police stations across Delhi seeking relevant information about the missing mini-truck. But as the IO had to go out on another case, Kishen Singh was kept detained in the thana.

In the meanwhile, the mini-truck was found by Karol Bagh police station abandoned on the road, at about 1.30 pm of that day (16 March). The drunken driver had left the vehicle in the middle of the road and had gone home. However, there was some deficient communication and the message did not reach Shahdara thana.

During this whole time Kishen Singh was detained in the thana. In the evening, an SI of the Shahdara thana, who is a relative of the owner of the truck, came to the police station, and said that if he had duty that day, then till that time the truck would have been recovered, indicating that Kishen Singh had been dealt with too softly. After this, Kishen Singh was taken to the yard of the police station, behind the SHO's room. This was the place where vehicles as well as other large things involved in cases are kept. In this open space, Kishen Singh was stripped naked, his hands and legs were tied, and then several policemen and a driver of the SHO started beating him. All this was happening before the eyes of Kishen Singh's sons and Balbir Singh. While the policemen were asking Kishen Singh where he had kept the vehicle, Kishen Singh was replying that when he did not know anything about the vehicle how could he answer, no matter how much they beat him up. Balbir Singh and the sons had been asking the police not to beat him up so harshly, as he was a senior person. However, the policemen were relentless. When the IO came and Balbir Singh asked him to inquire if the vehicle was found anywhere, he replied that he had sent wireless messages and had it been found, the message would have come. However, after sometime, the IO called up somebody and was told that the vehicle was found by Karol Bagh thana in an abandoned state.

After the news came, the family wanted to take Kishen Singh home. However, police asked them to leave him in the police station, citing reasons that he was badly injured, and that if women in the family saw him in such a state they would be frightened. They wanted to take care of his wounds and said that they would let him go the next morning. Balbir Singh and the sons brought some milk and bread for Kishen Singh, and then left. They thought that as the truck had been recovered, there should not be reasons to worry about more beatings, and thus they left the thana despite Kishen Singh's request to not leave him alone.

They were more concerned about the truck that was recovered. Balbir Singh did not have a very good image of police, and he had a suspicion that police might show the truck as recovered by them after confession by Kishen Singh. So he went to the place where the truck was found, and when police came, he showed them that the boot of the vehicle was locked and the goods were intact.

The next morning Balbir Singh did not accompany Kishen Singh's sons to the police station as he thought that only the formality of bringing him home was left. However, after a while he got a call from the son asking him to come to the Shahdara police station immediately saying that his father was very unwell. When Balbir Singh reached the thana, policemen told him that Kishen Singh was taken to the hospital. However, Balbir Singh did not believe them and went inside the thana. Once inside, he saw that Kishen Singh was lying under a small table.

When he made him sit and sprinkled water on him, Kishen Singh said, 'I've been beaten up a lot, you shouldn't have left me alone.' Then he took a sip of water, and passed out.

Balbir Singh ran out of the thana shouting '*mere aadmi ko maar dala*' (my man has been killed). Someone tried to stop him, but he was too frightened; he stopped only once he reached the main road.

Later, media covered the story. Relatives from their village came to condole with the family. There were a lot of people. The local thana of Sarai Rohilla deployed police in the area to ensure that no one protested or sat in dharna. Balbir Singh was associated with the Congress Party as a worker. However, his links did not yield much. According to him, the leaders talked to the Commissioner, etc., but at that time Congress Party was unable to do anything, because, 'It was a Congress government, how will they talk against themselves? The government cannot displease the police.' Rather, BJP leader Madanlal Khurana found it an issue and organized a meeting in the park in front of their house.

Despite all the media attention and the political involvement, however, the family could not go far with the case. They filed a complaint about the custodial death of Kishen Singh, but later backed out of it. They were frightened. They did not receive any summons from the court as the court's peon was stopped on the road by police. When they reached court on a few occasions, they were threatened with pistols by policemen in civilian dress inside the court. Police said, Balbir Singh reported, 'If the case continues it wouldn't affect us, but it would affect you. So you decide whether you want to go on with it.' The case was being heard in Karkarduma court, not in Tis Hazari court, where the family would have been more comfortable. They did not hire a lawyer, and had a lawyer given by government. He said: 'When we were not even allowed to come to the court, who would think of hiring a lawyer.' After some time they decided to give up. They said in the court that they did not recognize anyone. Therefore, the case went in favour of the police: all the policemen who were arrested were acquitted on 5 October 2005, by the court of ASJ Shri Chandar Singh.

The post-mortem report of the body, accessed through an application under the provisions of the Right to Information Act, 2005 listed 21 external injuries to the body, all of which were ante mortem. The opinion of the doctors at Aruna Asaf Ali Government Hospital conducting the post-mortem stated:

- Cause of death is shock due to haemorrhage occurring as a result of cumulative effect of injuries on the body, caused by repeated assault by hard blunt object directed upon the body by other party and is consistent with beating.
- All injuries are ante mortem in nature and fresh in origin.
- Cumulative effect of all injuries are sufficient to cause death in ordinary course of nature.[20]

It appears that the family had a strong case in the form of a supportive post-mortem report, but they never had access to it to know of the strength of their case.

The sons of Kishen Singh refused to meet and talk about the incident. One of them said in a telephonic conversation: 'Whatever happened had already happened; now we don't want to remember it again.' Balbir Singh said that though they could not win the case, the fact that the accused policemen stayed in jail for six months was a big lesson for them, because: '... the one who keeps others inside, how difficult it would be for that person to be inside himself'.

During that time, the neighbours of the family stood in support with them, and protested. The relatives from their ancestral village also came to sympathize. However, things have now come back to 'normal'. Kishen Singh's sons have shifted to Uttam Nagar where they have bought their own house. Balbir Singh continues to work in close collaboration with the police in Sarai Rohilla, something that he has been doing since 1972.

He is a member of the police committee also known as the Resident Welfare Association (RWA).[21] In the RWA meetings, however, nobody can talk of the misbehaviour of the police, but complain about minor things, like traffic congestion in the roads, absence of patrolling in the locality, etc. The beat policemen ask the local people not to complain, because they do not want complaints to go up. They say: 'If there is a problem then tell us, don't speak in the meetings.' The police of Sarai

[20] FIR 89/05.

[21] Both the terms were used by Balbir Singh interchangeably, and when asked he said that RWAs and police committees are the same entity.

Rohilla, however, do not trouble his family. He is known to police and they maintain a good relationship.

Balbir Singh, the only person who agreed to even speak of the incident looks at it as a problem of a few erring and corrupt policemen. He stated that the SHO was not guilty, as he was not present when the episode of beating up Kishen Singh took place, and hence was wrongly implicated: 'He was not even present in the police station during that time.'

He also had a reasoning about sufficient punishment for policemen based on their way of life and profession. What was palpable, was the disinterest to get involved with the police in any manner challenging their authority. This however, did not mean complete detachment from the police. On everyday matters, they have to coordinate and engage with the police. However, this also happens only to the extent that the police explicitly or implicitly asks for and approves. The things that the beat policemen ask them not to raise in police RWA meetings are not raised.

The rule of law was not the framework of understanding authority for Balbir Singh. If the police 'who keeps others inside' is tried, then that itself is a big achievement in his understanding of authority. On the other hand, despite the fact that Kishan Singh was tortured in front of him, and died while in the police station in front of him, pursuing the case against the torturers responsible for the death was not their first priority, for understandable reasons.

The RWA meetings that the police portray as a way of socializing the force, or making common people feel active partners in policing, thus appear to be performances organized for creating an image for consumption, where the people would come up and speak what the state wants to hear. They would not speak the things unspeakable by the standards of the state, as it is the strongest body around. The life here is one of accommodation and adjustment. Balbir Singh still continues to work as a Congress worker. One's past is set aside, at most as an unfortunate memory, about which nothing could be done, and all attempts are directed towards living lives at the present safely, lives that are precarious every day. In a way, the death is not as important as the lives that are still going on. Such sentiments, interestingly, also have an official version, as articulated by a judicial magistrate inquiring into another case of police custodial death in the year 2010. The overburdened judiciary, he said, has '... more important cases which are to do with the living, then these which have to deal with the dead.'[22] The deaths of people like Kishen Singh end up being no more than a tragic family history, being looked at almost like a natural calamity.

## Violence and Ambivalent Acceptance

The attempt of this chapter has been to understand how the institution of police interacts with the people from the margins, and in what role the police is acceptable to them. If we reflect on the anecdotes and the narratives of this chapter, several insights come up.

At one level, these narratives persuade us to revisit a unified idea of the state and a binarization of acceptance or rejection of it. The fact that the people often want the police to intervene in cases of petty quarrels or domestic violence, but do not want to enter into the legal procedures, shows that the institutions of the state are seen as capable of acting independently.

Further, the institution of the police, which occupy a central space in the life-worlds of people from the margins, does not receive a univocal acceptance or rejection from them. While some aspects of the institution are found to be useful to fulfil their own purposes, most often the same institution is target of widespread criticism due to its alleged partisan and corrupt nature. However, interestingly, some of these perceived negative aspects themselves enable the popular classes to utilize the institution. This observation is linked to a second finding.

The practices of the subalterns, while creating spaces for themselves, also help in letting the state further reach the locales. When the state is accepted as a part of the familial and the social, its legitimation is not a question of presence or absence, but is a question of legitimacy on what grounds. The nature of the interaction between the people and state indicates to an observer the grounds of such legitimation. The narratives of this chapter show that the ambivalent and the fractured acceptance of the authority of the state are shaped centrally by a figure of violence which spins out resentment and acceptance depending on the varying contexts.

[22] Interviewed at Rohini court, November 2010, as a part of the PUDR fact-finding team on a case of police custodial death. PUDR came up with a report on this custodial death. See PUDR (2011).

The narratives of life after deaths in custody, as discussed in the second part of the chapter, on the other hand, point towards an acceptance with resignation in the face of an understanding that the violence of the state is inescapable. The continued participation in the activities of the state, whether in the form of cooperating with police committees, participating in party politics or demanding benefits from the government, indicates that deaths in custody, do not evoke feelings of resistance strong enough to sustain a disaffection of the state.

# PART TWO

# 5

# Of Blessings and Banes

## People, ULFA, and the State in Lakhipathar

We have referred to Das and Poole's (2004) assertion that margins are spaces that are not fully ordered by the state. One such margin that we have looked at was the places and lives of the urban poor in the city of Delhi. Another margin, to which we turn now, is defined by both its lack of 'order' and its precarious physical location at the edges of the proclaimed territory of the nation-state. Lakhipathar, located in the fringes of the territory of the Indian state, in the easternmost district of the north-eastern state of Assam, has been a site of contending claims of authority, over Lakhipathar and over Assam in general. Lakhipathar is this unruly margin, where extraordinary laws are the standard procedure in an attempt to bring in peace and 'order', and violence in the process is a daily routine.

During the late 1980s the rebel organization United Liberation Front of Assam (ULFA) had its biggest camp in Lakhipathar in the Tinsukia district, known as the Lakhipathar camp. The ULFA was one of the most potent armed revolutionary groups of northeast India during the peak of its popularity. It was a political and social movement, an armed force, and an authority—all at the same time—having its influence in a major part of at least northern and eastern Assam. Nani Gopal Mahanta, a leading scholar studying the movement, has commented that ULFA vocalized 'a suppressed voice which is deeply engrained in Assam's psyche', it represented 'the unmet aspirations of the innumerable tribal and ethnic groups of Assam' (Mahanta 2013: xvi).

Having maintained its independent status much beyond the rest of colonial India and coming under British rule only in 1826, the undivided colonial Assam joined the Indian movement for independence and subsequently joined the Indian union in 1947. The early enthusiasm and allegiance of the freedom struggle era, however, waned gradually. The consciousness of an Assamese identity—which had its historical roots in British policies of bringing in educated Hindu Bengalis for jobs, and of settling Muslim Bengali farmers to increase production of food grains—reached its culmination in the form of an anti-foreigners movement in the 1970s, popularly known as the Assam movement. The ULFA movement could be seen as a radical faction of this movement, which wanted to break away from the upper caste Hindu Assamese leadership of the movement, emphasizing the 'colonial rule' of Indian state over the indigenous population of Assam (Talukdar and Kalita 2011: 29). The high point of the ULFA movement was during the late 1980s and the 1990s when it was relatively new, and with large numbers of cadres.

The Lakhipathar camp, it has been reported, was equipped with all amenities, such as a lecture theatre for training purposes reportedly with a seating capacity for 250 people (*Hindustan Times*, 14 December 1990: 7), a library and a six-bedded fully functional hospital, with the total capacity of the residential camps being 700 people (*Dainik Asam*, 4 December 1990: 1). The camp was, however, evicted after found abandoned, during an Indian army operation in the year 1991.

In this chapter, I discuss the socio-cultural background of the ULFA camp in Lakhipathar and go on to discuss through media reportage, the first moment of conflict between the state and ULFA in Lakhipathar. The discussion of the socio-cultural background draws on memory based oral narratives and personal observations in the field, archival sources, and literary works, apart from secondary literature. I also give a brief ethno-historical description of the various communities of people presently living in Lakhipathar. This part of the chapter is more in the nature of introducing the field site, before looking into state making and penetration practices of both ULFA and the Indian army in Lakhipathar, in the later chapters. The second part of the chapter in which I give a glimpse into the events of what is called the first 'war' of Lakhipathar through a reading of newspapers of that time, prepares the reader to delve into, comprehend, and place the oral narratives of the past experiences with violence and authority and their contemporary attitudes towards it.

## Choice of a Field Site and Lakhipathar

I went to Lakhipathar for the first time in the beginning of April 2012. The area is a reserved forest falling under the Lakhipathar range and the Upper Dihing division of the forestry department. Amid the thick forests, there are several villages which are also known as Lakhipathar collectively, though each village has its own name. Away from the settlements and deep inside the thick forest, the ULFA had its General Head Quarters (GHQ), roughly between 1988 and 1990. Towards the end of 1990, the central government, after declaring President's rule in the state under section 356 of the constitution, sent in the Indian army in an operation named Bajrang to tackle the growing activities of ULFA in Assam. Operation Bajrang had a concentrated focus in the Lakhipathar area due to its specific status as the site of the rebel army's headquarter. President's rule and the army operations first came between the end of November 1990 to June next year, and the presence of the army in Lakhipathar has continued since then.

In choosing Lakhipathar as a field site for my research, my major concern was whether Lakhipathar would be an appropriate field site to probe the question raised in this work. The attitude of the people of Lakhipathar towards the state—which violated them through its armed forces in the name of suppressing an armed movement that enjoyed popular support—should be predictable. Rodney Barker (1990) in his work two decades back has stated that states generate and retain legitimacy in the eyes of those who are not coerced, and its legitimacy is rejected by those who are coerced or threatened with coercion. However, field experiences in Delhi which revealed to me that those who suffer in the hands of the state are not always in a conflictual relation with it, meant that I needed to test this statement further for which I needed further field-based evidence. Lakhipathar then appeared to be the ideal place for my purpose: to investigate the effects of violence on the attitude of people towards the wielders of such violence. It appeared a valid exercise to examine the grounds of support that the rebel ULFA movement enjoyed, and to study how such a support base of ULFA responded when met with violence by the state over a period of time.

It also appeared to be a useful site, for the reason that it is very different from the sites of police violence in Delhi. In terms of structures of the institutions of violence, reasons of violence and form of violence, these two appear to be distinct. Such distincness of the sites, however, helps us to theorize, because despite such differences the two sites are bound by violence of an actor that represents political authority and which seek acceptance of itself and its political–institutional set-up. The actor that I refer to here is the claimant of political and territorial sovereignty, which is the state in most occasions, but also the ULFA as a proto-state in the pre-Operation Bajrang period in Lakhipathar.

Lakhipathar is an area of about 15 square kilometres including thick forests and villages—22 in total—within it. The area does not figure in any revenue map of the government. The forest department has a map of Lakhipathar reserve forest as part of the Upper Dihing division reserve forest, but the areas where people live in the forest, that is, the forest villages, are not marked on this map. The Google map search engine has only recently—and much after my stay—started showing 'Lakhipathar forest village', but not the individual villages.

Until the year 1971, Lakhipathar was a part of the undivided Lakhimpur district of Assam, and in 1971, after creation of Dibrugargh out of Lakhimpur district, it fell in the undivided Dibrugarh district, to be further shifted to Tinsukia, when the new district of Tinsukia was carved out of Dibrugarh in October 1989. The area is surrounded by oil towns of Digboi and Duliajan on two sides, and tea-garden strongholds of Makum and Tingrai on the other sides. To reach the villages in Lakhipathar, one can take a road that enters the forest from the east, coming from Digboi through Balijan *tiniali*,[1] and further passing through dense forests. Alternately, one can also move through a clearing between Mamoroni and Lakhipathar forest villages, and reach from Tingrai. On the road from Digboi, three privately owned minibuses, popularly known as 407,[2] ply, each three times a day. I was told that some ex-ULFA cadres, commonly known as SULFA (surrendered ULFA), also arranged for an Assam State Transport Corporation (ASTC) bus to ply from Lakhipathar to Dibrugarh for some time, but

[1] An intersection of three roads.

[2] These are Tata 407 model minibuses.

ASTC has now stopped the service due to the stated reason that they do not get enough passengers. The three minibuses, however, always run fully packed. People often travel on the top of the buses, though they get down and squeeze themselves into the bus once it enters the limits of Digboi town.

Digboi is an oil town. Oil was discovered here for the first time in India when some English officials traced oil in the footmarks of an elephant. The first commercial oil well of India was dug here in 1889 and the first refinery was started in 1901. The head quarter of the Assam Oil division of the Indian Oil Corporation (IOC) is located in Digboi. Many people from Digboi and its surrounding areas work in one or the other odd job with the IOC. To have a job with the IOC is considered to be very good fortune.

The logic of extraction of natural resources seems to have played a crucial role in the development of infrastructure in this region. It is one of the areas where railway tracks came very early. Tea leaves were collected from various parts of upper Assam, the plywood boxes to carry them were made in veneer mills in Margherita (16 kilometres from Digboi) extracting the deep forests of the region, coal is mined from Ledo (26 kilometres from Digboi) and oil is dug out from Digboi. Ironically, the railway tracks stop at Ledo even today. A non-passenger track runs until Tirap colliery—a little further east from Ledo—where train coaches are loaded with coal and are transported out.

The development of these industries and the railways perhaps had an effect on the demography of the area. Digboi town has a lot of residents who are not ethnic Assamese. People of Bengali and Marwari communities dominate business ventures. The centrally located residential areas, such as Borbeel, are inhabited mostly by Bengalis, while ethnic Assamese people living in the town are located in outlying areas of the town like Muliabari and Itabhata. There also are the residential colonies of the IOC, located next to Muliabari and the Central Military Hospital (CMH) area. The town also has an elite school of the Delhi Public School group, a rarity in a sub-divisional town like Digboi, where mostly the children of IOC employees go. All sorts of provisions starting from fish, meat, and vegetables to sweets and clothes are more expensive in Digboi in comparison to neighbouring towns.

It takes about an hour to reach Maaj Lakhipathar, that is, central Lakhipathar, from Digboi in one of the minibuses which run from the

Borbeel bus stand. Maaj Lakhipathar is the area where the only high school of Lakhipathar is situated, in close proximity to an Indian Army camp. The minibuses that ply from Digboi to Lakhipathar take one through the arterial road of Lakhipathar. While a few of the villages are by the road, to reach most of them, one needs to walk some distance after getting down from the bus. All the three minibuses were previously owned by surrendered ULFA cadres who bought these vehicles utilizing the rehabilitation package money that they received from the government after their surrender, and later sold off to local entrepreneurs who are their preset owners.

The bus journeys to and from Lakhipathar, as well as within Lakhipathar—where one can travel free of charge—have been very crucial for this work. My first meetings with several important informants were in the bus, and some very resourceful references came out in the casual discussions in a fully packed bus. The minibuses running through Lakhipathar's villages and forests and connecting it to the Digboi town, in fact, was a 'sphere' of debates and discussions. It may not fall into the strict category of the Habermasian 'public sphere' where 'learned' discussions on issues relating to public life take place. However, it definitely is a 'space' where the everyday men and women of Lakhipathar form their identities, opinions, and politics.

From Digboi towards Lakhiapthar, till Balijan, it is a regular pitched road out of a small town. Once the bus turns right at Balijan tiniali, however, the view begins to change. After moving past a few newly built *pucca* houses dotting the roadside together with older thatched huts, come expanses of fallow land covered with small shrubs. After a while, the land gives way to a marsh, swelled from heavy rains in summer, covered with water shrubs. Passing through these swamps, the road then goes across a small rivulet, the Digboi *nodi*. There is a wooden bridge which is functional, and another half constructed, but appears to have been left in that state for a long time.

The forest begins about a minute after crossing the rivulet, starting with waist-high shrubs at the roadside but thick growth further inside. After a while, a thick jungle on both sides begins. Creepers lie hanging from the trees. Vision is limited to a couple of feet through the dense and dark forest. The greyish, broken—and thus bumpy—gravel road is narrow and its sides are covered with felled leaves. Narrow tracks opening into the road from inside the woods could be seen if one looked carefully, which, however, one can follow with the eye only for about a metre. Tracks probably used by animals; elephants? I heard a lot of stories about trouble created by wild elephants during the time of the year when paddy is grown and about to be harvested. The tracks once used by the ULFA cadres were probably similar, my imagination says. I try to imagine how this forest hosted the biggest camp of ULFA in Assam, and how it was surrounded by tens of thousands of Indian army jawans. The army could trace some of the jungle tracks used by the ULFA cadres, not all of them. Those which were not found were the ones through which the last ULFA cadres from the camp fled, I was told, after blowing off land mines and killing many army soldiers in booby traps.

The first bus stop of Lakhipathar is at the beginning of Laupoti village. The bus stop has a pucca shade, constructed by a family from Gondhia village further down, in memory of their mother, as the dedication written on top reads. Some faint red slogan writing in Assamese is visible through the repainted pillars and half-walls: the only word that is legible is *chatra* (student) implying that it is a slogan by any of the student bodies active in the area. It is impossible to read which chatra body: *xodou axom*, Sonowal kachari, moran, tai ahom, gorkha or *axom jatiyotabadi yuva chatra*.

Lakhipathar is known as one of the most 'dreaded' places in Assam. In my initial days, the people of Lakhipathar expressed their surprise in finding an outsider, that too a woman, in their villages by telling various stories and jokes that ran. One was that no one would pick up a fight with you in Digboi town if you tell them that you come from Lakhipathar. On the reverse, it is also said that no good people from outside would want to come to Lakhipathar unless it is extremely urgent. The stated reason for this is that 'everyone in Lakhipathar is ULFA'.[3]

Such dread of Lakhipathar is related to its history of the last 20 to 25 years: following the tales of gory killings in the ULFA camps and the

[3] A few people who specifically highlighted their surprise were Deepak Gogoi and Dimbeshwar Gogoi of Pandhowa village, and Durgeshwar Dutta of Kenduguri village. Some people, however, were also a little suspicious and tactfully inquired whether I had gone only for research, or had some other motives as well.

army operations thereafter. Lakhipathar existed, however, even before that, before the reach of the state, beyond the media glare, and even beyond the knowledge of most people in Assam. Lakhipathar is a group of settler villages, resulting from migrations mostly from the undivided Lakhimpur district in the 1940s and 1950s. Most of the migrations were preceded by various natural calamities and the loss of land and livelihood in their original habitats, which forced people to come to a forested area like Lakhipathar in search of cultivable land. A large chunk of people came after the great Assam earthquake and subsequent floods in 1950.

The story of how Lakhipathar forest came to be inhabited was told in Lakhipathar widely by the elders. All of those who came looking for land did not settle down in Lakhipathar immediately. The forays to Lakhipathar for cultivation began before the earthquake of 1950, in 1948–9, mainly in the form of camps in forest clearings during the farming season. These farmlands were known as *paam* and those who cultivated in these paams were called *pomua*. Gradually the pomua people started to move into Lakhipathar permanently with their families, as the earthquake and the floods left nothing for them to live on in their native places.

The forest was swarmed by wild elephants, but people chose the lesser evil between mad rivers and wild elephants. The saying goes: *hati potit bohiba, pani potit nobohiba* (trans. Settle on the path of the elephant, but not on the path of the river). People migrating from a particular place tended to settle down as neighbours, and villages were named after their original villages.

One of the stories that run in the villages is that of a sadhu named Janaki Ram Das who entered into the forests of Upper Dihing and lived there in a wooden hut, in the present day Rangsangi area of Lakhipathar. Sadhu Janaki Ram persuaded the people who came for *paam kheti* (cultivation of farmland at a distance from home, generally by clearing forested areas) to settle down in the area. While going around begging alms, he talked to people in nearby areas and spread word about the fertile land inside the forest. According to this story, Janaki baba did a puja with a ritual fire of *hom* with 108 coconuts, in the presence of those whom he convinced to settle in the area. He chanted that this place would be known as Lakhipathar, as goddess Lakhimi or Lakhmi resided here. According to another popular saying, the name Lakhipathar fell on the place because the produce of paddy was excellent both in terms of quality and quantity. The land which was lying fallow for hundreds of years was very fertile, and if a grain fell somewhere, paddy plants grew on their own without any effort. Therefore, people started calling it Lakhimi Pathar: the paddy field based by the goddess Lakhmi. With passing time, nobody knew when Lakhimi Pathar became Lakhipathar.[4]

Though families in most villages of Lakhipathar today have land for cultivation, they do not have ownership rights over such land. During the early days of settling down in Lakhipathar, the forestry department was evicting the pomua people of Lakhipathar as illegal encroachers to forest land. Archival records document the phase of migration and settlement in Lakhipathar after the floods of 1950 as one of conflict with the Forest Department. A letter dated 9 January 1953, from the then Deputy Commissioner of Lakhimpur district, M. Sultan, IAS, urges the Secretary to the Government of Assam, Revenue department, to take necessary action for settlement of land in this Forest Reserve to flood-affected people on an urgent basis, while noting the non-helpful attitude of the District Forest Officer. The Deputy Commissioner also sent trace maps of the area to be deforested for the purpose of settlement of people.

A response from the Secretary K.C. Baruah, IAS, dated 6 March 1953 asks the DC to ascertain whether the land with big trees will be fit for settling people, and takes a sympathetic note of the Forest Department's position on not agreeing to deforest the reserve. A noting in the file by the Secretary of Forest department dated 16 March 1953 is thus: 'The forest cannot be de-reserved further, has already passed order I think in some other file. Revenue has also informed DC that these forests will not be available' (File No. AFR 119/53).

The people, however, took a representation to Shillong, the then capital of Assam, to meet the first Chief Minister Gopinath Bordoloi and the forestry minister Rupnath Brahma, and submitted a memorandum.

[4] The second version is widely told by people in Lakhipathar. The first version involving the Baba Janaki Nath Das was narrated to me by Mr Lalit Chandra Gogoi, retired headmaster of Lakhipathar ME School. This story is also narrated by Shivani Bailung (2005), a native of Lakhipathar, in a monthly magazine from Lakhipathar, which came out only for two issues, in the year 2005.

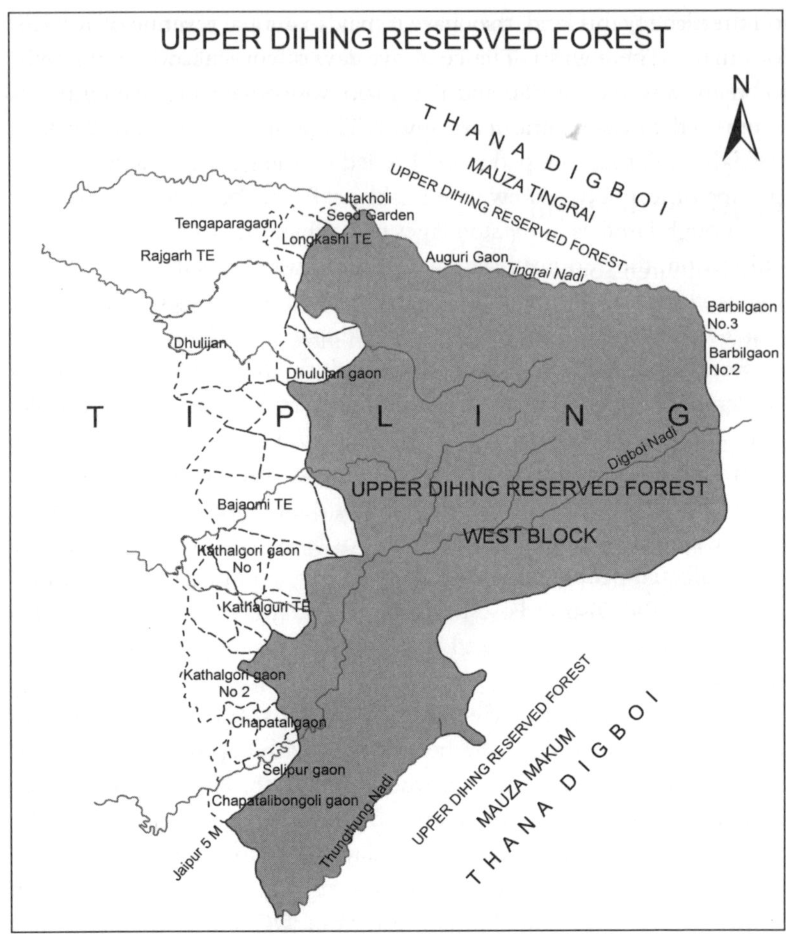


**Map 5.1** Upper Dihing Reserved Forest
*Source*: Assam State Archives; File No. AFR 119/53
*Note*: Map not to scale.

As an outcome, the forest department allotted 10 *bighas*[5] of farm land and 5 bighas of homestead land to each family. This land was given only for the purposes of living and cultivation and the people were given no proprietorship rights over it. They cannot sell it, mortgage it, or lease

[5] By measurements followed in Assam, one bigha of land is equivalent to 0.33 acre or 0.13 hectare.

it. In return for this land, they have to pay an annual revenue of Rupees four to ten. There was a practice of five days of corvée labour per family to be given to the forest department too, which has not been enforced in practice for last several years now.

## Arrival in the Field

I reached Biren Sonowal's house in Laupoti village for the first time on a rainy April morning. Biren Sonowal was the only person who spoke to me. The conversation started with an introduction of where I come from. He asked my surname and said, 'So you are a Kalita'. I corrected him saying I was actually a Koch.[6] He replied that in Lakhipathar people from the Koch community think of themselves as Kalita only.

There was a clearly visible feeling of unease on both sides. I tried to gear the discussion generally around the situation in Lakhipathar. I told Biren Sonowal that I wanted to study the events of the army operations, but he spoke more about wild elephants. After quite some time, a girl in salwar kurta came with tea and Good Day biscuits on a plate. Biren Sonowal introduced her as his elder brother's daughter, Dolly, and that families of both the brothers live together. To initiate a conversation, I looked at Dolly and said, 'So I'll come and bother you.' Dolly just smiled and went inside.

Everyone did not seem really very excited about having me. Therefore, I asked Biren Sonowal, that though I had thought of staying there, I would like to know what they thought about it. 'We have an extra bed, you can stay,' he said, 'but don't know how you will adjust … we eat only cabbage and eggplant, and our house is, as you see, not so good.' Though I assured him that these were not issues of any concern, it was a strange feeling, of imposing oneself as a guest on somebody.

I wanted to go around the house. Sonowal took us to the backyard, and showed the tubewell. There were a few pigs lying on the slushy mud in a corner of the backyard. There were thorny palm bushes by

[6] While the Kalita caste is considered as an unreserved category for the purposes of jobs and education, the Koch community is enumerated in the official list of Other Backward Classes (OBC).

the boundary fence. The thorny bushes prevent elephants from coming into the compound, Sonowal explained. After some time, when it seemed that there was nothing else to talk about, I fixed Sunday 8 April as the date when I would come and stay, and then we left.

My return to Lakhipathar after this first visit was a bit hesitant. The entry from my diary a day before I moved in with the Sonowal family reads thus:

> Saturday, 7th April, 2012:
>
> ... The endless forest on the way without any human visible, and then in the village the stories of elephants killing families, the muddy backyard of the house with pigs, the pungent smell of *laupani* cakes[7]—I am not so sure I really want to go back and live there. Even my phone was not receiving signals.
>
> ...
>
> 7th is ULFA foundation day. There may be troubles in the area.

The next morning I decided to go anyhow. It was drizzling that day too. When I reached Biren dai's house at Laupoti, by that time they had already had lunch, and had visitors: his younger brother's family who works in the IOC and lives in Digboi. I was introduced to the guests and I felt much more comfortable than the first day. In the evening when the guests were gone, I sat with Dolly, Kopou aai/khuri (Biren dai's wife), and Borma (Dolly's mother). Though Kopou aai started with, 'We are embarrassed to talk' and Dolly with 'We don't know how to tell the stories', gradually they started talking. In the evening, there were a few more guests: the colleagues of Bou (Dolly's elder brother's wife) in the Anganbadi centre who are on pulse polio duty.[8] I chatted with everyone, and by evening, I was taken by Dolly and one of Bou's colleagues to the next village, Dhonda Nahor, to talk to a retired teacher from a Lower Primary school.

That evening I was given pork curry and rice for dinner, though earlier in the day I was asked about pork and I had told them that pork is not something I usually eat. I felt as if they were testing me, but had it

[7] Small round balls prepared from a mixture of rice and herbs which is used as a base for preparing rice beer.

[8] Pulse polio is an immunization programme of Government of India. Children under the age of five are vaccinated against the polio virus under this scheme free of charge.

without asking anything. The nights are longer in Lakhipathar. It was still cold in April. The dinner was served at 6.30 in the evening, and by the time everyone in the family of 11 members ate in two batches, it was past 8 pm. It was time to sleep. I had a bed in the room where Dolly slept with her niece. Before we went to sleep, two of us had a hearty chat. The next morning was very different. I was no more feeling like a stranger.

## People and Society of Lakhipathar

Two decades back, parts of the road that splits to the right from Balijan tiniali (an intersection of three roads) towards Lakhipathar forest, did not get sunlight even during the day hours. The branches of huge trees—coming from both sides and joined in the middle—covered the road like a sheet. There was just one bus service which used to go out from the arterial road of Lakhipathar in the morning and come back in the afternoon from Digboi.[9]

Things have changed a lot now. The forest has thinned; it has been denuded over the years by whoever is mighty. People talked about a thriving ULFA-supported timber business at one point of time, which ran quite openly. In more recent years, it is mostly the army who is denuding the forest. In the last eight–ten years, I was told, the army had felled one tree every other day. They use it as firewood and also to make furniture for the camp. The tall Hollong[10] trees are chosen, as having a high oil content they catch fire easily.

Despite being communities living inside forests, the Forest Rights Act of 2006,[11] has not substantially affected or benefitted the people of

[9] Based on descriptions heard from various people and on a novel with the background of Lakhipathar of late 1980s authored by Dr Mrinal Kumar Gogoi (2004), a native of Lakhipathar and now a lecturer in Digboi College.

[10] Hollong is the state tree of Assam and Arunachal Pradesh. It is a tropical medium hardwood tree that grows to about 45 metres of height. The botanical name is: *Dipterocarpus macrocarpus Vesque*. In the year 2009, the Moran community, mostly living in the Tinisukia and Dibrugarh districts of Assam, declared the Hollong as their traditional tree and had raised their voice for its conservation. See *The Telegraph* 2009.

[11] The Scheduled Tribes and other Traditional Forest Dwellers (Recognition of Forest Rights) Act, 2006.

Lakhipathar. The Act provides that if a family belongs to a Scheduled Tribe and have been living in the forest land since December 2005, then it would get a patta, the document certifying entitlement to land. For other forest dwellers, the requirement to qualify for a patta is either 75 years or three generations of inhabitance. There are about six villages of Lakhipathar which are inhabited mainly by tribal people. In one of those six, land of a few families have been surveyed. They are hoping to get a permanent patta. But most other people in Lakhipathar, who are non-tribal, do not even qualify for a patta. Having migrated to the area in and around late 1940s and 1950, they have missed the 75 years mark by a few years. Interestingly, though the people are disgruntled about this matter, their worry is not that they would be evicted. Rather they are upset that while there was 'no such difference amongst the people', the government was making such unnecessary divisions based on caste and community. The most prominent reason cited for the need of a patta, again, is not about securing their land, but that it would enable them to take loans from banks, or would stand as a surety if they needed to bail someone out from jail. A popular young man who is one of the very few CPI (M) workers/organizers in the area was the only one to voice concerns of independence, that now they are living at the mercy of the forest department: the forest department dictates at every step. Getting a permanent patta would liberate people from that drudgery.

In earlier times, cultivation alone was sufficient for livelihood in Lakhipathar. The quality of the produce was excellent due to the fertile land. The sweet and greasy Lakhipathar rice was in high demand in the market in Digboi. These days Lakhipathar rice does not sell much. The market for good quality rice is captured by basmati brought in from outside. So, except for those who are left with small holdings due to partition among brothers, there are many families who can manage with a year's produce of rice for next three years. During my fieldwork in the rainy months of April, May, and June, when the process of cultivation begins, I heard families discussing whether to cultivate or not.

There are others who do not have that kind of land and need to look for sources of income elsewhere. Even those who have land need to look for other work, as the needs are many. Contractual engagements with the oil company are generally looked for. A permanent job in the Indian Oil Corporation (IOC), like that of a watchman, security guard or a driver, is considered to be a very good catch.

Some families have started small businesses—like grocery shops, or poultry farms and piggeries. A lot of people also prepare liquor-making cakes at home and sell those in the Tingrai market. In recent years, men from some families have joined the Indian state's armed forces. Many youngsters of the present generation are going to Digboi for further studies after completing 10th from Lakhipathar high school. The people from an earlier generation, who are parents of young kids now, regret that they could not finish their education because of the conflicts in Lakhipathar.

According to data provided by one of the three village headmen of Lakhipathar, Mr Chandrakanta Koch, the number of voters from Lakhipathar panchayat area for the 2007 panchayat elections was 5,024. This number, however, includes 1,044 voters of the two revenue villages of Mamoroni area, which are clubbed with the forest villages of Lakhipathar to make it an area for panchayati raj governance. There is one high school, three Middle English schools, and 11 primary schools, one of which is managed by the forest department. The 22 forest villages are home to people from six communities, with several sects/religious diversification within them. These are: Kachari (Sonowal and Mech), Ahom, Moran, Koch, Nepali (Brahmins, Chetri, Bhujel, Limbu, Gurung, Tamang, etc.), and tea-garden tribes (Hindu and Christian).[12]

The Ahoms are probably the largest population group in Lakhipathar. Seven out of the 22 villages of Lakhipathar are Ahom villages, which are also comparatively larger in terms of population than other villages in the area. Six villages are populated by people from the Kachari community, two by Morans, one by Koch, three by Nepali, and three by people from tea garden tribes. While the first four communities have a history spanning back to several centuries in these lands, people from the Nepali and the tea-garden tribal communities form a group of relatively recent migrants. While the origin of the Nepalis could be traced to the Himalayan country of Nepal, the tea-garden communities of tribal ethnic root were brought during the British colonial rule as tea

[12] Apart from these there were a few Bodo families in one village, one Bengali family and one Hindi mother-tongue family, and they are not enough in number to form a community of their own.

plantation labourers, mostly from the hilly areas of the central Indian region. These two communities are socially and culturally quite distinct from rest of the communities in Lakhipathar, and from each other. Nepalis are Vedic Hindus with practices of idol worship of various gods and goddesses, and people from the tea garden community follow Hinduism or Christianity—either Catholic or the Protestant GEL Church.[13] The other four communities of Lakhipathar, on the other hand, follow various sects of Vaishnavism.

Settlers coming from the north, the Ahoms are traced variously to a Tai or Shan tribe of Myanmar or a tribe from a Tai state of south-western Yunnan county of present-day Guagdong province in China (Barpujari 2007: 49–50; Gait 1926 (1981): 76–8). Their entry point to present-day Assam was at the valley of the Brahmaputra River near Tipam, a place that still holds this name, near Naharkatiya town of Dibrugarh district. The Ahom royals established their kingdom at Charaideo in Sivasagar district (Barpujari 2007: 53). The chronicles or *buranjis* which act as sources for modern historiographers of the Ahom community are accounts of establishment and expansion of the Ahom empire, which was known as Axom. The Ahoms ruled a large part of present-day Assam for 600 years starting from 1228 until 1826, when the British rulers of India had to be called in to fight an invasion from Myanmar and the treaty of Yandaboo was signed. The Ahoms established their empire not simply by invading but by mingling with the local population, and had followed Shaivism and Vaishnavism at various points of time. The Ahom people of Lakhipathar are descendents of the subjects of the old Ahom empire and could be traced to various parts of Tinsukia district in present-day Assam.

The Kacharis and Morans are two of the earliest aboriginal tribes along with the Barahis that the Ahoms met when they entered into the Brahmaputra valley in the thirteenth century. Both these groups are a few of the early inhabitants of Assam plains. The historiographical sources suggest that the Ahoms initially won over the Moran chiefs by tact and diplomacy of offering gifts, friendship, and goodwill, and engaged them as suppliers of various materials including elephants to the Ahom court (Barpujari 2007: 53, 60). The Kacharis on the other hand, were avoided by the first Ahom ruler Sukapha, due to their large

[13] Gossner Evangelical Lutheran Church in Chotanagpur and Assam.

concentration in parts that he came across on his way to Charaideo (Barpujari 2007: 56).

While there is no clarity regarding the origin or early history of the Kacharis, it is suggested that they belong to the great Bodo race. Some sources suggest that the Kacharis are originally from the south-west parts of China, migrating to the Brahamaputra and the Barak valleys through Myanmar, Tibet, Bhutan, and Nepal (B.M. Das 2007). In the thirteenth century, the Kachari kingdom controlled a substantial tract along the south bank of the Brahmaputra. In later confrontations with the Ahoms, they lost their territories and after a period as a dependency of the Ahom Empire, retreated to the North Cachar Hills (Barpujari 2007: 56–8; Gait 1926 (1981): 248–9).

Originally, non-Hindu animists, the Kacharis were influenced by the Vaishnavite wave of reformism brought to Assam by Sankardeva and Madhavdeva in the fifteenth and sixteenth centuries. The Sonowal Kacharis, a sect of Kacharis said to be associated with the profession of finding *son/xon* or gold in the Xuonxiri river, started to convert and accept the *ek xoron naam dharma*[14] from the seventeenth century onwards. Most Kachari people, however, still observe many of their tribal rituals, despite accepting the ek xoron naam dharma. The Kacharis of Lakhipathar are mostly Sonowals, living in five villages, with one village of Mech Kachari people.

The early history of the Morans too mostly remain undocumented, and for lack of sources, it is difficult to form an accurate account of Moran community's society, polity, and religion in its early days. The early habitat of this community is supposed to be the Doomduma–Kakopathar area in the present-day Tinisukia district, based on fossilized traces, and some state-like unions or chiefdoms are assumed. Despite the early subjection by the Ahoms, the community is known for their sense of an independent identity (Barpujari 2007: 60–1).

The Ahom rule introduced feudal land and agricultural relations in Assam, and under their stringent revenue policies life of the lower peasantries were getting very difficult. In such contexts, the Ahom monarchy faced several bouts of rebellions, often garbed as religious discontent. The widely known Moamoriah *bidroh* (rebellion) which saw three upheavals within a period of 37 years in the last days of the Ahom

[14] Literally, recourse under one god.

monarchy was one such prominent state-subversive instance, where the Moran people played a very crucial role. This 'bidroh' or rebellion was organized under the Mayamora *satra*[15] or the Moamoria satra which fell under the *kalaxanghati* order of Vaishnavism, most of its followers coming from tribal and so-called low-caste converts to Vaishnavism from upper Assam. Those who rose in rebellion against the Ahom monarchy under the Moamoria satra are known as Mataks—literally, those who are of one opinion. All Moran people were followers of the Mayamora guru Anirudhadev, and took active part in the rebellions, though people from other ethnic communities also became Mataks and participated. Though early historians like Edward Gait termed the rebellions of the Moamorias to be religious fanaticism or uprising against the royal family's intolerance, later historians like Amalendu Guha (1993) and Debabrat Das (1969) concur on the character of the Mayamoria bidroh as a class war.

In Lakhipathar, there are two villages of Moran people, most of whom migrated from nearby Moran-majority areas like Mamoroni and Makum.

Like the Kacharis and the Morans, the origin and ethnic character of the Koch people too are not decisively determined. Historians like Gait (1926 [1981]) and Barpujari (2007) argue that Koches are a Mongoloid race with very close ties with the Meches and Garos and Dravidians. The Koch royal power was founded by Visva Simha (1515–40), and during the reign of king Naranarayana and military general Chilarai, both

[15] Satras are institutional centres of the Ekasarana naam dharma tradition. Numbering in hundreds, these centres are generally independent of each other and under the control of individual *adhikaras* (or *satradhikars*), though they can be grouped into four different *Sanghatis* (orders). These centres, in the minimum, maintain a prayer house (Namghar), initiate lay people into the Ekasarana tradition and include them as disciples of the Satra from whom taxes and other religious duties are extracted. The mushrooming of Satras in the seventeenth century and patronage extended to them by first the Koch kingdom and later the Ahom kingdom was crucial in the spread the Ekasarana religion. Many of the larger Satras house hundreds of celibate and non-celibate *bhakats* (monks), hold vast lands and are repositories of religious and cultural relics and artefacts. The Satras extend control over their lay disciples via village Namghars.

sons of Visva Simha, reached its pinnacle, and controlled vast tracts of present day western Assam and West Bengal. They had several confrontations with the Ahoms, both sides winning occasionally. However, with the defeat of the Koch king in the hands of the Padshah of Gaur (Sultan of Bengal), and death of Chilarai, the expansionist moves of Koches came to a close (Gait 1926 (1981): 48–58). Naranarayan was a religious man. He first patronized Shaivik sects of Hinduism, but later patronized the Vaishnavite reformist movement of Sankardeva (Gait 1926 (1981): 57–9).

The persistent wars between Koch and Ahom kingdoms led to some movement of populations. Artisans and craftsmen such as potters, goldsmiths, and blacksmiths from both sides were taken to the other side and were settled. The Ahoms also sent artisans to Koch Behar to learn the art of making earthen images of Durga and other deities (Barpujari 2007: 82–3).

The name Koch, however, became a bit ambiguous in later periods. While the Koches are known for their early adoption of Hinduism, in eastern Assam, it became the name of a Hindu caste, taking converts from other tribes such as Kachari, Lalung, and Mikir, etc. In North Bengal and Goalpara, the nomenclature of Koch had largely been abandoned in favour of a more vaunted appellation of Rajbanshis (Barpujari 2007: 69–70; Gait 1926 [1981]: 46).

Though, within the caste hierarchy of Assam the Koches are kept at the lower rung, in Lakhipathar, they are not seen as low caste. The Lakhipathar Koches follow a sect of Vaishnavism known as Srimanta Xankar Xangha, which prescribes a highly social form of worship, but which at the same time, is also highly restrictive and exclusive.

With the co-existence of all these communities, the society of Lakhipathar is ethnically heterogeneous. Though there is physical proximity, however, some amount of distance remains intact between the communities, as the villages are internally homogeneous in terms of community and distinct socio-cultural practices are maintained.

If we attempt to reflect on why the ULFA chose Lakhipathar for its biggest camp in the home territory, it appears that the community specification(s) of the people of Lakhipathar could not possibly be a crucial factor. People from diverse communities with a very short history of settlements does not possibly offer a community based support base, though one may argue that the diversity of Lakhipathar may have helped the organization to connect to various communities. However, a more probable reason appears to be the simple geographical factor of the impenetrability of the forests and the lack of reach of the Indian state.

The ULFA, however, within the span of a couple of years, left a very deep mark in the history of Lakhipathar. All subsequent events of Lakhipathar's history are, in one way or the other, related to ULFA's rule over Lakhipathar in the late 1980s.

Before going to the filed-narratives in the next chapter, in the following, an attempt is made to reconstruct the experiences Operation Bajrang in Lakhipathar through newspaper sources: the only available written source for the same.

## When Lakhipathar became *Juddhar Pathar*[16]: Media Coverage of Operation Bajrang

> Teacher: What is imported to Assam in large quantities?
> 5th standard student: Sir, CRP[17]
> - A joke published in the Assamese daily, *Dainik Asam*, on 2 May 1991.
> Collector: Shri Deepak Das

On the midnight of 27 November 1990, Assam was brought under President's Rule, and the whole state was declared a 'Disturbed Area' under the Armed Forces Special Powers Act (AFSPA). ULFA was declared a banned organization. The situation was tense, however, for some time preceding this. It was common knowledge that many parts of the state were not being 'governed' in practice by the Assam Gana Parishad (AGP) run state government. Stories of abductions and extortions by ULFA were making rounds everywhere in the state, and the talk of President's rule was going on for quite some time. The rumour was that the power equations at the central level were delaying things. The V.P. Singh government at the centre had the AGP as a coalition partner, and so it was difficult to dismiss the AGP government in the state and impose President's rule, as it would have destabilized the central

[16] Trans. War field.

[17] My translation from Assamese. The commonly used expression CRP, a shortened version of the abbreviation for Central Reserved Police Force (CRPF), in general parlance used to refer to all kinds of security forces beyond state police.

government. However, when V.P. Singh's government was ousted by the Chandrasekhar government, the possibilities for President's rule became real. The AGP government was about to complete its term and it was asking for elections. However, on the advice of the Governor of Assam Devi Das Thakur, the centre decided to impose President's rule, as the situation was said to be not conducive for free and fair elections (Talukdar and Kalita 2011).

In the morning of 28 November, the streets of Assam were swarmed by security forces personnel. According to the newspapers, around fifty four thousand jawans under the Indian army's fourth core penetrated into every corner of the state. The Janata Bhavan in Dispur, which houses the state secretariat, was locked down, and the streets of Guwahati city saw heavy movement of army vehicles. The countryside of Assam woke up to see army at their gates, their houses and their fields. Helicopters were hovering over villages, fields and forests. The Assamese daily *Dainik Asam* commented that it was already known that the centre was considering the option of President's Rule for Assam. The Prime Minister had a meeting with the Assam chief minister on 27 November itself, but in the meeting he was not given any idea about the impending President's Rule in less than a day. All these things and the manner in which President's rule was declared at midnight as if in a hurry, a newspaper commented, clearly portrayed the attitude of the centre towards Assam, and the status of the federal principles in practice (*Dainik Asam*, 29 November 1990: 1).

Around Lakhipathar, the troops started moving from the daytime of 27 November. The soldiers formed human rings attempting to block all passages into and from the forest. However, utmost care was taken to keep the plans and movement of the army undisclosed, with careful movement of trucks, to ensure that the ULFA cadres were not alerted. The villages of Lakhipathar were filled with soldiers speaking alien languages incomprehensible to the common villagers.[18]

[18] I was told by Biren Sonowal of Laupoti village and Deepak Gogoi of Pandhowa that the soldiers spoke Hindi with a south Indian accent which most people could not understand, and those who understood a bit, it was difficult even for them. In any case, those were days when the television had not reached the villages, and the radio broadcasted Assamese songs and news. Therefore, even a Hindi spoken with a standard diction perhaps would not have worked well.

The ULFA, however, proved to have had better intelligence than expected. When the army moved into the forests, they faced intermittent firing from light and sophisticated weapons as well as land mine explosions and booby traps. Finally when they reached the camps inside the forest, not a single cadre was found there. Some wooden guns suspected to be used for training purposes, huge amounts of food rations and some documents and books were found. After a few days, 15 decomposed bodies were found when land around the camps was dug up. It also appeared that ULFA had about seven different gender-differentiated camps with capacity of accommodating about 100 people in each, with a six-bed furnished hospital. In some of the camps the copies of an order issued by the Commander-in-Chief Paresh Baruah on 19 November, asking the cadres to leave the camps as soon as possible was found. It indicated that the plan of the army operation was leaked to the ULFA from some very high level, as it was kept a secret at the home ministry level (*Dainik Asam*, 4 December 1990: 1).

Apart from penetrating deep into the forests, the army also entered the villages. They searched for the missing cadres of the camp in the homes of Lakhipathar. The area was sealed and no one was allowed to go into or out of Lakhipathar, including media persons. The adviser to the government of Assam under President's rule P.P. Srivastava, in response to a question by journalists, said that Operation Bajrang was qualitatively different from earlier famous operations like Bluestar or Black Thunder and hence the media was not taken to those areas (*Dainik Asam*, 2 December 1990: 1).

In this scenario, the reports that the newspapers carried, about incidents of Lakhipathar, were based mostly on the army and the state briefings, and a few narratives here and there came from people who had fled from the villages and had taken shelter in the Digboi town. This was with the sole but crucial exception of the reporting of Dilip Chandan, a journalist working with the weekly newspaper *Sadin*, who slipped into the villages and reported from first hand observation, though his reporting was refuted as exaggeration by many.

The papers were, nonetheless filled with stories from all parts of the state, and even after strict control of the flow of information, killings of civilians and other atrocities by the armed forces were not unknown. Places like Lakhipathar for the first time became headlines in the local press, and had found place even in the national and international media.

In the period immediately preceding the 1990 operations and the President's rule, the ULFA enjoyed a relatively supportive press in Assam. Uddipan Dutta's work (2008) on the representation of the ULFA in the Assamese language media between 1985 and 1990 argues that such representations both reflected and shaped the perception of common people. In such a scenario, it is not surprising that when the President's Rule was declared and the Operation Bajrang started, many of the newspapers were critical of both, and scathingly reported the damages done by the army. Even those papers such as *Sutradhaar* and *Agradut*, and those intellectuals such as Homen Buragohain, Hiren Gohain, Kamala Saikia, and Kanaksen Deka, who advanced critical analysis of the working, organization and goals of the ULFA in the erstwhile period, commented negatively on the President's rule and the army atrocities. The media strongly condemned the imposition of President's rule as well as the Disturbed Areas Act which brought in the army under AFSPA, through editorials, and the mood was also reflected in the tone of news reporting. While the state newspapers continually covered stories of the army operation, casualties on both sides, the overall warlike situation, the fate of common people, and the comments of the leaders of various political parties and groups, in the national media the issue got prominence only for a few days.

During this phase, apart from the telling reportage and editorial pieces, however, the Assamese press—both English and Assamese language—also carried some brilliant cartoons, which captured the mood of the time. Cartoons generally being exalted representations of a popular mood, giving it an effect of irony and sharpness, are critical inputs to understand the politics of a certain time and space. On another front, the very *presence* and the *sharpness* of such cartoons in a specific temporal–political location signifies the level of political engagement of the people with a specific issue, the degrees of trust upon various political actors and the environment of outwardly expressing these attitudes. In the following, I attempt to narrate the happenings around this period through some of such cartoons published in the leading dailies.

While reports of torture, rape and other army atrocities upon civilians in the name of finding ULFA cadres were coming in, the leaders of the Congress party, who were in favour of the President's rule ending the run of the AGP government, and central government bodies dismissed such reporting as exaggeration. In the context of such blame

FIGURE 5.1 News versus rumours

*Source*: *Dainik Asam*, January 1, 1991, p. 1. The flying news says, 'rape and torture by army, people terrified by merciless beatings.' The government yielding a gun and with a suspected ULFA member pinned into it says, 'don't believe in those rumours.' The common man replies, 'in new year you should not either believe that all such allegations are rumours'. (a loose translation of the meaning by me).

games between political parties and leaders, however, there was no respite for the commoners. Young men were detained for 'interrogation', and tortured. Many people went missing and some others were reported to have died in the custody of the armed forces. Fact finding missions of people with varied loyalties had varied stories to tell. While Congress leaders including Hiteshwar Saikia downplayed the allegations, he also blamed the AGP government for making army operations inevitable. Some independent fact-finding groups also went to ascertain the reports of mass rapes and torture.

In such a situation, the comment of S.K. Sahai, the then minister of state for home affairs, that in the conditions of an anti-insurgency army operation, the cases of rape are not unusual, raised furore. Interestingly, no clarification about this comment was seen to have come from Mr Sahai in the newspapers (*Dainik Asam*, 6 March 1991, 16 March 1991).

FIGURE 5.2 ULFA by unlawful assembly
*Source*: *The Assam Tribune*, 14 December 1990, p. 1.

FIGURE 5.3 Suspect revolutionary
*Source*: *The Assam Tribune*, 6 January 1991.

People were brought in for interrogation and were arrested for the smallest of the suspicions. The terrifying scenario was captured well through satire in some cartoons that I found in the English news daily *The Assam Tribune*.

In the newspapers, there were reports from local correspondents as well as letters to the editor from common readers. There also were news of protest rallies, organized either by the All Assam Students Union (AASU), or those organized at local levels by groups and associations of women. Protest by women is seen and has proven to be an effective and visible form in the India's north-east over time.

In this context, the leader of a regional political party named the Purbanchalio Loka Parishad (PLP), Nibaron Borah, filed a writ petition in the Gauhati High Court describing the atrocities committed by the army and appealing for justice to the victims. He, personally arguing in

FIGURE 5.4 Terror of indigenous explosive device
*Source*: *The Assam Tribune*, 16 January 1991.

FIGURE 5.5 Business as usual
*Source*: *The Assam Tribune*, 20 February 1991, p. 1.

the court, portrayed the history and culture of Assam as different from that of mainland India, and appealed for the repeal of the AFSPA and the military rule. The proceedings of the Court were covered in the local dailies in great detail (for example, *Dainik Asam*, 17 December 1990: 1, 6).

While the army atrocities became well known, the court condemned some of its actions in its orders in specific cases. The army also presented a 'making up' face and held court martial of two soldiers who were then expelled from the army for charges of rape. These steps were welcomed, but suspicions never ceased (*Dainik Asam*, 6 March 1991; *The Assam Tribune*, 8 March 1991).

In the *Dainik Asam* of 7 January 1991, a letter from one Mr Nagen Saikia, an ex-air-force man, was published which clearly doubted the report of court martial of two army jawans for the crime of rape. He stated that as far as his knowledge of armed forces laws goes, the crimes of murder, attempt to murder and rape cannot be tried in a military court and have to be referred to a civil court. In such a situation, he raised doubts if the reports of punishment by a military court are just an eye-wash (*Dainik Asam*, 7 January 1991). Figure 5.5 tells a lot about such doubts.

Such suspicion and aversion was responded to by the state, both its armed and civil bodies under the President's rule, through publicity and other measures attempting to correct its public image. The government of Assam under the governor attempted to do it by influencing common people through messages printed in prominent spaces in the newspapers, and by promising more employment avenues. This was sharply commented upon by the media through cartoons like the one here (See Figure 5.6).

The military was also attempting to portray a face of 'social service' through programmes such as cleaning up government hospitals and washing hospital clothes and blood donation programmes. While these programmes of the army were commented upon, there also was reporting of people's rush to buy tax-free goods from the army canteens being opened to the public (*Dainik Asam*, 13 February 1991).

While the whole of Assam was burning, news was gradually seeping in from Lakhipathar too. Lakhipathar attracted great interest because it was reported to house the biggest cluster of camps of the mysterious organization, that is, the General Head Quarters of ULFA. The remote and unheard of villages of Lakhipathar suddenly became famous. The interest and curiosity about Lakhipathar was perhaps intensified by the nature of news that was coming by. The area, as mentioned above, was cordoned off for any non-military person for several days, and the news based on secondary sources had variations at best and contradictions in many cases.

While the news that Lakhipathar camp was being targeted was there in the news papers of 29 November, the actual coverage of the incidents taking place began to appear from 30 November onwards. The *Dainik Asam* of 30 November reported that in the refugee camps set up in Digboi town there are around 1200 people from Lakhipathar and nearby areas. It also reported that the sound of fierce gun-battle could be heard coming from the Lakhipathar forests, which is suspected to

FIGURE 5.6 Militancy and jobs
*Source*: *The Assam Tribune*, 2 January 1991, p. 1.

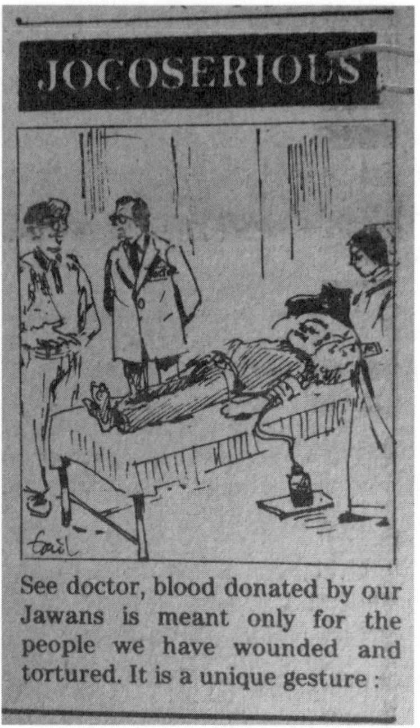


FIGURE 5.7 Gestures of goodwill
*Source*: *The Assam Tribune*, 25 February 1991, p. 1.

be surrounded by a joint force of Indian army and commandoes. The *Hindustan Times* reported on 30 November what Lt General S.K. Brar of the Indian army had divulged to them the previous day about the Lakhipathar area. He was reported to have said that the Lakhipathar camp, south of Digboi oil field of upper Assam, was situated in a thick jungle and that it was extremely difficult to approach the camp in the absence of firsthand knowledge about the terrain and logistics. The trouble was enhanced by explosive devices laid by the ULFA, including booby traps. He was also reported to have said that the people in the surrounding hamlets had been trained by ULFA to pass on advance signals about the movement of security forces. Further, he also mentioned about an instruction of the commander of the camp to the cadres, many copies of which were found in the abandoned campsite, to vacate it by 19 November (*Hindustan Times*, 30 November 1990: 1).

While the local papers put the number of people taking shelter in camps at 1,200, the national papers put it to be 700. It was also reported in the local press that the number of people taking shelter in the camps is only a fraction of the total number of people who had fled from their homes. In addition, it was reported in the local media that government relief to camps came in only on the third day. In the national newspapers however, it was reported that adequate relief was provided to such people. The issue of use of tanks and helicopters was another controversial one. The newspapers reported use of tanks as described by some people who had fled from these areas, some had seen movement of army tanks outside Lakhipathar, and a reporter of the Assamese weekly *Sadin*, who sneaked into Lakhipathar, even sent back photographs of tanks in the

**Figure 5.8** War tourism
*Source*: *The Assam Tribune*, 18 December 1990, p. 1.

**Figure 5.9** Anti-insurgency strategizing
*Source*: *The Assam Tribune*, 5 January 1991, p. 1.

paddy fields of Lakhipathar. The army however denied use of tanks by holding a press meet in Guwahati. While most papers reported the army as saying that helicopters were used for surveillance purposes, *The Hindu* of 3 December 1990 reported that helicopter gunships had been used during the action launched by security forces. Some reports said that tanks were actually used in Nambor reserved forest near Nagaland border. Overall, the pictures depicted by the news reports were confusing, and often contradictory. It was also reported in many newspapers that the civil and military authorities worked almost on counter-purposes during the initial days of the operation, as the army was not taking anyone into confidence. *The Hindu* of 3 December 1990 reported that the national media had suffered because of that, as international media like the journalists of the *Time* magazine of America were flown into Operation Bajrang areas like Lakhipathar, while the national media was not allowed access.

Dilip Chandan, the young reporter from the news weekly *Sadin* who slipped into Lakhipathar jumping a strict cordon, was reporting from inside that young men from villages of Lakhipathar like Kenduguri, Borjan, Dhadum, Bhekula, Rangsangia, Laupoti, etc., have all fled. The army jawans were moving with an air of war-like urgency, detaining people on slightest of suspicion (*Sadin*, 7 December 1990: 1).

Chandan also reported the visit of the Congress (I) president of Assam, Mr Hiteshwar Saikia, to the relief camp in the Central School of Digboi on 3 December, which created a controversy later. It was reported that when Hiteshwar Saikia faced the people at the relief camp, a young woman named Sewali Neog studying in Class 11, asked him to remove the army telling how much they had to suffer while fleeing through the jungles at night. She said that she had lost all her educational certificates. She also asked him to deploy Assam Police instead of the army and that they are not afraid of the Assam Police. Hiteshwar Saikia reportedly replied to her, asking why they hosted the ULFA in their villages, and that all these would not have happened had they not sheltered the ULFA. After this, Anowara Taimur, a woman leader of the Congress (I) tried to console Sewali by caressing on her face. Sewali retorted by saying, '... first you open army in our villages and then you are trying to show that you care!'[19] Visibly uncomfortable, when the Congress (I) leaders tried to leave the camp, people, old

[19] My translation from Assamese.

and young, men and women, gathered behind them shouting slogans that President's rule should be revoked and military atrocities should be stopped (*Sadin*, 7 December 1990: 1, 14). Later in a press meet, the Congress leaders accused the journalist Dilip Chandan of exaggerating facts while narrating their visit to the camp, and said that nothing of such nature happened. Chandan however protested by reiterating the veracity of his narrative (Reported in *Sadin*, 14 December 1990: 1, 4).

It was reported that in and around Lakhipathar, around 18,000 army jawans of the mountain division under the 4th corps of Indian army had been deployed. The scene inside Lakhipathar as depicted by Chandan gives us a picture no less than that of a war zone: alert soldiers lying on the ground behind embankments, some others busy communicating through their wireless sets, trucks carrying soldiers, and armoured tanks. There were some huge craters on the road just before entering Laupoti village: reportedly, results of dynamites planted by ULFA to resist army operations. Villagers were quoted as saying that four trucks carrying Indian army jawans sprung to the height of 10–12 feet into the air in the impact of the landmines. People were also quoted saying that tanks ran over paddy fields of Kopohua village, and that people from the village had fled through jungles. Mukheshwar Sonowal of Laupoti had a bullet in his thigh. A boy from Pandhowa, Phanindra Gogoi, said that his mother was slapped by the army jawans and a pair of earrings and two finger rings were taken away. 'Is someone raped?'[20] asked Chandan. Most people fell silent; somebody said, 'See, which Assamese girl will publicize that she has been raped? But definitely there have been torture.' It was reported that the atrocities on women were maximum in Laupoti and Dhunda Nahor villages (*Sadin*, 7 December 1990: 1, 4).

*Sadin* was the only paper which could give such a vivid description of the lives of the people of Lakhipathar during those days. However, the authorities came upon heavily on the media house. The office of the newspaper was raided and the issues between January 1991 and December 1992 were seized.[21]

[20] Quotations in this section are translated by me from the news report originally published in Assamese.

[21] These issues are now not available with the media house, and could not be found in any other library in Guwahati.

## The Unending War?

Lakhipathar saw violence even before Operation Bajrang. The memories of being uprooted, the fear of eviction, of elephants, and of 'aliens' during the Assam movement, were all violence of different sorts and degrees in their life-worlds. The Operation, however, seemed to have marked a break—a break from all earlier experiences of violence—this was a violence to the degree of a 'war'. There were two clearly marked parties involved, and the third group of people whose loyalty was sought and divided between both the warring groups.

This war ended for most people in Assam after the gunfights were over, and the ULFA camps of Lakhipathar were captured by the Indian army. Some others thought the war to be on till the time the President's rule was intact. The people of Lakhipathar too refer to this first moment only, as the 'war'.

However, one is curious; did the 'war' really get over?

# ULFA in Lakhipathar

## Perspectives and Perceptions

From here, I see only one side of the tree,
Don't know
Which flower blooms on the other …
Heard, that the clouds dance with their wings in the spring
The river flows with passion,
Taking the coo of the cuckoo
Crossing the reeds
And riding the wind,
Butterflies emboss every flower.
Here, now
In the spring of night the drum weeps and yells
The evening moos
For the morning
The poisoned river brings dead fish
The taste of freedom in the *khorika*.[1]
…
From here, I see only one side of the tree,
Don't know
Which flower blooms on the other …

—Jehirul Hussain[2](n.d.)

[1] Khorika means a very thin stick usually pinned to a fish to roast it or to pick it up.

[2] Jehirul Hussain was a progressive Assamese writer and poet. Translation mine.

In this chapter, my attempt is to mark out different perspectives from which ULFA was looked at and understood in and around Lakhipathar, and to analyse the implications this divergence in perspectives has for the emergence and strength of an alternative source of authority. More generally, the attempt is, to inquire into the question of how authority structures are generated and belief systems are evolved, through a study of ULFA–people interactions in Lakhipathar, and to study how various sections of people in the area relate to this holder of power and physical violence. Apart from existing scholarly works that I rely on, the primary material that I work with in this chapter is mostly drawn from the field, complemented by a few interviews with movement leaders. The chapter enables us to understand the specific legitimate space of authority that the ULFA had occupied in Lakhipathar in the pre-operation Bajrang years, despite the fact that all its policies, practices, and mannerisms were not liked by large sections of people in Lakhipathar. This observation parallels with an observation of people's relations with the army in Lakhipathar that I discuss in Chapter 8, and forms the ground work for the larger argument that I offer, about acceptance of power structures and wielders of violence, however fractured that may be, despite experiences of suffering in its hand.

*Those days we used to feel that we have already got independence.*

That is the most common response from anyone who lived in Lakhipathar during the late 80s, when asked how it felt during that time. The independence here did not mean the independence that India won from the British. Until that time, the only permanent sign of the independent Indian state inside Lakhipathar was the Lakhipathar range office of the forest department. Apart from that, they knew the state through the police actions during the Assam movement between 1979 and 1985. Therefore, the independence they referred to was the independence of Assam, experienced through having a structured set-up of governance provided by the ULFA. The ULFA virtually ran a parallel government in this area along with many other parts of Assam during that time. While the police and the forest departments had no role in the day-to-day life of the villages, the 'social reform' programmes organized by the ULFA were actively implemented and its public meetings were highly attended. No policeman of the Assam Police dared to come to Lakhipathar during those days of 'independence', I was told. As a man from Laupoti village narrated, if any policeman met Paresh Baruah—the self-styled Commander-in-Chief of ULFA—in the Tingrai market, he would salute Baruah. While the ULFA was very active in most parts of the Brahmaputra valley in Assam starting from the late 80s, how it was perceived by various sections of people, however, was not uniform. The social–cultural position of a given group or a person influenced the ways in which the person in question and the rebel group engaged with each other. Whether the ULFA activities were seen as experiences of 'independence' or of 'insurgency' depended on the *perspective* provided by varied subject positions.

After the Asom Gana Parishad (AGP), a regional party which was an outgrowth of the Assam movement, came to power in the state in 1985, the ULFA operated quite openly and with tacit government support. The mass base of the ULFA and the AGP was more or less same or overlapping. The AGP could not afford to dissatisfy its base by turning against the ULFA. And under AGP rule the civil machinery of the state including the police preferred to look the other way when ULFA was spreading its organization in different areas, recruiting cadres, collecting money and implementing 'reforms' as well as doing moral and social policing.

The increased influence and capacities of ULFA were not experienced in the same way by different sections of people. While the major concern of this chapter is to understand these varying perspectives and how the distinct image, role, and mode of operation of ULFA influenced such perceptions, a brief note on the genesis of ULFA as a movement would not be out of place here. An understanding of the origin, history, and goals of the organization and the socio-political background of its leaders would help us place the organization in the larger socio-political milieu of the time.

## The Political–economic History of Assam and the Genesis of ULFA

The genesis of ULFA cannot be attributed to any single reason. Though at an immediate level ULFA is understood to have grown out of the more radical factions of the Assam movement, a deeper analysis shows that there is a long historical process of the formation of an Assamese consciousness behind it, many of which also contributed to the Assam movement. Talukdar and Kalita (2011: 3) have listed factors such as geographical separation of the north-east from the mainland India, the aspirations for independence of some communities since pre-independence times, the end of Ahom rule, the large-scale immigration to Assam, the Assamese nationalist thinking that became increasingly intense under the leadership of the Assamese middle class and their attempt to keep power centralized in their own hands, the overly centralized character of the Indian state and the feeling of deprivation nurtured by Assamese people, and last but not least, the influence of nationalist consciousness and the idea of self-rule developed through various anti-colonial movements around the world.

Before the British came, the post-independence geographical territory of Assam did not exist as such. Until the arrival of the Ahoms, the land was controlled by numerous small kingdoms. The Ahoms who arrived in the thirteenth century, with the help of their superior military power and agricultural skills succeeded in bringing together large areas previously under the rule of other small rulers. The first seed of the idea of an Assamese nationality was developed under Ahom rule itself. Later, after the British took over Assam through the Yandabu agreement of 1826, the interests of the British colonialism and Ahom nobility gradually came into conflict. The princes of the erstwhile royal families challenged the British within a couple of years. The British managed that first attempt tactically, by putting Purandar Singha, a royal prince, as a subordinate king in Upper Assam. Later, when the tea plantations started, large numbers of labourers were brought in from Bihar, Orissa, Bengal, the Central Provinces, the United Provinces, Madras, etc. The population of Assam was less and a sufficient workforce of cheap labour to work in the gardens was not available. However, when the labour force was brought in from the outside, there arose the problem of food grain shortage. The minimal population of Assamese people could not produce sufficient food, and vast lands were lying uncultivated. For this reason, and also because a major source of British earnings was land-revenue, the authorities encouraged the immigration of Bengalis and Hindustanis on very easy terms. While the people of Assamese aristocracy like Maniram Dewan were offended by the discriminatory treatment shown to Assamese tea-garden owners by the British, the conflict between the common Assamese and the common immigrants was a phenomenon of later years. In fact, initially, the immigration of outsiders was supported by the Assamese people.

The conflict started when the British brought in educated Hindu Bengalis for various administrative jobs. The middle-class Assamese had no conflict with the Muslim Bengali peasants coming from Eastern Bengal. However, when the educated Hindu Bengalis came, it was a direct conflict of interest for them, as they saw that the jobs under the British went from the hands of educated middle class Assamese to the Bengalis.

The seeds of Assamese nationalism under the leadership of the Assamese middle classes were sown at that moment. Later, the conflict with Bengalis was extended to conflict with the Banias and other people coming from various parts of India. After independence, this conflict has also assumed a cross-border character, as the stream of immigrants now became illegal immigration of foreign nationals, due to partition and re-partition of the British–Indian empire into India and Pakistan first, and the further creation of Bangladesh later (Talukdar and Kalita 2011).

The Assam movement started in the year 1979 with the main demand of expulsion of 'foreigners' from Assam. While the definition of who is a foreigner and who is an Indian remained contested[3] throughout the movement and afterwards, this movement basically used the legal–constitutional provisions of the Indian state, to shame the state on its

[3] While the movement leaders had taken a stand where the definition of a 'citizen' would be decided by following the benchmarks established by the Constitution, the National Register of Citizens of 1951, the Indian state was ambiguous about the grounds for deciding who is a citizen and who is a illegally residing foreigner. While the National Register of Citizens of 1951 was based on the Nehru–Liaqat pact, which allowed citizenship rights to people entering the country till 31 December 1950, effectively pushing the Constitutional deadline of 19 July 1948, there were several other official documents which brought some ambiguities to the status of people, specially Hindu Bengalis entering from Eastern Pakistan/East Bengal after that. The Immigrants (Expulsion from Assam) Act of 1950, which was repealed in 1957, and a secret government/administrative order from 1965 made implicit distinctions between Hindu 'refugees' and Muslim 'illegal aliens', which was withdrawn in 1971 were two such orders. Though both were repealed, however, these two became sources of contention while defining the category of a 'foreigner' between the movement and the government. See Baruah (1999 [2008]: 118–19).

own words, and to solve the issue of illegal immigrations to Assam (S. Baruah 1999 [2008]: 118–21).

According to most accounts available in the public domain, it is around this same time that the ULFA was founded. The date was fixed at 7 April of 1979, when the then young founding members supposedly gathered in the historic Rong Ghor premises in Sivasagar: a palace of the erstwhile Ahom rulers of Assam (Baruah 1999 [2008]: 148; Talukdar and Kalita 2011; Saikia 2015). However, based on some personal memoirs of a police officer serving in the region during that period (Rammohan 2005) and conversations[4] with a top leader of the ULFA presently engaged in talks with the Indian government, it appears that though the idea of such an organization was formally structured out in 1979 for the first time, the real functioning of the organization began sometime in

[4] In a personal conversation on 10 May 2012, the Finance Secretary of ULFA Chittraban Hazarika, now an important leader in the pro-talks faction, narrated to me the early years of ULFA: In the year 1979, Bhimkanta Buragohain and Arabinda Rajkhowa along with some others thought of establishing an armed organization for the demands of an independent Assam to get rid of the 'colonial rule' of the Indian state. Initially they were organized as two separate groups with similar ideology, one led by Bhimkanta Buragohain (known as *Mama*, meaning maternal uncle), Suren Dihingia (an advocate from Naharkotia), etc. The other group was led by Arabinda Rajkhowa and Pradip Gogoi. Both the groups merged to form ULFA. Through contacts of Bhimkanta Buragohain, linkages with the Naga secessionist group NSCN were established and arrangements for training were made. The main work of ULFA started from about 1982. Before that, the work was of preparatory nature. In 1982/1983, the Arabinda faction met in a remote village in Jorhat for the first time. The Mama faction was operating in the meantime. Their Deputy Commander-in-Chief was Buddheshwar Gogoi. Other people were Suren Dihingia, Ponaram Baruah, Soneshwar Gogoi, Bhadreshwar Gohain, etc. The Arabinda faction approached the Mama faction about a merger and asked if they would lead. The Mama faction said that they would not be able to drag so much and asked Arabinda to take over. The elders wanted to give moral and political support while not being actively involved in the armed struggle. At this time, Arabinda was the Vice Chairman of his faction. In 1985, the merged ULFA met for the first time in a General Council level meet at Barpeta, in an abandoned hospital. Arabinda Rajkhowa was selected as the chairman of the United Liberation Front of Assam (ULFA) in this meeting (C. Hazarika 2012, pers.com, 10 May).

the early 1980s. Baruah (2005 [2007]: 152) has argued that the failure of the Assam movement to negotiate a deal with the central government and the holding of assembly elections in 1983 amidst widespread cries to correct electoral rolls, have had an impact on the growth of ULFA in the early 1980s. The ULFA made major inroads, he suggests, during the largely unpopular Congress (I) regime led by Hiteswar Saikia that came to power after the 1983 elections which was boycotted in majority of ethnic Assamese strongholds. It has also been argued that due to the degeneration of the AGP, an outgrowth of the anti-foreigners movement led by student leaders, when it came to power in 1985, getting involved in deep corruption and nepotism, and not keeping the promises that it made on the issue, Assamese nationalism took a militant turn in the form of the ULFA (Menon and Nigam 2007: 144).

Though the ULFA is known to have emerged out of the more radical factions of the Assam movement, there were, however, some fundamental differences in the ideology and principles of both the movements, as seen from some early publicity documents of ULFA. The core difference was that while the Assam movement depended on the procedures available within the legal–constitutional framework of the Indian state, ULFA had set out with an ideology which disbelieved that any substantive changes could be achieved within the framework of the Indian state and the constitution. Their stated goal was to establish scientific socialism in an independent Assam. They saw the Yandaboo Treaty of 1826 between Burma and the British colonizers of India, whereby Assam was brought under the company rule, as the moment when Assam lost its independence, and stated that their struggle is to restore the independence that is lost since then. They also made it very clear that by independence they do not mean any form of partial autonomy, but meant full political, economic, social, and cultural independence that is the right of every nation in the world (ULFA 1989).[5]

[5] Over time, however, sections of ULFA cadres who had come out for talks had agreed to go for a compromise/solution within the Indian constitution. Most importantly, through the present talks which began in 2011 after the arrest in the year 2010 of almost all the leaders from the topmost level except for the Commander-in-Chief Paresh Baruah/Paresh Assam, the pro-talks faction of ULFA has redefined their notion of sovereignty, and now is willing to accept a solution within the Indian constitution.

Further, the organization also gradually distanced itself from the immigration issue that was at the centre of the Assam movement, and advocated for the rights of 'Axombaxi' (that is, people living in Assam) rather than the 'Axomiya' (natives of Assam) (Baruah 2005 [2007]: 151; Menon and Nigam 2007: 144). In a total negation of the ideology of the Assam movement, a statement of the ULFA from July 1992 addressed to 'East Bengal migrants', stated that the hardworking east Bengal migrants are to be considered Assamese, whereas the Indians (identified with people from Bihar, UP, Rajasthan, and other parts of mainland India)—and not only the Indian state—are the real enemies of Assam.[6]

While the public documents of ULFA talked about political, economic, and social and cultural independence, the working of ULFA in locations like Lakhipathar spoke a lot about their values of independence and ideals of self-rule. Though depending on time and place the position of the *xangathan* (organization) and the space it occupied in people's lives varied, the ULFA appeared to have run, if not a parallel state, than at least a parallel in-the-process-of-genesis state.

Baruah (2005 [2007]: 151–2) notes the engagement of ULFA in various forms of 'social agenda', such as conduct of trials for people involved in drugs and prostitution rings, punishment of corrupt and negligent government officials, prevention of 'corruption' of Assamese culture and social life by asking people to refrain from Hindi film songs and disco music, and so on.

Uddipan Dutta, discussing the media representation of the ULFA between 1985 and 1990, shows how the organization was virtually running a parallel administration in Assam through activities such as public humiliation of and physical violence against those who were considered to be 'offenders' by the ULFA, or constructive works like building of roads and river embankments. Reports of such activities found frequent coverage in the media, until a diktat came from the organization warning the mass media not to publish anything about it without its permission. The media reportage not only described what the organization was doing at the ground level, but also published news about satisfaction of the common people about such activities. The newspapers carried photographs of people kneeling at busy road intersections or in front of public offices or cinema halls, as a punishment

[6] Based on Routray's translation of ULFA (1992) leaflet.

ordered by ULFA. The organization was so much legitimized that, as reported by *Dainik Asam* of 26 February 1990 and discussed by Dutta (2008), a top leader came and spoke in the 59th Annual Conference of the Srimanta Sankardeva Sangha surrounded by one-and-half a dozen body guards, in full presence of the Assam police force (Dutta 2008: 51–9).

During the late 1980s, the government run by the AGP was in a complex relationship with the ULFA. As a system–party, it should have resisted the growth of an anti-systemic movement like ULFA; but ULFA being an organization sharing ideological roots with the party, which was also seen as a radical fringe of the same movement out of which the AGP party emerged, the government was in practice unable to curb the growth of ULFA (Baruah 2005 [2007]: 153–4).

In the following section, we would examine how this parallel governance by ULFA was perceived by various sections of Assamese people in and around Lakhipathar.

## Perspectives on ULFA

### Insurgency

In the late 1980s, under AGP rule the civil machinery of the state including the police preferred to look the other way when ULFA was spreading its organization in different areas, recruiting cadres, collecting money, and implementing 'reforms' as well as doing moral and social policing. Huge amounts of money were collected from the tea gardens, from corrupt government officials, and from businessmen (Hazarika 1994 [2011]). Initially even the ULFA cadres themselves were surprised by the ease in which the business community succumbed to their pressure: 'A simple telephoned threat, the display of weapons by tough-looking militants, "friendly advice", or even an occasional roughing up was enough to help local traders part with millions of rupees' (Hazarika 1994 [2011]: 185–6).

In such a situation of immense fear and uncertainty, most of the tea gardens were paying regular contributions to the ULFA 'war chest' fearing for the life of their officials. Individual business families were targeted too. A member of an Assamese business family from Duliajan town who had contracts from the various installations of the oil industry narrated to me their life in those days. The woman who spoke to me, probably in her mid-forties now, was fuming with anger while telling me the story.[7] She was newly married to a son of this rich family, and had a young baby. However, for her, life became terrible at that age. Her husband was an engineer in the oil company while the other brothers looked after the family business. However, it was her husband who became most vulnerable as he had to go to field sites as an engineer. She showed me an old letter from ULFA where 14 lakh rupees were demanded from them. The late husband of the woman gave up his job in fear. However, until they gave the money the lives of the brothers were under threat. 'I used to go out when they would come', she went on, 'because they used to be softer with women, and my sister-in-law won't dare'.[8] Finally, they gave the entire amount in a few instalments. However, even after that the 'bastards' did not stop with their demands. Once her brother-in-law was taken away to a nearby house and was roughed up, because he entered into an argument with those who came to put a demand. They had no option but to concede. Regular supplies of rice, wheat flour, sugar, etc., in large quantities, 'a bus-full of them',[9] had to be sent to the Lakhipathar camp. One of their ambassador cars was never returned. A gypsy was recovered after a lot of requests, which was in such a bad shape, that they repaired it and then sold it off. And police was, of course, of no help; the ULFA boys 'would ask you to deliver the ransom money to an official in some police station', at times.

The midnight 'rescue' of the tea-garden officials of Doom Dooma division of the Uniliver group preceded the Lakhipathar operations immediately.[10] Those officials lived under threat for a long time.

[7] Personal interaction at her home, 4 June 2012.

[8] Such statements indicate that culturally rooted ideas of respect for women and their chastity influenced the cadres of the xangathan, which restrained them from treating harshly even a woman whom and whose family they wanted to intimidate and coerce upon. This is in stark contrast with an episode of how the attitude of the Indian army towards women was perceived, as discussed in the next chapter. See Chapter 7, p. 212.

[9] She clarified that she meant a TATA 407 model mini-bus.

[10] On the 8 November 1990, at midnight, the non-Assamese officers and their families of the Doom Dooma tea estate owned by the multinational Unilever group were evacuated to safety in Calcutta, by a special Indian Airlines

Sanjoy Hazarika narrates the modus operandi of the organization while making demands to the tea gardens (Hazarika 1994 [2011]). When several companies in Calcutta received summons from the ULFA to visit them and hold talks on the 'economic' development of Assam, several executives from various companies went to Dibrugarh. From Dibrugarh they were taken by a young man to meet the leaders of the xangathan.

> The ULFA contact man … sat in the front car, directing the small motorcade as it bumped over the town's small lanes and then to a small tea garden in the neighbourhood. As they approached the plantation, young men in military uniform armed with automatic weapons stood at attention on either side of the path.

Not only was the road completely under the control of the ULFA, but the manager's bungalow itself was converted into a military base 'swarming with men and weapons'. The executives were taken to the ULFA negotiators in batches. The 'talk' is narrated by Hazarika thus:

> Tapan Dutta, the lean, young commander-in-chief of the Dibrugarh unit of ULFA led the questioning. Armed guards kept fiddling with their weapons behind the executives, clearly aimed at unsettling them.
>
> 'Aren't you ashamed of exploiting Assam all these years?' snapped Dutta, starting on an aggressive note.

When some of the executives tried to elaborate upon their company's welfare projects and their suggestions for future community oriented work, the ULFA leader Tapan Dutta responded 'with a sharp retort': 'Save us your lectures. We want one crore rupees (about 300,000 dollars) from you.' (Hazarika 1994 [2011]: 192–4).

And that was not all. Some members of the tea industry's apex body, the Indian Planters Association, had earlier that month complained

---

aircraft, by the central government body named the Research and Analytic Wing (RAW), after a request for the same from its officials at London and Delhi came to the Central government. The state government was not aware of this until the whole process was completed. The company had initially approached the state government when threats to its officials came from ULFA after they did not relent to a demand for contribution to the rebel organizations 'war chest'. However, when the state government was not helpful, they approached the Central government directly. (Hazarika 1994 [2011]: 192; Talukdar and Kalita 2011: 93).

to the Chief Minister. So they were warned on this night, 'We know you have complained about us to the Chief Minister. We know everything that happens in Assam and if you go and spread the word about this meeting, the consequences will be very severe' (Hazarika 1994 [2011]: 194).

This modus operandi of funds collection was accompanied by political assassinations and 'social reform' policies in the form of public humiliations and punishments of 'offenders' in towns and villages. Political assassinations carried out by ULFA during this period targeted mostly the leaders, members and relatives of leaders of the Congress (I) party and the leaders and workers of the United Reservation Movement Council of Assam (URMCA)[11]. There were some major attacks on people from law-enforcing agencies as well, such as the killing of the Superintendent of Police (SP) of Dibrugarh district Daulat Singh Negi or a Sub Inspector (SI) of Laluk police station in Lakhimpur district Atul Sarma (Dutta 2008: 47–9).

While the Assamese dailies condemned such attacks, there was this frequent rhetoric of a '*nyasta swartha sokro*', a circle with vested interests, being behind such assassinations, acting to block the socio-economic development of the state. The assailants were often termed as 'unidentified gunmen' but not as ULFA cadres (Dutta 2008: 44–6).

## Freedom

The very years of the late 1980s were experienced in Lakhipathar as the time of peace. Though, like the majority of Assamese people the people of Lakhipathar got involved in the Assam movement under the All Assam Students Union (AASU), and there were some clashes with some Bengali and Bihari families most of whom left Lakhipathar thereafter,

[11] United Reservation Movement Council of Assam (URMCA) was an apex body of more than 37 Scheduled Castes (SC), Scheduled Tribes (ST), Other Backward Classes (OBC), More Other Backward Classes (MOBC), Jharkhandi, and some democratic organizations of the state. As the Assam Police remained a mute spectator to the activities of ULFA during the height of ULFA activities, URMCA had put a up stiff resistance to ULFA and its high-handed activities in many places, armed with traditional weapons like bows and arrows (Dutta 2008: 71–2).

very few people outside the neighbouring Digboi town knew about this place. The children studied in the schools that the villagers themselves set up in their villages, and the adults worked in their fields. Very few went out to study in the Digboi College. And even after that, most of those who went to college chose to settle finally in Lakhipathar, mostly as teachers in the local schools. A few more, without sufficient land, went out to work in Digboi town as daily wage labourers. 'We so much enjoyed living there at that time that no one thought of coming out and settling elsewhere' recalled a man from Lakhipathar in his late thirties who has now settled in the outskirts of Digboi town (N. Sonowal, 2012, pers.com, 10 May).

The villagers of Lakhipathar noticed a rush of motorbikes in their area by about the middle of 1989. They saw unknown faces, but did not initially know very well what the matter was. Gradually they started hearing rumours that ULFA had established a camp inside the forest.

In the summer, or the autumn, of 1989, a public meeting was organized in Lakhipathar. Chandrakanta Koch, one of the present headmen of Lakhipathar, presided over the meeting. By that time, those who took interest in the happenings had seen a few issues of the ULFA mouthpiece *Swadhinota*. One of the prominent speakers in the meeting was ULFA's founding member and advisor Bhim Gohain (known as *mama*). 'Bhim Gohain was their Foreign Secretary at that time', an elderly Mr Gogoi of Pandhowa village recalled. Before Bhim Gohain established this new organization, Gogoi personally knew him. In 1977 they 'became Janata together' (members of the Janata party), and went for meetings to Sadia. Prior to the Janata Party, Bhim Gohain was with the Ujoni Axom Rajyik Parishad, a body which asked for an Ahom state in upper Assam. While in the Janata party, he was the secretary of the Sadia constituency. In the following elections to the state assembly, he sought a Janata Party ticket to contest from Sadia, but was denied. Gogoi said, 'I knew him to his bones ... He was a simple man'. He had a graduation degree, but did not have a job. His family was affluent with a lot of land, and he was a good artist. He was unmarried, and about 50 years old at that time. He left the Janata party after the party ticket was refused, and slowly started working with the idea of ULFA. Gogoi meanwhile joined the CPI(M) and was not in touch with him. When Gohain came for the public meeting in

Lakhipathar, Gogoi went to attend it. He saw and also spoke to Bhim Gohain, but by that time 'Gohain had become a leader, he was the foreign secretary, and I was just a simple villager. He had acquired an "ulfio style[12]"'.

After this meeting the villagers began to see the cadres of ULFA in Lakhipathar openly moving around. The central camp was established deep inside the reserve forest. The location of the camp was, as rumour says, decided based on the strategic advantage provided by Lakhipathar's thick forests and its near inaccessibility from the outside. Initially, Gogoi thoughtfully said, the plan was to perhaps set up the camp in the Tingrai forest. However, they had probably realized that it was not a good location with the 38th national highway passing by adjacent to it. Therefore, Lakhipathar was chosen (Mr D. Gogoi, 2012, pers.com, 22 May).

At that time, for most people of Lakhipathar, what ULFA meant to do and what was its political line, was far from clear. As the contact with the people gradually grew, and the cadres started coming to the villages to buy supplies of pork and chicken for their camps, they developed their own understandings of the organization.

One prominent way through which the people of Lakhipathar got to know the xangathan was the game of football. The ULFA had a culture of sports, and several of its leaders were very good footballers, including Paresh Baruah, the Commander-in-Chief, who happened to be a state-level player earlier. People of Lakhipathar had been seeing ULFA boys going to and from the forest in their jeeps and bikes for some time, and had heard them in some public meetings called by the organization, but had really grown affectionate towards them through some celebrated and now widely remembered football matches.

The extraordinary stories of competence in the football field were also accompanied by other fanciful stories about the organization and their leader. The 'boys' mingled with the local people. They came to buy pig or chicken, and would sit and talk to the people who would gather around. The content of their stories ranged from the mysterious powers of their leaders to the narration of epics like Mahabharata and Ramayana (C. Hazarika, 2012, pers.com, 10 June). Paresh Baruah was

[12] ULFA-ized mannerisms. He probably implicated the authoritative attitude that Mama had assumed by that time.

a mythical figure and was looked up to with awe. People talked about his magical skills, gossiped about his power and authority—how even police worked under his command—and were enthralled by the stories of his extra-human powers. Baruah would occasionally give a rare visit to a family in the villages and people would gather around him, to listen to this tall young man with a very fit body.

The leaders urged the villagers to join the organization through public meetings as well as door-to-door campaigns. When I asked some of those people who enrolled into the xangathan about what pushed them to join, they said that it was an exciting thing to be in ULFA. Every young man and woman wanted to join it. Neela Sonowal of Dhadum was stopped from joining by his family. Durga Dutta's daughters also wanted to go, but the strict father was very clear that his children would not join the organization. However, many youngsters like Jotin Koch and Dipen Sonowal went ahead.

There also was a perception among people that the organization was some kind of an employment avenue. There was a story from one of ULFA's meetings. The leader urged people for names of volunteers to join the xangathan. One middle-aged man gave the names of all his three sons one by one. At this the leader asked, 'Are they from the same family?', and when the father replied in the affirmative, the leader had to again make it clear that only one member from each family was sufficient. In another meeting, a boy raised his hand when asked who all wanted to join, though he was not very serious about it. However, later he was taken from his home as he raised his hand in a public meeting. Many also had some notion that if he or she died working for the *dex*[13] then ULFA would look after the family.

Despite heightened emotions, most of the recruits from Lakhipathar were only lower level cadres and were not given any armed training. They were mostly engaged in running errands, to patrol the roads of

[13] The term dex would translate to country/state and interestingly not 'nation', for which the Assamese word would be *jati*. The usage of this word appears to be interesting in the context of the history of an Assamese identity movement in the 1960s and '70s, the focal point of which was that of jati: an ethnic/linguistic Assamese national identity. Whether there was a clear shift in focus from a linguistic/ethnic determinant to a political–territorial determinant in visualizing the ideal political community would be an interesting area of research.

Lakhipathar at night, and to signal to the camp gates if any unusual movement of persons or vehicles was seen. Jotin Koch of Kenduguri said that he was mostly given the job of polishing shoes and washing utensils. Only on some lucky nights did he get to do patrol duty with a telescope and a torch.

Most of these recruits never reached the main camps where the leaders lived. They had access only until the checkpoints. The villagers were not allowed either. Perhaps the awe of the villagers and building up of the mysterious 'characters' of people like Paresh Baruah, which so much captured the interest and imagination of the people, was also helped by such distance. People knew that they lived inside the jungle, but how they lived and what they did there, were always matters of speculation and gossip.

The villagers of Lakhipathar did not wonder much about the goals of the *xangathan*. Everyone had heard of *swadhin Axom* (independent Assam) but no one put much thought about what the ULFA actually meant by it. Most people perhaps somehow equated what they *had* already at that time as the swadhin asom, as statements about feelings of independence in those days indicate. Even those who were not enrolled as members of ULFA, recognized their authority, by cooperating with them. Biren *dai* recalled how on some days when he would go fishing in the Digboi river flowing inside the forest, the ULFA boys would see him and exchange pleasantries. 'They would ask what fish I've caught and sometimes ask if I would sell it.' If he refused, they would not insist. Rather they would ask, '*Kiba xunisa neki daiti*? *Sab raasta clear ase ne*?' (Have you heard anything, uncle? Are all roads clear?). By this, they would mean if any policeman had been around, Biren dai explained. He would assure them nobody was around. So they would leave.

Later, in an interview with Chitraban Hazarika—the Finance Secretary of ULFA who is now engaged in peace talks with the Indian government—he said that it was important for the ULFA leaders to talk to people and to talk influentially. He himself used to talk quite a lot. He used to tell various stories including stories from the Indian epic Mahabharata. He said that an emotional bond was formed with people through such story telling in friendly sessions. In addition, for an armed struggle, 'emotion is very important', he went on saying, 'how else do you think you can make someone to join a dangerous life, or make a suicide squad member? Raising emotions is crucial.' (Mr C. Hazarika, 2012, pers.com, 10 May).

## ULFA as a Proto-state

During the first public meeting of ULFA in Lakhipathar in 1989, questions were raised by attending journalists about the nature of the independent state that ULFA aimed for. They said, 'We can understand that there exist even smaller independent sovereign states with even lesser population. So from that perspective the notion of an independent Assam is not irrelevant. But what about the future form of the state? Would it be a socialist state, a capitalist state, or would it be a monarchy? What manifesto do you have about that?' Bhim Gohain, the ULFA Advisor himself took that question but only to respond by saying that ULFA would decide on that matter once independence was won (D. Gogoi, 2012, pers.com, 22 May).

Despite such indeterminacy regarding the form or structure of the independent state that ULFA was fighting for, the ongoing practices of power by the organization at that time showed clear marks of stateness. Going by a definition of state as the entity which claims supreme power in a given territory and where rules laid down by this entity are adhered to, the organization was operating in the interiors of Assam, if not already like a fully formed state, then at least as a state in the making.

In this proto-static form, the authority of the organization worked through a mix of the personal and the social, the religious-cultural and the national, the benevolent and the coercive, all of which constituted the political in Lakhipathar of that time. The xangathan in Lakhipathar was involved in various affairs of the daily living in the villages. It had a programme of social reforms, influencing the lives of people in their most intimate spheres such as drinking, dressing, and love relationships. Probably influenced by the teachings of Sankardeva, and under the ethical norms of a Matak belief popularized by the Mayamora/ Moamoria sect saint Anirudhadev, of which the military chief of ULFA Paresh Baruah was a follower, the ULFA in those years actively advocated against alcoholism. 'Probably Paresh Baruah asked the ULFA boys to control alcoholism in the villages a bit,' Deepak Gogoi from Pandhowa, who himself happened to enlist in the organization during those days, said. 'But the boys felt as if they had got the authority of Paresh Baruah and started acting indiscriminately. Even those who had a drink in the quiet were beaten up.' For Kachari people rice-liquor is an essential item even for their rituals. However, the 'boys' would vandalize their houses even when they prepared liquor for such customary use.

Another area of ULFA's intervention came with a moral code for women in the matter of dressing and for youngsters in the matter of love relationships. Dipan *bai*,[14] a woman probably in her mid-thirties, narrated the fears of her girlhood. Dipan bai liked to keep her hair short, but she was too frightened to keep it that way, because people said the ULFA boys would not appreciate it. She was about 13–14 years old at that time. She and her friends fancied wearing salwar-suits. However, the diktat of ULFA was that, if you were young then wear a frock or a skirt, and if you thought you were too old to wear a short dress, then switch to *chadar-mekhela*, the traditional attire for Assamese women. Salwar-kurta was a banned dress, as it was seen as representing Indian-ness. Further, in a relatively open society that Lakhipathar was, the socialization of young men and women came to be strictly monitored. If they went a bit too far in their behaviour as per the notions held by the ULFA boys, punishments like beatings for men and chopping off of hair for girls were executed.

After the passage of more than 20 years, the villagers expressed their diverse take on such 'reform' measures, speaking from their own caste and community produced locational subjectivities. Durga Dutta, a prominent Xankar Xanghi and a self-declared critique of the ULFA even during the times of its high popularity, spoke favourably of ULFA when it came to such 'reforms': 'They did a very good thing by evicting the liquor joints in Lakhipathar. They taught the drunkards a good lesson.' Further, '… they also punished if somebody gave an illicit proposal to a girl' (D. Dutta, 2012, pers.com, 9 April). Biren dai, from the Sonowal community, who was present with me when this comment was made, did not confront Durga Dutta immediately, but on our way back told me: 'He is a *xoron guru*,[15] I can't confront what he says. But most people obeyed such rules only because they had to.' The sentiment that was

[14] *Bai* is an Assamese word for elder sister.

[15] A religious leader who has the authority to induct another person into their faith.

expressed was: after all who would risk going against the wielders of guns?

Deepak Gogoi of Pandhowa had a similar take on the 'reform' measures:

> In ancient times it happened that the father would walk down to a distant village, see a girl, and the son would marry that girl without questioning. But it no more happens. A girl and a boy would get married only when they know each other, talk to each other and fall in love. In that process, no one can draw a fixed line of limits as to what to do and what not to do. Sometimes they would get a bit closer than usual. But for that matter beating up boys and chopping off the hair of girls was not fair.

Deepak added that, despite being a member of the organization, he tactfully avoided being part of such campaigns.

Apart from such policing of personal spaces, the xangathan also organized people to do public works such as repairing of roads. It advised villagers on better methods of harvesting, and financially helped students from weaker backgrounds.

Sanjoy Hazarika in his brief description of the Lakhipathar incident in his book *Strangers of the Mist* (1994 [2011]) writes that he was told by a villager that the ULFA did not interfere in their lives, and they did not interfere in ULFA's. The narratives from my fieldwork, however, indicated the opposite of this. It appeared that ULFA penetrated into almost all spheres of life in Lakhipathar. The organization symbolized the superior physical force, keeping the police at a distance. They intervened in how people lived their daily lives, influenced their social practices, and tried to shape their emotions: all the functions that a 'state' tries to do with its population. Of course, the process was not complete, as the time was short, but the process started nevertheless.

The story of a lone policeman of Lakhipathar working in the Assam Police department was telling in such contexts. He was describing how he chanced upon a few ULFA cadres at his own home. This was a day in the early 1990, and was before ULFA was banned and the army operation came. He, however, was cautious while talking about this experience even now, and requested anonymity. This person, who worked as a policeman and was posted elsewhere, used to come home only when he got leave from work, and on such days he used to see the ULFA boys on the roads, but never spoke to them as such. However, once he met them at his own house. They were staying at his house that night, and when he reached, he was asked who he is and from where he had come. After he gave them his identity as a policeman, one of them asked, 'What will you do if someday you come into a confrontation with us, what if we meet in an encounter?' That was a difficult question. They had their weapons, and in Lakhipathar it was only their command that ruled. The policeman answered that such a thing will be decided by the circumstances only. 'You have your guns,' he remembered to have said, 'and I also have my gun. If we meet in an encounter as opposing parties, obviously I won't be able to surrender my life to your bullets. I'll have to fire too.' At that point, another ULFA boy intervened and admonished the one who asked, 'Why are you asking such things? We are living at his house and have found no troubles. So let it be.' Then this guy turned to him and asked, 'You are with the police, so do you tell your officers about us?' He replied that he did not tell anything to anyone, and that he knew that if he said anything it would also bring trouble to him. After this conversation, he was allowed to go to sleep.

But that night he could not sleep. He held his small bag of clothes close to him, and kept lying on the bed, ready to flee to the forest in case something happens, or in case a police party arrives, though he knew that was unlikely. He was afraid, thinking what would happen to his job if he was discovered with ULFA cadres at his own home. Somehow, the night passed and he left home early in the morning next day.

Such incidents reflect the confidence that the ULFA cadres had about their standing in the society of Lakhipathar. They did not bother even to find out beforehand whose house they were staying at. When they came to know that the host was a policeman, they passed a veiled threat by asking if he played the role of an informer, but did not move out from his house. Their decree ruled Lakhipathar: they knew it, and so did the policeman.

## Dissent and Freedom

Though the ULFA operated in Lakhipathar almost unchallenged during these times, it did not mean there was no dissenting opinion. The questions raised by the media in ULFA's first public meeting in Lakhipathar echoed in the minds of some who had the opportunity to think. It led to other questions regarding the viability of an organization with such ad hoc and indeterminate focus. However, despite having doubts, many preferred to stay silent, as speaking out did not seem to matter when one was not a 'voice'. Dimbeshwar Gogoi of Gondhia village had one such silenced opinion. He decided to wait and watch, rather than speaking out.

The grounds of allegiance to the xangathan's rule from some others, were divided between a trust in intentions and a mere tactical strategy. While some of the organization's goals, principles and operating mechanisms appeared attractive, participation in its activities were also often egged by the need to be seen as patriots as opposed to traitors.

For many common villagers, it was an acceptance based on mutual understanding and accommodation. The ULFA offered some order and some excitement to the remote village life of Lakhipathar, and in return, the people accepted its authority.

Dissent as a political act and freedom as a political space are precarious. They may get erased, suppressed, or co-opted so well that what begins as dissent to oppression may change and start looking like cooperation in freedom. The meaning of freedom is constituted after all by the categories of the discourse in which one lives. This is not only true in the case of Lakhipathar, but when we reflect back on narratives of custodial death in Delhi and the acceptance of the everyday life of co-existence and cooperation with the police, a similar discursive construction of freedom appear to be operative. Freedom in the slums of Delhi is to learn tactics to avoid police torture and to be able to use it for one's own needs.

In the next chapter, while delving deep into the memories of those who lived through the times of ULFA and the subsequent years of conflict, we would see how dissent and acquiescence, protest and legitimation flipped like two sides of the same coin. The choices that people made are so embedded in their contexts that trying to find meaning in their actions outside these contexts may be bewildering.

7

# Bearing Witness

## Memories, War, and Life in Lakhipathar

The sphere of the political penetrates into the mundane living of a people or a community too. Starting from the division of work at the family level, to the settlement of disputes at a community level, the working of a mechanism of social living is a statement in the sphere of the political. And these mechanisms are mediated, bargained, accommodated, refined, and rationalized through experiences of such political living in the past and the anticipations of the future. In a previous chapter, we referred to Kleinman and Kleinman's (2009) argument that collective experiences of suffering shape individual perceptions and expressions. It appears that collective experiences of suffering also shape collective practices of communities.

In this chapter, my attempt is to bring to the fore the conflict and armed violence in Lakhipathar, both at the moment of the Operation Bajrang and the subsequent years, as remembered and interpreted by the people of Lakhipathar. I have included lengthy narratives and deeply personalized memories that I collected during my fieldwork. A lot of these conversations were emotionally taxing, not only for the narrators, but also for me as a researcher/listener, and while these narratives have a crucial place in elaborating the larger argument of this work, this chapter also has an additional aim of contributing towards an open conversation about an episode in the history of the Indian state that is often buried and forgotten. The narratives of violence, giving a picture which amounts to no less than an Agambenian 'state of exception', lets us at the same time see and be alarmed at how such exceptional states are normalized and accepted, as we discuss the routinization of the army's presence and its blending into the socio-political life of Lakhipathar as an authority in the next chapter.

When I was in Lakhipathar in the year 2012, the days were quite ordinary. People say, since the then group of army from the Gorkha regiment had come to Lakhipathar, life has become much easier. Living in the villages, I saw jawans jogging on the road in front of their camp in the mornings. I also saw army trucks moving on the road regularly. People said that the jawans occasionally came to their houses and asked them questions, but did not physically harm or bother people unless something serious happened. There are some Assamese-speaking jawans amongst them and thus interactions have become easier. Though they beat up people if found drunk on the road, in the regular course they did not unnecessarily bother the local people. The descriptions sounded strangely similar to the presence of ULFA in the 1980s.

The apparent image of normalcy in the present given out by people, however, has developed through numerous negotiations with life conditions, power, and authority over two decades. This aspect of the normalcy comes to bear on one's mind when life stories of people are heard, both from the present and the past. The extraordinary past that is almost hidden in the everyday workings of people, becomes visible when one talks of the 'days of suffering'.

The narratives of the extraordinary past, and how it fades into an ordinary present, however, holds answers to questions of how political authorities are established.

## Recollection of the Past in a Time of 'Peace'*

When I went to Lakhipathar, I stated my purpose openly. So while talking to me everyone initially had a specific frame of mind, knowingly or

* As discussed in chapter one, terms like routine and extraordinary, normalcy/peace and war are contextual. While to a lot of people it would seem that the continuous armed presence and surveillance of an armed unit basically meant for fighting external wars amidst a civilian citizen group amounts to an extraordinary situation, to the people of Lakhipathar, having the army amidst them has come to be a regular part of their day-to-day lives.

unknowingly shaping what they said and how they said it. Narrations were filled with emotions: of pain, hurt, and surprisingly even of humour, always talking of a 'then' which is distinct from the 'now'. Gradually that performance of remembering *for me* died down to some extent. I was accepted as a 'regular' guest with whom they could live 'normally', by sharing everyday concerns and joys. It was then that I started seeing how even this everyday living is tangled with the extraordinary past in subtle ways, that how they react and relate to the specific life conditions and situations that emerge in the present is intricately linked, in ways which are sometime apparent and other times not, to their varied pasts of suffering.

Listening to the narratives of past sufferings was for a researcher, thus, not merely a tool to know what happened to the narrators in the past but it also gives a key to analyse why and how they live in the present. The expectations from and the conditions of a daily living shape what people remember and how. Thus, remembering an event of the past was not only about the past as such, but it was very much a political act in the present.

## Collecting Memories

The newspaper versions of the happenings in Lakhipathar give a linear chronicle of events. They were portrayals of the events by the media soon after they happened. The news reports were mediated in terms of *experience*: reports were not based on first-hand observation and experience of what happened to the people of Lakhipathar. The reporters collected their stories from army, police, and other state sources, and from people who managed to flee the area and came to the *xibir* (refugee camp) in Digboi.

The narratives collected from the field were mediated in several other ways. They were mediated through time, through experiences (or their absence) and through expectations. When I started to talk to people about the events of Lakhipathar, many of them said they did not know what to talk of. I had to give reference to what I had read, or what others had told me, and then gradually their versions began to come up. The stories often travelled back and forth in time, many times the confusion being whether a specific incident happened before 2000 or after 2000. Many times, I also stopped trying to find out when exactly a thing happened. The attempt to place it at the exact temporal frame and doing that with certainty seemed to make the narrators nervous of themselves. They could, however, distinguish between the stories from the first army operation, which was often referred to as the *juddha* (war), much more clearly from events in the subsequent period. The narrations were also pieces of the individual narrators' own personalized histories, conditioned and shaped through their experiences of social existence, feelings of self-worth, practices, and notions and expectations of what is to come. Hence they do not come together to give a linear and rounded narrative of what happened in Lakhipathar, but provide only fractured parts of a whole.

## The First War: Operation Bajrang

In early April 2012, the intermittent rains were making the Lakhipathar roads muddy. People were usually home by evening from all kinds of engagements. The annual paddy farming had not started yet. In the Sonowal family, while Kopou aai and Bou would cook dinner in the *paakghar* (kitchen), I used to sit by the fireplace together with Borta, Borma (Dolly's parents), and Dolly, in the mild warmth coming from the fireplace. Borta would do some work, like repairing a bamboo basket, or roasting a piece of meat on the fire. He is mostly silent. Borma would start talking, laughing at every little thing. Dolly would give her comments in between. After a while, Bou would come and give Borta and Borma their regular bowls of *haaj* (home-brewed rice wine).

I would ask Borma about her time during Bajrang. The years 1990–1 were the worst period. The army has been here forever since, but nothing can beat that first time. Borta was coming back from the field in his bicycle. He did not reach home; he was picked up by the army midway. Borma was at home with her hump-backed mother-in-law and a neighbour. Everyone else had fled to Digboi. They stayed back because the mother-in-law could not walk so far to Digboi. They were very frightened, '*hoga muta ulua obostha*' (the condition was like peeing and shitting in one's clothes out of fear). '*Gotei khon pil pilai ukonir nisinake army*' (The army was everywhere like lice in the hair). All the men had either fled or the army had taken them away. The next morning some army men came and took Borma and other women to the school where the detained men were kept. She saw Borta there. His face was swollen with the beatings. After she identified him as her husband, he was given medicine. She was also asked why she had not come with food and warm clothes for her husband. She said, 'I didn't even know where he was the night before; I thought he might even be dead.' It was the month of *Aghon* (a month in the Assamese calendar in the beginning of the winters), and it was very cold. Her husband's vest was torn by the army. He passed the night with a bare torso. The army however gave him roti to eat. Everyone was beaten up while being interrogated. They were asked if they had seen an ULFA cadre or if they were in ULFA. People were beaten until they answered in affirmative, but if they answered in affirmative, then they were killed, and then the news went out that an ULFA cadre was killed in an encounter. People chose the beatings over death. At night, when they were allowed to come back home, Borma with her mother-in-law and a neighbour, silently slipped away to a neighbour's house to spend the night together. They had no sense even to shut the doors. In every house, there were army jawans. Some army men camped in their house too. They had a *bongali*[1] boy who worked in their fields. He knew a little Hindi. He catered to what the army people wanted. People in the village were forced to sell their chickens and goats. The army was also supplied food from outside which were brought in huge pans and pots in army trucks.

There was a man from the village named Mukheshwar Sonowal who was shot in the leg. He was fleeing when he saw the army. Borma saw this man. He was bleeding, and army jawans were dragging him on the road. He used to wear a dhoti like most men, and his dhoti was taken off. He was naked, and bleeding, and he was brought near the women's group. Then his leg was bandaged by the army. The women were made to sit in a dry ditch by the roadside.

After a few bowls of haaj, Borta too added to Borma's story, remembering times that he found difficult to talk of when not drunk. 'We did not understand what they asked. What will you say if you don't understand what they ask? I was coming back from the field. Actually, I saw that the men were taken away by the army, and so was trying to come home. But then they got me. They had beaten me up a lot. My back and my legs pain till date.' Borta is in his mid-60s now. Though he

[1] She was referring to a tea-garden tribe boy. The tea-garden tribal people working as casual labourers are commonly called bongali.

tries to forget the past, his body and its pain act as constant reminders of what happened.

Borta and Borma were digging things up from some distant past, and I was immersed in some wintry cold night of 1990, when Borma was going to the backyard again and again unable to control her bowel movements impelled by fear. Under the yellow light of the 40 watt bulb, all four of us were consumed in the conversation.

However, dinner was ready soon, and we sat on wooden *piras* (low stools) on the earthen floor of the dining room in a semi-circle. Bou and Kopou aai ate after others had eaten. Maina, Bou's four-year-old younger daughter was whining over the food. Probably she was too sleepy. Bou asked her to stop complaining; threatening her that the army would come and get her. She shut up and ate. After I was done, I waited and sat there while Bou and Kopou aai were eating. That was a daily routine. In the meantime, Dolly used to clear out the used utensils and pile them up in a corner, to be washed in the morning. Tales about the army operations were wrapped up too, to be brought up in other conversations the next day.

The Sonowal family in Lakhipathar are among those people who do not view the events of Operation Bajrang as having any major impact on their present lives. When they talk of the past events, they do not talk in an accusatory tone. Events of violence and horror were depicted as if they were some natural events, as if they were things that were unavoidable.

Operation Bajrang was lifted a little ahead of the Assam assembly elections held in June next year. Though Lakhipathar has never been left free of armed forces since then, the impact and memory of this first encounter with state violence is remembered distinctly from all later phases.

## The Army Cordon and the Walks to 'Safety'

When the army cordoned off Lakhipathar to search for ULFA cadres, and many were detained and tortured, people wanted to leave their villages fearing for their lives and for the 'honour' of their wives and daughters. People in the villages near the main road saw things which induced tremendous amounts of fear in them. The Sonowal family, practically being one of the first families that the army encountered when they entered Lakhipathar, saw both the ULFA cadres fleeing, and the army personnel arriving in trucks. The elder Sonowal brother Borta, and his wife could not flee from Lakhipathar as they had their elderly mother, who could not walk to Digboi, to take care of. The younger brother, Biren dai, fled along with all the children in the family and his wife. He has a story of walking past the army check post, out of Lakhipathar. Many others from the villages near the main road, have stories of arduous flights to what they felt was 'safety', away from the terrors of Lakhipathar.

## Laupoti: Biren Dai, Kopou Aai

Laupoti being the first village on the approach road of Lakhipathar, the villagers had directly witnessed many moves of both the warring parties immediately before and after the army entered. A few days prior to the army operation, Kopou aai and other women cutting paddy in the field saw the movement of ULFA cadres from their camps. They saw files of young men in uniform carrying guns walking through the paddy fields crossing into the forests. They also saw 'sacks full of money' carried on elephant back by a mahout named Baang from Mamoroni village. 'Even Paresh Baruah passed through the field in front of our eyes', Biren dai interjected in a pretentious way.

Soon after that the army operation began. Biren dai went on to discuss the techniques of the army jawans and the manoeuvring by the rebel cadres in great detail. The army jawans were standing 5–6 *nuls* (about 20 meters) apart from each other, lining the road. Through that small gap, the ULFA cadres would swiftly jump across the road and pass over to the forest and emerge in Tingrai station and from there would go to Nahoroni village.

Neither Biren dai nor his wife were there to experience what happened once gun-fights ended and the army entered the villages. He got quite frightened after a bomb went off ripping through an army vehicle at Laupoti tiniali. He had seen those who implanted the bomb, as anything that happens at Laupoti tiniali is clearly visible from their house. The day when the bomb went off, he saw the ULFA men, loitering around. The bomb was planted earlier. People in Laupoti knew that there was a bomb planted at that place, just did not know when would it go off.

That day, when the bomb went off, Biren dai was at work. It was noon, about the time when children come back from school. Biren dai and his colleagues fell off on the ground on impact of the blast. The noise made him very curious. He wanted to come out to the road and see what was happening, but his Bihari colleagues stopped him. They were saying, 'The army will not do anything to us, it is you who would get trapped.' However, finally all three of them came out to see what was happening. There were two army vehicles and the first one was blown off. They saw a deep crater that opened up on the road. The jawans from the second vehicle were picking up injured people.

'Did anyone die?' I asked. Biren dai said that he did not know how many of them died, but the condition of the vehicle was so bad that he thought whoever was there in that vehicle had died. The doctor was giving some treatment to some of them. He saw the doctor tearing his own shirt and bandaging the wounded soldiers with it to prevent blood loss. Later, when the group moved, three jawans with some metal poles moved in front of the remaining truck, knocking on the road checking for more bombs, and the truck followed them slowly. While moving they kept firing towards the forest on the Tingrai side for about half an hour, targeting any possible ULFA cadre who fled after setting the bomb off, '*Dhrdhrdhrdhrdhrdhr* ...' Biren dai showed how the firing happened.

He had described in great detail and in a vivid manner about the use of arms and violence by the warring groups. The emphasis was on details, like the doctor bandaging the wounded, or how the guns were fired. In the same manner, he described in great detail the techniques and manoeuvres of the ULFA cadres. His narrative often sounded not to be a narrative of suffering, but as an expression of awe and surprise effected by competitive power/force of the warring parties. His awe of power was also reflected in how he narrated his flight to Digboi from Lakhipathar. His narrative was imbued with statements implicating his 'relation' with people in power, and his encounter with previously unseen weapons, again emphasizing the dimension of awe of power more than the trauma of suffering.

After the bomb blast Biren dai believed it would not be safe to stay put in the village. However, he was scared to escape through the hidden jungle paths. He decided to walk on the main road, leaving it up to fate as to what would happen. On the road, near Borbil tiniali, he saw a strange thing which he later came to know to be an army tank. It was his first encounter with an army tank. An army jawan was standing on top of it, and some tree twigs were perched on it. Biren dai, from a distance, was wondering if it was an elephant. There were other people whom they met on the way, and though they were nervous, they kept walking. When they reached the army check post, he saw that many other people were detained there hidden behind some bushes.

At the check post an army jawan asked him, '*Kaha se aata hain*?[2]' (from where have you come?). '*Lakhipathar se aata hain*' (I have come from Lakhipathar), Biren dai replied. Then he was enquired about the person who had just passed by before him. Biren dai said that he did not know, 'I've not seen anyone, how can I say?', he explained to me. However, the jawan gave him such a hard slap that his body turned around. Biren dai, however, thought, 'Let it be.' Then he was asked where he was going. He said that he had to go to a doctor as his son had fever. He was also asked what he did, but when he showed his IOC security guard's identity card, he was told that such cards were available in the market. When Biren dai insisted that his card had the genuine signature of an officer, he was sent to the commander.

The commander asked him to sit on the ground. It was about six in the morning.[3] The sun was gradually becoming strong as the day advanced. Hungry, tired, and frightened, they had to wait there the whole day. Biren dai's youngest son started crying in hunger, '*Maa bhaat de, bhaat de*'. But 'where will you get rice in the forest?'. A forest guard from Makum, Rajon Moran, whom Biren dai knew, was also there. He asked Biren dai if he should get some rice for the child. Biren dai

[2] Biren dai acted out how the jawan asked him and how he replied. He was one of those rare people in Lakhipathar, who had some exposure to Hindi-speaking people, owing to his job in a PSU having employees from all over India.

[3] Though the whole of India is in the same time zone, in reality there are huge differences in real time amongst diverse areas of India. Assam being in the north-east, and Tinsukia the easternmost district of the state, sunrise is at about 3.30 am even in the winters and the sun sets as early as 4.30 or 5 pm.

looked around and said, 'Leave it, you don't need to get rebuked for me.' Also, there were so many other children, and all of them were sitting hungry since morning. So how many would he cater to, Biren dai thought, and hoped that they would reach Digboi soon. After seeing the child crying, the jawans offered him roti, but the child did not take it and cried louder, saying, 'I don't want roti, I don't eat roti at home also, I want rice.' They had to sit there till seven in the night, when they were finally let off. But they were stopped again at Balijan tiniali, where there was another check post. But Biren dai had a relatively easy time there. The officer was Punjabi, and Biren dai told him that his brother's wife was Punjabi too and told him her name. Then the officer said, '*Theek hain theek hain, hamara aadmi hain naa*' (fine, you are from our side), and let him go.

Biren dai and his family's escape, was one of the easiest escape stories that I heard. The stories of people from villages that were further inside, and who stayed for a little longer before they decided to leave, were marked by trauma and suffering at a much deeper level.

## Sewali Neog and the Night Walk through the Jungle

When I came back home after the day's work in the villages, I used to rest for a while and then sit with Borta, Borma, and Dolly as they made liquor cakes from rice powder mixed with some herbs collected from the forest. They make cakes—which is not legally permitted—of about a quintal of rice every week, dry them in the sun and then Borta carries them to the market in Makum bundling it in the carrier of his cycle, to sell it to shopkeepers.

While the preparation of the cakes goes on in the Sonowal household, we talk of diverse things. They were always keen to know what I had done during the day, and who I had talked to. Then they would give me their suggestions about who I should talk to, and would analyse what a specific person had told me and why.

In one such conversation, Dolly suggested that I should meet Sewali Neog. Bou seconded her. 'Sewali is a very brave girl', both of them said, 'During the first operation she shouted at Hiteshwar Saikia', the foremost leader of the Congress (I) party in Assam during that time. Later she joined the xangathan but came back after some time for reasons which were not clear to them.

Sewali works in the ME school of Maaj Lakhipathar, next to the Lakhipathar High School, and lives in the suburb of Digboi. I first met her in the Lakhipathar bus. Someone told me that Sewali was sitting a couple of rows behind me. I turned back, and shouted over the noisy conversations and the rumbling of the bus that I wanted to meet her, telling very briefly who I was. She agreed to meet.

The day when I actually met her came much later. I was in the ME school to talk to the teachers, and Sewali came from her class after a while. She first agreed for a conversation there itself, but when I began to ask things, she said, '(H)ere I am in a different mood. (T)alking of those things will take me somewhere else. So you better come home.'

I reached her home one day, as pre-decided, at around 3 pm, after she was back from school. The driver of the shared tempo in which I was travelling from Digboi knew her house and dropped me just in front of it. Her husband and their six-year-old son were also home.

Though she earlier agreed to share her experiences, this time she began by saying that it had been a long time since she had last discussed these things, and that generally she avoided talking of those times. While I did not insist, she, however, started to tell her story in a while, in a conversational mode with her husband Neela Sonowal, who also hails from Lakhipathar and has his share of experiences.

That year she had just passed her matriculation examination[4] and had joined the Digboi College for a higher secondary course. She was a keen student and aimed to earn a master's degree, a degree that is a rarity for a place like Lakhipathar. There were a lot of expectations that she would do good from her family and community. What happened in the months of November and December that year changed her life forever.

At about 4 am in the morning of 28 November 1990, the sound of gunfights coming from the forest was heard for the first time. The people of Lakhipathar had not heard such fierce gunfights before, and they were both confused and worried. They were worried about the army entering the villages. Many such terrified people fled Lakhipathar on the night of 28 November, through hidden jungle paths.

[4] As the High School Leaving Certificate (HSLC) examination (10th board examination) is commonly called.

During the day, there were discussions and plans about leaving the village. By evening, some boys from Digboi—some of them associated with the All Assam Students Union (AASU), and others who stayed in Digboi for work—came to smuggle out young boys and girls from Lakhipathar. A group of about 100 to 150 boys and girls from the villages Pandhowa, Kopohua, and Laupoti got ready to flee. The elder people were not taken along. 'Only young boys and girls', the leaders of the group gave strict instructions, 'old people will stay back.'

It was a very tragic day, Sewali remembered. When they prepared to leave, they did not know what was lying ahead for them. Neither did they know what was in stock for their parents and grandparents and uncles and aunts, whom they were leaving behind. It seemed as if they were leaving the elder people to die while themselves fleeing to safety. It seemed as if the separation was forever. The atmosphere was heavy with everyone crying, fearing that this might be their last moment with their dear ones.

The group started at dusk and walked the whole night through the forest. The boys who led them knew alleys through the thick forest. While walking, they had to use their hands too, to clear the road of creepers and tree branches blocking the track.

They had neither the time nor the sense to dress properly for the cold night of November. On the way, they had to cross a small rivulet inside the forest, which luckily did not have much water during that time of the year. At another point, they had to crawl through a culvert, as crossing the road above was not safe. To add to the difficulties, leeches covered everyone's hands and feet. In these parts of Assam, it rains even during the winters, and the jungle is always damp and has leeches and other insects. The fear of elephants and other wild animals was imminent too during the harvesting season.

Sewali said that they had to use the jungle track because all the main roads were blocked. Lakhipathar was made into a *sunor temi.*[5] Neela said: 'Anyone can enter it, but no one can go out of it.' But though the army was doing its best to seal off the Lakhipathar area, they did not know about the possibility of people tracking through the jungle.

[5] A container with a small mouth and a broad base used to keep lime paste eaten with areca nut and paan leaf.

However, even when one went through the jungle, at one place they had to cross the main road. That was a risky part of the journey. The armed forces were given special powers, to shoot at sight in case of suspicion, and army vehicles were moving on the road. They kept lying on the low ground on the side of road in the biting cold of November over water that had accumulated, waiting for an opportunity to cross it. They were thirsty and some people were drinking water from puddles formed in elephant footmarks. There was a little baby in the group, a three-month old girl with her mother. She started crying, and everyone got anxious, because the army vehicles were moving very closely. The mother pressed the mouth of the baby to muffle the sound.

Once the vehicles passed, the group hurriedly crossed the road and entered the forest again on the other side. The group also split into two somewhere on the way. After walking for a few more hours, they finally entered Digboi.

Though many people thus fled Lakhipathar, some people, mostly those who were old, stayed back. Walking so far was the concern for some; some were just unable to decide. That night, while Sewali and others were walking through the jungle, the army entered the villages. Several married and unmarried women were raped from the villages of Dhonda Nahor and Roadside Kopohua. Old men and women were tied to army trucks and dragged on the road behind running vehicles.

Sewali's outbursts in the refugee camp in Digboi, when the Congress (I) leaders Hiteshwar Saikia and Anowara Taimur visited them, were reported in the newspaper and were referred to in Chapter 5. I asked her, what happened to her mark sheets and other documents, which were reported in the papers as lost while fleeing from Lakhipathar. Sewali laughed when I mentioned this and said, 'At that time I was very angry, and thought that it is the only way to make them realize what we were going through.' She had not really lost her documents, though she feared losing them. The trauma of this experience left deep marks on Sewali's mind and she joined the xangathan in subsequent years, but only to be left with further experiences of pain, fear, and frustration afterwards.

## Army at Home

By the intervening night of 27 and 28 November, Lakhipathar was filled with army jawans. They blocked all roads to Lakhipathar and entered and stayed in the villages searching for rebel ULFA cadres. While men were taken to makeshift interrogation centres in school buildings and *namghars* (community prayer halls), many families had to accommodate stays of jawans in their houses. Others had to let them use their houses for various other purposes.

## Dhonda Nahar

Dhonda Nahar is one of the villages that run parallel to the main road of Lakhipathar. The front door of Lalitya Gogoi's house in Dhonda Nahar was not opened for a month during the army operation starting on 27 November. Cows remained in the cowshed. Sometimes an old man from a nearby house took the cows out, as, owing to his age, he was subjected to less suspicion. Mr Gogoi was a schoolteacher. He was telling the story of the first army operation calmly, as if he was narrating it from his memory of reading a book, and his wife was inserting little details in between. His wife sounded more emotional, and brought up more personal details.

It was the harvesting time. At the tiniali where the road coming from Tingrai joins the road coming from Balijan to enter Laupoti village, there was a bomb blast. A vehicle of the army was blown up. Mrs Gogoi remembered her part of the story from that first day after the night of the 27th. They had no meals until two in the afternoon. The last meal was at 2 o'clock the previous afternoon. The army jawans were delivered food by army vehicles. Gogoi's family was also offered food, but they were scared to eat. Therefore, the leftover food was given to dogs, cats, and cows.

'Tank gari's' were run from one end to another in the paddy fields over crops about to be harvested. People were in the fields. They were first made to stand on a line. Then the women were sent back home and the men were taken away to the school. Some army men lived in the school, many others stayed in people's houses. They kept asking: 'Where is ULFA? Where is ULFA's camp? Do they come to your place to eat?' The women were so frightened that they used to hide under their beds. Many people fled through the forest and went to relief camps in Digboi. Gogoi's family did not go, because they did not know how it would be to live in a camp, having 'never lived in a camp before'. They stayed home thinking that they would die at home if they had to.

We were sitting in the small veranda of the old Assam type house by the main road. An army vehicle passed by. Everyone remained silent for a moment. They started speaking only after the vehicle disappeared from vision at a distance. Mr Gogoi broke the silence, 'That's an army vehicle. The camp is now a little further, about three kilometres away. The army always has had a camp in Lakhipathar since that first war, though the location of the camp had kept changing … doesn't matter even if they hear us saying this.' The wife added, 'Now they have Assamese guys in there. This group is good, not like the earlier ones. We suffered a lot earlier.'

Though they said they were not afraid of this group of the army, the low, almost whispering voice in which Mrs Gogoi talked, and the way they became silent while the army vehicle passed by, spoke a lot. The jawans in the present batch of the army have not harmed them, but the fear of the army was still palpable.

She also talked of her children, remembering the old days: 'Our children could not study at all. They (the army jawans) used to come at dawn. They'll come at 4 in the morning.' Once they came at 12 in the night, took her second son. The son came back after some time and told her that they would come at 4 am to have tea. Several times, she had prepared food and tea with supplies provided by them and served them.

The coming of the 'they', the army, the 'other' was haunting. Even when they had come only for tea or food, these visits were remembered as moments of fear and violence.

On the night of 27 November, some army jawans stayed at the Gogoi household. 'They gave sugar and tea leaves asking to make tea for them' Mrs Gogoi remembered. Gogoi intervened, 'Some of them were good people, but amongst them only there were some bad guys. The good ones identified the bad ones for us.'

It was crucial to note how even during an armed operation which saw rapes and torture of civilians, the people talked of individual responsibility of the jawans for the atrocities. Many of such statements, it appeared to me, were not instant observations or feelings at the time of the first encounter with the army, but developed through the more than 20 years of living with the army thereafter. This was evident from how people while narrating their stories, drifted from one point in time to another. But gradually the driftings themselves started to make sense as a part of the story: of how the moment has been remembered not through some exact unchangeable memory, but through a memory that gradually developed, shaped, and reshaped.

Army personnel were living in almost every house. The higher officers like Major were the ones who lived in people's houses, and the jawans used to give two hourly guard duties in front. When the army asked for space to stay at Gogoi's house on the night of 27 November, they left one of the two rooms in their house for them. The next morning another group of army jawans entered the house and took Mr Gogoi away, saying that they needed to talk. Some from the group which was in the house were having a bath by the bore well. The group that came asked Mrs Gogoi how many members were in the family. She replied seven, but two of her sons were not home. One of them fled from home the previous night when the army entered Lakhipathar, and stayed with somebody else. When the army inquired about these two members who were not there in the house, the jawan who was bathing by the bore well 'saved her'; she remembered him saying, '… the other two are in the *xibir* in Digboi'. Those who were not found at home were counted as ULFA members, but Mrs Gogoi said, this jawan saved them by speaking on her behalf to his fellow man. Several women from Dhonda Nahor village were raped those very days, and men, old and young alike were tortured publicly. The remembrance of such little acts with a sense of relief and gratitude on the face of violence all around was something intriguing.

Gogoi spoke more on behalf of others while his wife remembered things that happened to her and her family. 'The people of Lakhipathar suffered a lot', Mr Gogoi said. When his wife talked of the army taking him away for the first time, he recalled it: 'That day, I was left back at home at two in the afternoon. They asked me many things, things that I never knew.' He however skipped any account of torture. Only his wife added: 'He suffered in such ways that it is too much to talk about.' Gogoi remembered that the teachers could not teach at all. They were taken away several times, to different places, and were asked many questions, while detained for whole days. Again, he skipped any account of violence on the body. However, the woman who accompanied him by repeating: '… he suffered a lot', expressed without uttering it in words, things that were perhaps unspeakable. The violence on the body seemed too difficult to pronounce in words.

## Laupoti

Jethai is Biren dai's elder sister who lives towards the end of Laupoti village with her three unmarried daughters, one son, and his wife. When she talks of her experiences with the army during the Operation Bajrang, though it is quite detailed with personal experiences, it also sounds a bit distant; though she narrates episodes of trauma and violence, one cannot read the intense pain one would generally expect from a sufferer while remembering such events.

The moments of Operation Bajrang were recollected with a laugh, by adding how funny and foolish it was of them to hide under the bed in the fear of the army, as if it was an earthquake, or that she even stopped cooking properly out of fear.

One night they had skipped dinner and were sitting huddled together listening to the fire fight that was going on. Then at around three in the morning, the army came and asked them to come to the namghar immediately. No one had time to eat or bathe. When they reached the namghar, there already were a lot of people sitting there. The women were inside the namghar, while some men were kept tied to the pillars. Some others were being beaten up in the open yard.

All the young men who were still staying in the village were tied with a single piece of long rope in a line and were made to squat in the *murga*[6] position for the whole day. When any of them lost balance and fell, all of them would fall in a line. It made a very funny scene, Jethai was laughing again. So were all of us, who were listening to her. Whoever would lose balance in that squatting group was, however, beaten up with rifle butts and thick sticks, she added, as if to make up for her laughing at them. The others already knew the story; surely, Jethai has narrated it to them many times. The daughters were adding whenever Jethai was missing out on any of the funny parts. The story of the beatings, the sleepless nights, the terror of getting caught by the army, all these were remembered as things from an unrelated distant past.

Whether we look at Biren dai's narratives of fleeing from Lakhipathar, Borma's narrative of terror-filled nights while Barta was being beaten up by the army, or Jethai's stories of fearing the army

[6] An awkward and difficult position resembling a murga or a chicken.

like an earthquake, their stories are limited to the period of the first blow of the army. It is often remembered in Laupoti like a fable, rather than any tragic and unjust past making them grieve even today. The mode of telling the stories of hardship was a mix of drama, glorification, and humour. But the intense feeling of pain one could sense in the narrations of Sewali, for example, or coming from people like Jotin Koch of Kenduguri or from the Moran villages that we discuss later, was not there. Laupoti had *intimate* exposure to the ULFA for a longer period than to the army, and the people were impressed by the skills, tactics, and the arms of the ULFA boys which were openly displayed. When the army came, the first days of Operation Bajrang were intensive but the period was relatively short, when compared to years of torture and suffering of people in some other villages. Those in Laupoti who did not experience this phase, such as wives who had came from a different place, or people who fled from home during those days, nevertheless participated in the stories, indicating that they heard the stories many times.

## Arrest and Torture of Lower Level Cadres

### Deepak Gogoi, Pandhowa Village

Deepak Gogoi was a member of the Left students group, Students' Federation of India (SFI) before he joined the ULFA in late 80s. As a lower-level cadre, when the army came in the winter of 1989, he was entrusted the responsibility of keeping a Kachin-trained but ailing cadre named Robert safe. Deepak hid him in Lakhipathar itself, slipping in and out of the forest. In the initial days, Deepak met the army several times, but by using his presence of mind, he saved himself.

However, after giving the army a miss on several instances, Deepak faced what he called 'the most difficult day' of his life. It was sometime in late March 1991. Amongst the over-ground political cadres of ULFA in Lakhipathar, a man called Kamala Moran was the chief. That day Kamala Moran was arrested somewhere outside Lakhipathar. When the news reached Lakhipathar, Deepak and rest of the cadres in hiding got frightened. Kamala knew all their hiding places. They feared that he would divulge everything under torture. 'It was a Saturday; and it was the most conflict-ridden day of my life', Deepak sighed. That night all the houses where he usually took shelter in were raided by the army. Kamala Moran was dragged along to identify safe houses. Deepak was tense and was not able to decide what to do. It was a very dark night. At about 11.30–12, he came out, thinking where he could spend the night. While walking aimlessly on the road, he met a man standing at his *poduli* (entrance to a traditional Assamese home's compound leading to the dwelling house), who asked Deepak where he was going to stay. It was not one of Deepak's usual shelters. The house was just by the village road. When Deepak told him that he was unable to decide where to stay, then this person asked Deepak to stay in his house. Deepak accepted the offer. He was tense and frightened. Whenever he tried to lie down and sleep, the sound of the army vehicles moving on the road did not allow him to.

At about 3.30 in the morning, when the first lights of morning came, the old lady of the house came to Deepak and softly told him, 'Diensi[7], army has surrounded everything, even our toilet is surrounded by army.' Deepak realized that he had no chance to escape. Somebody told him that the houses of those where he used to stay were in bad shape, and even the floors were dug up. He peeped through the window and saw that the place was full of army men. Kamala Moran was also with them. While giving up any hope of escaping, he still changed his clothes and wore a *chaador* (an unstitched piece of long cloth generally wrapped around the upper body by men and worn with a skirt called *mekhela* by women) from the family, the way elderly men wear it. After about an hour and a half, the large army group that came in 20–30 vehicles, left the place. They did not come to check the house where Deepak was staying, by 'sheer chance', Deepak said. But after the army was gone, the people of the village 'requested' him to flee from Lakhipathar and go somewhere else as it would be the best thing for him as well as others, Kamala Moran being already in the custody of the army. Paying heed to this suggestion, Deepak ate something at his host's house, and went out. There are two roads from Pandhowa to reach the main road of Lakhipathar on which the bus runs: if one takes the first one it reaches the road near Laupoti village, at the entry point to Lakhipathar; if the second road is taken, it takes one to the

[7] People in Lakhipathar know Deepak as Diensi.

road near roadside Kopohua village, which is further into Lakhipathar. It happened that day that Deepak chose to take the second route to the main road and board the bus there. So he remained unaware of the army troops who were waiting on the main road near Laupoti, taking position from their bunkers and checking everyone who passed by. Had he taken the first route to the main road that day, he would have seen the army bunkers before boarding the bus and could have re-planned his escape. Now, as it happened, he saw the army jawans only when the bus reached Laupoti. At the first check point at the Laupoti tiniali, 'Commander Joshi himself was sitting.' But Deepak crossed that check point safely without being identified. A kilometre further from there towards Digboi, inside the forest, there was the second check post. This time Deepak got really nervous. The army jawans were walking towards him from the opposite direction along with Kamala Moran. Kamala was in bad shape with marks of beatings and electrocution all over his body.

Deepak and other passengers in the minibus were asked to de-board the bus and were made to stand in two lines. Deepak stood at the third position from the beginning on the left row. By then he had no other option but to just hope that somehow Kamala missed him out. However, that did not happen. Kamala immediately identified Deepak. The army concluded that they had found a 'boss' and let the others leave in the bus. A handcuff was put on one of Deepak's hands, and a huge dog was tied to the other hand. Another rope was tied to his waist and a jawan held the other end of the rope. After interrogating him in the nearby camp in the Laupoti primary school, he was bundled into a truck and taken to a larger camp in Digboi. In his interrogation in both the camps he accepted that he was a lower-level political member of ULFA without engaging in any act of violence and convinced them that he joined the organization only because Kamala Moran persuaded him to. For reasons not completely comprehensible to Deepak, he was set free after that. The officer interrogating him said: '(N)ow you leave. Our operations will continue for some time, so you don't go back to Lakhipathar'. Deepak did not fully trust the officer when he asked Deepak to get off the truck and leave, he almost felt a bullet piercing his head from behind while taking unsteady steps forward. He did not go back to Lakhipathar for about a month.

On his way to the Digboi camp in the army truck, the jawans asked him why he joined the ULFA, and said that he should have joined the Indian army. There was only one of them who was poking him with a rifle. Once in Digboi, Deepak was looking at known faces to send home a message about his arrest as suggested by the jawans. Many of them were in the same bus that Deepak took that day, but nobody looked at him and pretended to be strangers.

The atmosphere was marked by suspicion, distrust, and fear. The regular life of Lakhipathar was stalled, when one could not even trust their neighbours. This image of fear and alienation came up in narrations by other people as well, when they talked of villages being marked as taking sides: either of the army or the ULFA, or about even the neighbours not coming out to see what was happening when wails came out from the next house at night.

## Jotin Koch, Kenduguri Village

Jotin Koch joined the xangathan only some time before Operation Bajrang was launched. He was impressed by the glamour associated with being an ULFA cadre, and was also motivated by the hope that it would be some kind of a job. As a cadre, however, he only got to do odd jobs like cleaning utensils and polishing shoes.

During Operation Bajrang, while he was hiding away from home, the army came looking for him in his house and his family members were beaten up and tortured. One night towards the end of *Sot* month (end of March), he along with two friends was walking near Dhulijan Laina gaon towards Makum through a jungle road, and they were stopped and arrested at a army check post set up at a forest gate. At about 12 in the night, after messages were sent through wireless sets, they were blindfolded with black cloth and all three were taken to the Nagajan forest camp. In the camp, somebody named Shankar was asked to note down the identification marks of everyone, like moles, cut marks, or eye colour, etc., on the body. After that, the commanding officer of Operation Bajrang known as Topa,[8] was called up, and he was told

[8] The character of Topa reached almost mythical dimensions during the operation and thereafter. More about this is discussed in the next section.

'*mil gaya mil gaya*' (found). Then Topa came over and took them to Tingrai camp at 1.30 am.

All three of them were interrogated at the Tingrai camp separately. They were still kept blindfolded. In the xangathan Jotin took the alias of Makar Khanikar, but the army had the name Jotin Koch in their records. Therefore, when he was asked his name, he said that his name was Makar. However, he was not safe. There were two other Lakhipathar boys in the camp already, Bajra and Lalit Moran, whom Jotin did not see as he was kept blindfolded. These two were beaten to pulp and when they were brought to identify him, they identified him as Jotin Koch instantly. So now it was Jotin's turn to face the tortures, doubled by the fact that he had lied.

Beginning to talk of the torture, Jotin laughed at his own fate, and said, '... after that they started to play the *madal*[9]'. But gradually he assumed a grave disposition, and kept telling me: 'I cannot describe what they did to me, what they did to me is beyond words ... no matter how much I try, I cannot tell you how I felt.' I sensed the restlessness in his voice as he tried to make visible the gravity of the suffering he had, while failing to capture them in words.

The other two who were caught with Jotin were beaten the whole night till they lost consciousness. In the morning at about 8 am they were taken in a truck and were dropped inside the jungle. Blood was oozing out from their heads, from their backs, from their legs and arms. The sun was high. They started walking towards their homes through Laupoti tiniali and then through Joipuria road. People on the way were staring at their bleeding bodies. They kept walking putting their last bits of strength into it, thinking that it was okay even if they died, once they had seen the faces of their parents.

The parents on the other hand, did not know anything till they reached home. They thought that the boys were safe somewhere. When they reached home, Jotin's mother fainted. His father and his aunt started crying, while trying to console him. Later, in the first 'surrender' ceremony of the Bajrang operation, Jotin, along with 200 other boys and girls from Lakhipathar 'surrendered' in the Kosujan ground. His tales of suffering, however, did not end there.

[9] Madal is a double-headed hand drum, slightly different from the Assamese hand drum dhol. Probably it is of Nepalese origin.

## 'Topa' and the Kosujan 'Surrender' Ceremony

Paresh Baruah was Lakhipathar's 'man of mystery' till Operation Bajrang. With Bajrang, another 'man of mystery' entered the history of Lakhipathar: Topa. He was an army major and the commander of the army in Lakhipathar area during the operation. Everyone in Lakhipathar had a bit to talk about Topa.

No one knew his real name. People were not sure which regiment he came from. Everyone had a different surname for him and a matching regiment attached to it. Topa was middle aged and bald, earning him the name *Topa*: the Assamese word for a bald man. He was remembered as the most shrewd and ruthless army man Lakhipathar had ever seen. Some people say that his own brother was killed in the hands of ULFA because of which he became so barbaric, some others attribute it to his 'ripe' age and vast experience.

While people remembered how merciless he was in torturing people, they also remembered his unparalleled memory. He was readily described as having a very 'sharp' mind. His memory was such, Durga Dutta from Kenduguri once said, that he knew who is whose son and whose daughter in every family (28 May, Mr Durgeswar Dutta, pers.com, 2012). Jotin Koch added to that, '… not only that, but he also knew in whose house a baby is born and what name is given to the newborn. Not only just people, he also knew in whose house a calf is born and what name is given to that calf' (Mr Jotin Koch, 2012, pers.com, 28 May).

Topa arranged the first 'surrender' ceremony of ULFA in Tinsukia district in the Kosujan ground, where about two hundred boys and girls from Lakhipathar were made to 'surrender'. These 'surrenders' were of a different nature. 'Whomever Topa had seen', Deepak said once, 'he became ULFA … he had never seen me, neither I had seen his face, so I never had to surrender, and thus I never became an ULFA, and more importantly never became a SULFA.' This was despite the fact that Deepak was a member of the xangathan. As much as Deepak was not counted by Topa in his list of ULFAs, many other young boys and girls, who had no links to the organization at all, many of them being school children studying in high school classes like 8th, 9th, and 10th, or at most in the higher secondary classes, were counted in his list of 'dreaded ULFA insurgents' and 'allowed' to 'surrender' in a public ceremony after these 'misguided' youths realized their 'mistake' under the 'guidance' of the army.[10] The rehabilitation packages were discussed well in the public domain, with the major news dailies carrying caricature of such measures in the form of cartoons.

In Lakhipathar, the issue of how fake these 'surrenders' were, is often discussed. No doubt, there were a few people like Jotin Koch and Dipen Sonowal who were affiliated to the xangathan in some minor way and thus could be counted as 'real' ULFA members, but the vast majority of those 200 youth were no ULFAs. Until the time they 'surrendered' in a public ceremony, neither did they really know what it meant. Neela Sonowal, who hails from Dhadum village of Lakhipathar, did not ever join the organization. His parents were sceptical of the possibility of success of the xangathan from the beginning and they consciously kept away from it. When the army entered the villages, like every other youth, he fled to Digboi, as any youth found in the village was tortured or killed and then it was counted as the death of an ULFA cadre.

However, before the Kosujan ceremony, the people in the village were told that an identity card would be given to all the young men and women, so that they would not have trouble from the army in future. Neela's parents specifically asked him to come from Digboi to go and collect the card. It was understood as some kind of certificate saying that the person having the card was not an ULFA cadre and that thus would keep the holder safe. It is only later that they came to know that the card meant that the holder was a member of the ULFA who had now forsaken links with the organization. The story did not end there. After Operation Bajrang, several other operations came to Lakhipathar, and the army has been an almost constant presence since then. Whenever a new group or a new regiment of army came, the list of those who held an 'identity card' as 'surrendered' was taken out, and they faced fresh atrocities.

[10] Another similar surrender ceremony was reported by the newspaper *Dainik Asam*, where a surrendering leader gave a speech in a ceremony organized by the army. He said: 'This is a plea from me after committing a wrong and then getting reformed later … my plea to everyone in the ULFA, do surrender, do lay down your arms … today we realize that independence cannot be achieved through the path of revolution. We have received this realization and experience from the armed forces' (*Dainik Asam*, 1 April 1991, p. 1, translation mine).

The fact that money was attached to this act of 'surrender' also complicates the issue. Thus Akon da, Durga Dutta's son, once said in the presence of several others that that it was a matter of luck that despite the money, his father remained rigid in the fact that his son was never a member of ULFA, and thus would never go to 'surrender'. Jotin Koch, who was around, became defensive at this and said, 'No one surrendered for the money at that time … such things happened later … the only thing that we wanted during that time was some relief, that our parents be able to live in peace.'

## Post-Bajrang: Two Decades of War and State

The assembly elections of Assam were held in two phases on 6 and 8 June 1991, and Operation Bajrang was called off before the elections. The ULFA was negotiating with the state in the meantime, and it offered to declare a ceasefire and consider the possibility of talks if the army operations were called off throughout the state. Further, the organization also declared that it would not interfere in the elections. While the decision to withdraw the army allegedly just when it was getting a foothold was looked at sceptically by many from the defence installations, the declaration by the ULFA came as a surprise too for most people at that time. It is argued later by ex-police officer E.N. Rammohan in his book *Simply Khaki* (2005), and was suggested to me[11] by Sunil Nath that an understanding was arrived at between the xangathan and the Congress (I) leader Hiteshwar Saikia, to this effect. Sunil Nath is an ex-ULFA leader, who joined as a cadre in 1983 under the alias Siddhartha Phukan and went on to become the Central Publicity Secretary of ULFA till he came out in 1992.

Though Operation Bajrang was not very successful initially in the Lakhipathar camp sites, as the cadres had already fled from there, gradually, as the army got hold on the terrain of Assam and developed its own information channels, it came down hard upon the organization. It was getting difficult for the ULFA cadres to keep hiding in villages, and many had to flee from Assam. The torture of common people was also reaching unbearable extents.

[11] In a semi-formal conversation, on 15 May 2012.

In the midst of all these, a major cordon and search operation was organized by the army in the Saraipung area near Digboi, where unknown to them, the ULFA C-in-C Paresh Baruah was hiding. Baruah, trapped in such way, immediately sent out a courier to Rebati Phukan, a man hailing from the same village as Paresh Baruah and close to both him and the then chief minister Hiteshwar Saikia, asking to send a message to the chief minister. The bargain was this: the army operation would be called off, and ULFA would not interfere in the elections. Without the knowledge that Paresh Baruah himself was trapped, this probably was a tempting offer for Hiteshwar Saikia. The next morning a meeting was hurriedly called in the Raj Bhavan with even the governor not knowing the agenda beforehand, and the Principal Advisor Prakash Singh, who earlier worked under Hiteshwar Saikia and had his loyalties for the ex-Chief Minister, convinced the governor for the withdrawal of the army. (Rammohan 2005: 166–70).

The elections went off peacefully.[12] Congress (I) won 61 seats out of a total of 106 in the Brahmaputra valley.[13] The AGP and the newly formed Natun Asom Gana Parishad (NAGP), a splinter group of AGP formed immediately before the elections, won 18 out of 103 contested and five seats respectively.

The election statistics from the districts of Tinsukia and Dibrugarh, both known as the strongholds of the ULFA during this time, with the backdrop of a brutal army operation which was portrayed as legitimate by the Congress (I) party, was interesting. In Tinsukia district, all the five assembly seats went to Congress (I), while AGP contested in 5 and NAGP in 3 seats respectively. Congress drew 52.84 per cent of the total votes. In Dibrugarh, out of a total of 7 seats, Congress (I) won 6 and CPI (M) won 1, while both AGP and NAGP miserably failed to win even a single seat contesting from all 7 constituencies. Here, the percentage

[12] As reported in the media. The villagers of Lakhipathar, however, talked of an incident near the Lakhipathar voting centre, where the ULFA cadres killed paramilitary / army jawans by throwing hand grenades on the day of the elections.

[13] The Brahmaputra valley is the area where the ethnic Assamese people mostly live. The Borak valley is mostly Bengali dominated, and the ULFA as well as the Assamese nationalist sentiments had very little popularity in the Borak valley.

of votes received was thus: AGP 21.34 per cent, NAGP 1.10 per cent, Congress (I) 41.22 per cent, others 36.33 per cent (C.N. Baruah 2009: 33–48).

The new Congress (I) government led by Hiteshwar Saikia took oath on 30 June 1991. The ULFA maintained a low profile and kept silent until then. But the very next day, 15 top government officials of various organizations, including a Russian national, were kidnapped by the organization from different parts of the state, and in return for their release demanded the release of all imprisoned ULFA cadres and other political prisoners from the jails (*Dainik Asam*, 5 July 1991).

The new government received a blow very early. The police was completely clueless and helpless about the abductions, while the ULFA was very rigid with their demands. Finally, most of the top leaders of the ULFA were released, but the organization failed to keep its word and two of the abducted persons, Russian mine specialist Sergei Grietchenko and T.S. Raju from the state of Andhra Pradesh were killed in their custody (Ahmed 1991). This created a lot of furore and killing of innocent people in custody was not taken very well by the people, though it was also seen by many as a failure on the part of the state.

During this time, several political assassinations also took place. Major targets were leaders of the Congress (I) party. Another assassination that shook Assam was the killing of social worker, freedom fighter, and journalist Kamala Saikia on 9 August 1991. Kamala Saikia was a vocal critic of ULFA through his writings.

In this context, on 15 September 1991, the Indian Army forces were brought in to the state again in the request of the state government and deployed in eight districts: Dibrugarh, Tinsukia, Jorhat, Golaghat, Sibsagar, Dhemaji, Lakhimpur, and Nagaon.

With this dramatic change in scenario, the army came back to Lakhipathar, this time in the form of Operation Rhino. In contrast to the army camp settled in Tingrai during Operation Bajrang, this time the army came closer and their camp was settled inside Lakhipathar first near Dhonda Nahor village, and then shifted to the present location near the High School and occupied the residential quarter of the ranger of Lakhipathar Range office of the Forest department. In this compound, they also constructed several other structures at different points of time by using the unpaid forced labour of the villagers, so that a whole unit of the army could be accommodated. Thus, another military camp was securely established in Lakhipathar, this time of the Indian army, instead of the ULFA.

## The Army in the Longue Duree: Surveillance, Violence, and Creation of the Enemy Within

The first moment of violence experienced by Lakhipathar in the form of Operation Bajrang was non-nuanced, random violence, and the people of Lakhipathar were one in their fears and sufferings. Post-Bajrang, the violence of the army and other state forces became more nuanced. With the forces always being around, and with rumours produced and having played their role, an environment of suspicion and mistrust was created amongst the villagers. After sunset, people stopped stepping outside of their houses. Only the army walked on the roads after dusk. A part of this process was also the complete cut off of some villages from others, avoidance of people from some villages by others, marking of some villages as ULFA villages, and others as 'informer' or 'CID'[14] villages. Thus during the late '90s and early 2000s, people did not visit Rangsangi village. The people of Kenduguri and the Nepali villages were thought to be army spies, and they were avoided by everyone. Even in 2012, people avoided going to the Moran villages—Rangsangi Moran gaon and Aamguri Moran gaon, as they were seen as ULFA villages.

The stories in these villages were not very different from the others though. They were just spread out over a longer period. In Rangsangi Moran gaon, in every family either someone died, houses were burnt down to ashes, clothes and jewellery taken away, or men and women were beaten up, tortured, electrocuted, and jailed under sections of TADA and UAPA. Some court cases were still going on. A mother showed me a picture of her son who was sixteen years old when killed by a group of unified command personnel of army, paramilitary forces, and the state police, while asleep along with a few others in the backyard, to avoid the army raids which used to pick up every male found at home. The body of the boy was later hung on a bamboo pole and brought near their house. The father was told by the unified command personnel that they had killed a *pohu*, a deer. Later when the family asked for compensation, they were told that the boy acted as ULFA linkman, and there is

[14] By 'informer' or 'CID', they meant informer to or spy of the army.

no compensation for the death of such people. No compensation was given after the paramilitary forces burnt down their house either. They were told, '(Y)ou host ULFA at your house, why should we compensate if your house is burnt down for that?'

The brother-in-law of Torali also died in the organization. She had experienced the forces several times, and was beaten up severely by iron rods and bamboo poles. If the army found an extra used plate in the dining floor, they would accuse them of hosting an ULFA cadre. When the raids started, as a married woman with a few unmarried sister-in-laws, she had to go and face the army. In a previous chapter, we noted how a young wife attended to the ULFA cadres coming to place a demand or to collect ransom, for the reason that they were generally softer with women.[15] In Torali's case, however, she needed to go ahead to save her unmarried sisters-in-law from any possible 'dishonour' in the hands of the army.

## Rangsangi: Surveillance of the Army

Purnanada Saikia of Rangsangi village is the ward member from the Ward no. 6 of the Lakhipathar *gaon* (village) panchayat. During Operation Bajrang, the army came towards Rangsangi also, from the Tingrai side. They came marching on foot, wearing different shades of fatigue clothes. The line was about one kilometre long. They carried everything with them, including pots and pans to cook. However, they turned to the main road and did not enter the village. The people were frightened and kept hiding inside their houses.

Soufalary, Purnanada's younger brother had to move his house because of the operation. His house was next to the forest. He had four daughters; and all the men in the village had to flee. Purnananda Saikia was the only man staying at home in the whole village. The isolated house of Soufalary and his four daughters staying at home was a risky thing. So they moved their house to a location near Purnananda's. Purnananda's sons had fled to their brother-in-law's house in Laina Dhulijan gaon.

Those days, all the women left in the village alone used to come and stay the nights at Purnananda's house. When the army would come,

[15] See Chapter 6, p. 172.

they would ask, why all the women were staying there. Purnananda would say, 'We are village people, and we get frightened if we hear bullet sounds. All the men have fled. So the women have come to stay with me out of fear'. During Operation Bajrang he was not beaten up.

On the day of the election of June 1991, two army jawans were fired upon and killed by ULFA. The polling station was near the high school/range office. That day, Purnananda was also a polling agent there. Once he reached home, he heard that two jawans were gunned down. The next day, he saw that everywhere it was just the dark uniforms of the army.[16] They came through the mud and water of the '*Xaun mahor pathar*'.[17] Purnananda thought that it would not be good if everyone fled. So he stayed at home. The jawans carried stout branches of the *gohora* (a kind of large tree) tree. They first met Momi, his daughter, and beat her up. Then they found Purnananda and beat him up with every question. Then they also went to the other houses. Everywhere there were only women. Girls and women were beaten up with the branches of the gohora tree. This continued for quite some time. After that incident Purnanda had severe pain in his whole body, and he had to go to a doctor at Digboi. His treatment continued for three months.

The young men of the village suffered a lot, even their regular meals were at stake as they had to stay away from their homes, in the fields, or in the jungles. Even those who were at home, they just had rice with salt. No one had either the courage or the enthusiasm to find vegetables to eat.

People would not go from their own village to the other villages of Lakhipathar. Rangsangi being located in one isolated corner, no one from other villages ever came there. People were frightened of two things, one was the fear of army jawans who they suspected were hiding in Rangsangi, and the second and more palpable fear was that of being seen as a spy. People from outside Rangsangi thought that if they went to Rangsangi, the Rangsangi people would think of them as spies.

[16] During this time, as per all written accounts including newspapers, ULFA was keeping low and was charged up with the kidnapping of officials only after the new ministry took oath. This version of the killing of the army jawans came only from Purnananda.

[17] Literally, the muddy fields of the monsoon season.

People were afraid to keep their lamps lit at night. The men would sleep in the paddy fields, in the *tongi-ghar*[18] or lying under the paddy crops. The army did not go to the fields looking for them. So hiding there was a way of escaping torture despite all the insect bites and the cold wind. Staying at other people's houses was not an option, as people were not able to keep guests. They were afraid that they would be penalized if somebody who was not a family member was found in their house. Even relatives were not able to come, as the army would think any extra person to be an ULFA cadre.

The army knew how many people were there in every family. On days, all the members from every family were asked to gather in the school field, but each family was made to sit separately from other families and they were not allowed to talk to people from other families. On such days, the army would note down how many members there were in each family. When the army would later come to the village for checking, they would count how many beds were there in a specific house. If there was a family of four, and there were more than two beds (which should be sufficient for four people according to the army's counting), then the family would be charged with sheltering ULFA cadres. If somebody had extra beds—kept for occasional guests such as married daughters and their husbands—then these had to be kept dismantled, and outside the house. When the army came for checks, they would carry a list of names of people in each family and their photographs. If there was some mismatch between the list and the people actually present, either in terms of presence or absence, then that family got into trouble.

What was striking in the narration of events by Purnananda, was that despite experiences of torture and restrictive impositions and memories of pain on the body, the way these episodes were remembered had more of emotions of fear combined with awe, rather than sentiments of injustice done to a people. Other than the violence on the body, the surveillance of the army was emphasized a lot. The tortures and beatings were narrated in a way as if there was no newness in those, as if they were the least interesting parts of the story, while the technicalities of surveillance were elaborated in great detail.

[18] A high platform commonly made of bamboo and hay amidst paddy fields to keep a watch on the crops.

## 'Unlawful' Lives

The violence on the bodies, and the arrests and detentions were given a legal status in these circumstances by interpreting them through provisions of various laws, ordinary and extraordinary. The imposition of President's rule in 1989–90 was one of the moments when a state of emergency was declared where the regular law of the state was suspended. Such an exceptional regime, however, did not end there, as the state of Assam has continuously been categorized as a disturbed area since November 1990 facilitating the imposition of the Disturbed Areas Act and the Armed Forces Special Powers Act (AFSPA). Further, there have been laws like the Terrorist and Disruptive Activities (Prevention) Act (TADA) and the Unlawful Activities (Prevention) Act (UAPA) in operation. Through these legal arrangements, the construction of random lives as 'unlawful' was a regular occurrence in Lakhipathar.

Two of the most well-known sections of law, producing unlawful lives in Lakhipathar, are UAPA sections 10 and 13, because almost everyone who for any reason ever had a case filed against him or her, had those sections in the chargesheet. While section 10 penalizes membership of unlawful associations, which includes participation in any meeting of the specified unlawful organization, section 13 penalizes actual activities.

Among the numerous cases under UAPA 10/13, one prominent case was that of two young men named Don and Petua respectively, who were killed at gun point by a Unified Command party of Indian Army and Assam Police accompanied by surrendered members of ULFA known as SULFA.[19] The conversations that took place before they were shot at were in public and many people heard the SULFA men saying that they could not to go back from Lakhipathar empty handed, and

[19] The government of Assam was trying to suppress the issues raised and demands made by the ULFA by attempts at maligning the organization and by dividing the cadres, apart from the physical coercion meted out to people in the form of army and paramilitary force operations. While the unimaginable levels of violence discouraged people from falling into the lists of the state, all kinds of incentives, including monetary benefits were offered to break away from the xangathan. Many times, these 'returned' cadres, SULFAs, were allowed to keep their weapons, for their 'personal security'.

hence should kill Don and Petua, despite the awareness that these two were mere daily wagers.

Petua's elder brother living in Dhadum showed me a worn-out piece of paper, folded and kept carefully, that he got from the Duliajan police station. It stated a case against Don Saikia and Petua Sonowal, as Duliajan PS case no. 98/1999 under section 120 (15)/121/122/124 (A)/353/307 of IPC, read with sections 10 and 13 of the UAPA as well as section 25 (7–13) (a) 27 of the Arms Act. Later the case as filed in the FIR was retained as true vide GR no. 25/01dt 21-10-2001.

I was told that most people charged under these sections are accused of being linked to ULFA. For most people the cases become a serious burden, even when they are out on bail, as hiring lawyers and travelling required a lot of money. Further, given the pace of our judicial system, the cases come up for hearing sometimes after a decade or even more since their release on bail.

## When Army Rule Became the Everyday

In Lakhipathar, the stories of violence are unending. Reference to such violence comes up in conversations even if the discussion is not apparently political. This is in contrast to the unwillingness and disinterest of neighbours of Mahir or relatives of Kishen Singh in Delhi in talking about those deaths. Partly the reasons may be the nature of the widespread violence which encompassed almost everyone living in Lakhipathar society, and the form of ideological constructions in

---

The state, however, used such surrendered cadres to hunt down or identify people who are still with the organization or anyone else linked to them, including relatives, in return for securing their personal safety. Their vulnerability was exploited by the security forces, in a major way during the period from 1998 to 2001, and sporadically afterwards, using them as a force against the ULFA (Talukdar, Borpujari, and Deka 2008 [2011]: xvi).

While in the period between 1991 and 1996 the SULFA cadres were used for identification purposes and they were already in the scene by establishing syndicates and big businesses exploiting the patronization of the governments, post-1996 they acquired a more deadly role, in the form of carrying out politically motivated murders which came to be known as *gupta hatya*, or 'secret killings' (Talukdar et al. 2008 [2011]: 5).

both contexts. While relatives of those who died in police custody in Delhi are very conscious of their constructions as criminals, those who suffered violence in Lakhipathar were not constructed as criminals. They were constructed as an enemy army or its collaborator. Even for people who refused any participation in the activities of ULFA, the constructed identity of a rebel supporter was not as morally questionable as that of, for example a 'thief' in Delhi. Even when they denied association, they did not look at ULFA or the army as moral opposites, rather as we would explicate in the next chapter, they are often perceived in very similar light.

The daily presence of the army today is not a part of the narratives on violence, its presence is not seen as out of the ordinary in Lakhipathar anymore. Like the past of ULFA-times are remembered as days of 'freedom', similarly, the present time is talked of as the time of 'peace'. Life in Lakhipathar moves at a regular pace. By reading through such everyday life and the unexceptional presence of the army in Lakhipathar, and comparing it to the days of ULFA rule, I attempt to make some arguments about formation of authority in the next chapter.

# 8

# The Making of an Authority

## The State versus the Non-state

> The chief foundations of all states, new as well as old or composite, are good laws and good arms; and as there cannot be good laws where the state is not well armed, it follows that where they are well armed they have good laws.
>
> —Niccolo Machiavelli, *The Prince*, Chapter XII

Machiavelli wrote these lines in his advice to the prince for consolidating a state that was not a democracy. Machiavelli argued that a prince has to have strong armed forces of his own to maintain law in his land, and without it, requiring to depend on mercenaries and auxiliaries, he would not be able to maintain his rule. The absence of an army was not considered as an option, but the stronger the armed force, the better the rule was considered. In the context of a state that follows the procedures of democracy, that is India, these lines still appear to be relevant. The territorial nation-state, an entity that is continuously in the process of consolidation, constantly needs to discipline and order its various unruly margins. The 'disciplining' of these margins through the presence of 'good armies', ensures that these margins are also 'ordered' by good laws. In this chapter, I look at Lakhipathar in its present, in the ways its everyday social life is shaped and influenced by what happened here in the past. I also examine the place of the army in the present, what 'peace' and 'normalcy' means in contemporary Lakhipathar, and how community and belongingness, right and wrong are conceptualized in the shadow of an armed force.

Like the previous chapters, I draw on ethnographic field material, some of which are in the form of narratives, while some others are based on my own observations in the field. Studying how the people of Lakhipathar perceive the army and the state in contemporary times, offers us answers to the question of legitimacy or its absence for a state that has been violent, and the grounds for such popular attitude towards the state.

## Bihu, Football, and Authority

In late May of 2012, the army unit in Lakhipathar organized a Bihu function, in the public auditorium built by them near the panchayat office, close to Kenduguri village. It coincided with an Assam bandh that the ULFA called, protesting the visit of the then Indian prime minister Dr Manmohan Singh to Assam. However, despite the call for the bandh, the Bihu function went off successfully. People from all over Lakhipathar came to watch and participate. Deepak Gogoi's daughter from Pandhowa village won the first prize in the competition for under-14 female Bihu dancers. The auditorium was so packed that many people had to stand outside the hall. The function went on well past midnight. The army jawans remained at the place all the while, the commander himself enjoying performances sitting in the front row.

The army now seem to have penetrated into the cultural life of the people, after making their presence firm and undisputed in Lakhipathar. One and a half months after the Bihu function, in the month of July, the army in collaboration with a youth club called Jyotipur Juvak Sangha of Lakhipathar organized a football tournament. Stretching over a week in the high school field, many teams from outside Lakhipathar and from all over Tinisukia district participated, and drew a lot of spectator crowd. The July rains were braved and the Lakhipathar high school field became muddy with footfall. The army also fielded a team. Their first team won one game. However, after that they probably got some orders from above to field a second, inferior, team. The rumour among the people of Lakhipathar was that the army thought that if in the tournament organized by the army, the army itself won it would not be well received. The second team of army could not proceed much. The prize money was taken by a team from a village near Makum.

The game of football over the years seems to have captured the imagination of political aspirants in Lakhipathar. In the 1980s, football was popularized in Lakhipathar by the ULFA cadres. Several of its leaders were very good footballers, including Paresh Baruah, the Commander-in-Chief, who used to be a state-level player, and they used to organize several matches in Lakhipathar every year. Whenever there was a football match, everyone—men and women, boys and girls, children and grandparents—was either an enthusiastic spectator or a participant. ULFA took on this enthusiasm and organized friendly football matches between a team of selected players from Lakhipathar and the ULFA team. A teacher from an ME school of Lakhipathar often used to play the role of the referee. People came out to enjoy the matches in full strength. For the final matches, people came from places as far as Dibrugarh and Sivasagar. 'We didn't know what interest all these people coming from afar had', remembered Neela Sonowal, who played football in some of such matches (2012, pers.com, 10 October). When there would be a match in the High School field at Maaj Lakhipathar and Paresh Baruah would be playing, the first check post of ULFA would be set up at the entrance of the first village, that is, Laupoti. Everyone going in would be checked at several check posts from that point. When Baruah would be playing, there would be armed guards standing by the field. Baruah is remembered as a magical player. His goals were straight, and when he passed the ball to someone, it reached exactly the place that he intended to, 'If someone missed the ball even after that, Baruah would severely scold him' (B. Sonowal, 2012, pers.com, 10 April).

The events of the football matches helped the ULFA penetrate well into the lives of common people in Lakhipathar, and at the same time displayed their governing capabilities through check posts and armed guards, thus successfully creating an image of authority—competent and charismatic. In the present, when the Indian army organized the football matches, they seemed to have served a similar function too.

Partha Chatterjee in *The Black Hole of Empire: History of a Global Practice of Power* (2012) discusses the football matches played in colonial Calcutta between the European teams and the Bengali teams as having imbued with political meanings. In the context of colonial Calcutta of 1911, when racist divides between Indians and Europeans were widely and openly prevalent, the victory of the Mohan Bagan team over the East Yorkshire Regiment meant a symbolic assertion of the capability of the Indians who were seen as an inferior race. Football was seen as a 'manly sport' and the 'manly' Europeans were projected as racially superior to the 'effeminate' Bengali men in the field. The Europeans, he discussed through several narratives of previous and consequent matches, attempted to maintain their perceived superiority through partial treatment of players and unfair tactics. The victory in a football match was not merely seen as a victory in a game of sport, but as symbolizing either superiority of one people over another, or as assertions of equality by the colonized.

In the context of Lakhipathar, the games of football seemed to portray images of 'manliness', power, and camaraderie at the same time. While the visible manifestations of power as projected by checking of civilian people at ULFA check posts, the presence of armed security guards when the leaders played, etc., produced an effect of awe amongst the people, the superb skills of its leaders on the playground led to the added dimension of charisma. On the other hand, people also felt proud to be participants in that practice of power, as they gladly remembered stories about 'playing a game with Paresh Baruah'. Association with authority was seen as lifting the status of a person. The element of awe and obeisance can be marked also from the fact that the detail of how Paresh Baruah would scold the players when they did not play well was also remembered. Every little action of the authority was registered in the minds of the people.

In a similar way, the football matches of Lakhipathar in the present can be seen as imbued with such political meaning too. The rumour that the army replaced their superior team with a second team, so that a civilian team could win the tournament, was telling in itself. If the rumour was indeed true, then it throws light on the army's self-perception in the given context. In a game of football, which is 'especially well suited to the competitive exercise of controlled collective violence' and where '(T)he deployment and movement of forces belonging to the two sides … each side defending a citadel that the other is trying to penetrate, easily lends … to the analogy of field warfare' (Chatterjee 2012: 293–4), the fact that the army did not feel the need to prove its superiority says the confidence it enjoys about its image. The act of withdrawing one's best team so that others can win can be seen as coming from a benevolent patriarch. On the other hand, if the rumour was not true, then that shows the depth that the authority of the army has achieved in Lakhipathar. The common people of Lakhipathar were so convinced of the superiority of the army that they could not think of a civilian team winning the tournament without some special relaxation.

This act of 'letting others win' was, however, accompanied by other symbolic performances. On the prize distribution day, the Digboi Divisional Forest Officer (DFO), and the Block Development Officer (BDO) came. The *gaon burha* (village headman) Chandra Kanta Koch chaired the meeting. The army and the Jyotipur Sangha also brought Bipul Baruah of Jeraigaon, the younger brother of Paresh Baruah,[1] to distribute the prizes. The ceremony started with a march past by the army, displaying their discipline and strength. That was followed by Bihu and Nepali dance performances. While space was given to express the cultural and sports talents of the villagers, all this happened with the background of a powerful armed force looking over things.

Bipul Baruah in his speech said that he had just been told that his brother used to play football in that very field. He made an appeal to his brother Paresh Baruah and his companions to come back to the mainstream, highlighting the fact that he was speaking from the same field from where his brother started the journey into the fringes about three decades back. The event was an assertion and expression of authority in its symbolic, as well as in its most overt ways.

Such engagements of the army with people in Lakhipathar today means that while it is still feared today, it is also revered. Apart from the Bihu function that the army unit organized, the villagers of Lakhipathar organized a Bihu function on their own too, during the summer of 2012. The Lakhipathar army unit was named as an important patron in the leaflet that was circulated (Lakhipathar Central Rongali Bihu Organizing Committee 2012), and the commander of the company was invited to the function. The fear of the army now does not come with distaste; it comes with a sense of awe. The day-to-day life of Lakhipathar gives a sense of ordinarity, where the army operates and is accepted as a normal but distinct part of the society.

Chandrakanta Koch, the 'most important' of the three gaon burhas of Lakhipathar according to the villagers, is from Kenduguri. During

[1] The C-in-C of the ULFA camp in Lakhipathar in the past, and the chief of the faction of ULFA still fighting for an independent Assam.

the ULFA days before Operation Bajrang, he acted as a publicity division leader of the xangathan, while his father was the gaon burha. His son Jotin Koch was a lower level cadre in ULFA. These days Chandrakanta works in close collaboration with the army, in his official credence as the gaon burha. However, he does not talk much of his past affiliations with the ULFA, perhaps because being the gaon burha himself, it contradicts his official role.

He was also tortured and jailed in 1995 for his alleged association with ULFA, but as there was no evidence, he was released in about a month. After coming back from jail in 1995, the forest department made him the gaon burha, as his father was getting old. Since then, he has been working as the gaon burha. He is also a member of the police station management committees from about the same time, earlier in the Duliajan thana, and now in the Digboi thana. As the gaon burha, he has to work in close collaboration with the army and the police, apart from the forest department and the gaon panchayat. When the army or the police need any information about anyone in Lakhipathar, they contact Chandrakanta Koch. During my stay in Lakhipathar, a local boy was killed in an encounter in the Sivasagar district. The gaon burha went to identify his body and also reported it to the local army unit in Lakhipathar.

Chandrakanta said that due to the army unit's continuous presence the people of Lakhipathar are living in peace now. Unlike the early years of the army's presence, they are not afraid these days. The present army unit is much better than the earlier ones. Not only this unit, but the Punjab Regiment before this one was also good. He told me of a dharna that people exhibited in Makum demanding removal of the 'evil' Bihar Regiment and how the people succeeded in sending them off. He talked of his appeal to the army commanders to love the people in the villages if they wanted the people to love them back, and that the army commander had shown understanding of the fact.

Now-a-days, if there is trouble sensed by the gaon burha, he asks the army to provide extra surveillance. So the xangathan is not able to do anything here, and thus the harassment of people has lessened.

But as a regulatory official, he has also come to face some difficulties due to the influence of the army. Due to people's eagerness to go to the army even for things which are to be resolved by the headmen, at times friction over the jurisdiction of the army and the gaon burha had occurred. Chandrakanta said in a complaining tone, 'Traditionally it is the area of the *gaon burha* if two brothers or a husband and a wife fought', but gradually people have started going to the army looking for a solution in such matters as well. Thus, some time back, he had intervened and asked the army to not take up such issues. He told them, 'This is not your job; this is not why you are here. I am here to handle such things, and if need be I'll take them to the police.'

It appears that Lakhipathar lives with several separate yet overlapping layers of authority. At one level, it is the communal forms of authority that people accept. At another level, there are the village headmen, the elected panchayat, and the army. Being forest villages, the gaon burha or the village headman, appointed by the forest department, often hereditarily, is supposed to look after the villages in matters akin to policing. The panchayat is, on the other hand, an elected body for the governance of Lakhipathar, in terms of building and repairing roads or in implementing any welfare schemes. The army is there due to the continued presence and operations of ULFA, as the Commander of the army unit stationed in Lakhipathar told me (a captain, who did not divulge his name, and went to the extent of removing his badge before I could see it, 2012, pers.com, 22 May). These bodies, however, do not always operate in accordance with their prescribed roles only, and in this context how people relate to these bodies offer interesting insights. Such working also brings to notice how the popular expectations from various institutions vary at different points of time, or how various public personalities orient their roles depending on the political contexts.

While the army is seen to be enjoying popular trust, making people approach the army over the gaon burha who is a fellow villager, not much trust appears to be placed on the elected body of the village panchayat. During the summer of 2012, popular dissatisfaction was high amongst the people against the panchayat.

Such a place of the army, however, has passed through moments of opposition and resentment in the decades in which it also gradually became a regular presence in Lakhipathar. As we discuss some moments of conflict and resentment in the next section, one aspect that is striking is that of an emphasis on specific people who occupy institutional positions at a given time. Such emphasis on specific people—who are seen as cruel—and thus opposed, in contrast to a general acceptance of an armed force at one's doorstep and active engagements with it, reminds us of how in Delhi too specific police personnel were seen as either corrupt or evil, whereas the institution itself often came in handy in taking care of one's own businesses.

## Protest Mobilization and the Issue of Responsibility: The Assamese Bihari Conflict

In Lakhipathar, the issue of personal responsibility and identity of the army jawans—which company or regiment one is from and what personalized qualities individual commanders have had—is a recurring one. The narrations of one's encounters with army personnel, both during and after Operation Bajrang, are filled with observations of such nature. Even when the people of Lakhipathar came together in protest against the army, the protests were against a specific regiment, and the violence against which the protests were organized was construed as being unleashed based on communal grounds.

In the year 2003, there was a major conflict between the people of the Assamese and Bihari communities, which drew a lot of national attention. It began in the form of a confrontation between 'locals' and 'outsiders' with demands of preferential treatment by 'locals' in Class III and Class IV job recruitments to the Northeast Frontier Railways, in the month of November 2003. Allegedly, the identity cards of those who travelled from outside the state, particularly candidates from Bihar and Tripura, to write the examination held in Guwahati were seized and destroyed by local job seekers. This led to a sharp reaction in Bihar and within days, passengers from Assam and other states of the northeastern region travelling in trains, who have to pass through Bihar, were assaulted and one woman was molested. There were unconfirmed and probably exaggerated reports of Assamese travellers passing through Bihar being killed and their bodies put back in trains going to Assam and of the gang rape of a Naga girl who was later paraded naked, in English language dailies. Reports of such incidents led to a sharp reaction in Assam, and soon led to assaults on so-called Biharis, that is, Hindi-speaking people (Prabhakara 2003).

The backlash began in Guwahati and spread to other areas of upper Assam, Tinsukia having the highest toll. After two weeks of the first outbreak, the officially released number of deaths was 56. The victims, which included women and children, were either hacked, stabbed, or shot to death. The ULFA gave a call asking all the 'Hindi-speaking people' to leave Assam. While the number of people internally displaced in the state is not known, about 20,000 persons were believed to have fled the state. In Tinsukia district, more than 5,000 Biharis took shelter in relief camps (Prabhakara 2003).

During this period, Lakhipathar had a unit of the Indian army from the Bihar Regiment. Amid such heightened emotions and real acts of horror, the repercussions of having an armed Bihari unit amidst a majority of ethnic Assamese people were quite predictable.

By this time, people of Lakhipathar were getting used to the army in their villages. Practices such as people needing to give a list of family members to the army, and having to put up the list of people staying in their house near the front door, or of informing the army if a family had a visitor, and so on, had gradually come to be accepted as routine and no big stories around them ran.

The 2003 incidents, however, interrupted this routine. The army unit took all the youths from the villages to the camp, and there they were brutally tortured and humiliated. They were beaten up until they bled profusely and broke bones, and when they cried out for water they were humiliated by giving water in buckets and asking them to lick it from the buckets in a manner that animals do. Some others were forced to eat soil. Such were the tortures, a woman told me, that the men could not come back and tell the women-folk what all had been done to them.

This time, however, the people of Lakhipathar did something that they had not done before. Women took the lead in this new form of activity. It had been a practice in Lakhipathar for sometime by then that when the men were taken to army camp and tortured, women came out in groups, with their sickles and asked the army to return their men. They did not move until the men were released.

But during the Bihari–Assamese conflict, the protests organized by the women took a much bigger form. The idea first came to Sewali Neog's mind. The army camp was located just in front of her school. From the grounds of the school, she saw young men covered in blood shouting for water. Seeing such torture she organized a few women and passed on a message to other women, asking them to spread it in the villages, that they would blockade the main road in Makum on one of those days protesting against the torture by the army (Ms Sewali Neog, 2012, pers.com, 10 October). Ukha from Kopohua village cycled to several villages and passed on the message. A day before the blockade, she along with others did it all over again: they cycled through the villages and passed a piece of paper to every village detailing the time and the place of the blockade.

The next morning, Ukha's husband was taken away by the army. After getting him freed from the camp after a couple of hours, she travelled to Makum in a truck. People went to Makum in large numbers. Some people went sitting behind mini-trucks that carried fresh tea leaves from the gardens, some others cycled, and still others walked through the jungle all the way. Villagers from nearby Nazirating and Tamulikhat also joined in, as the Lakhipathar army camp had created trouble for them as well (Ms Ukha 2012, pers.com, 23 May).

In the blockade, the women stood in the front, with their sickles. They blocked both the National Highways 37 and 38, and the railway track. The Intercity Express train that runs from Guwahati to Ledo was detained. There was loud sloganeering. The Deputy Commissioner (DC) of Tinisukia, IAS officer Sanjay Lohia was present there but was unable to do much to calm down the crowd.

While all this was going on, a contingent of the army coming from the direction of Doomduma going towards Betjan Bagan camp appeared on the spot. When the army group was passing by, the agitated people started pelting stones at them and the situation went completely out of control. The women were furiously raising their sickles. A jawan got injured by Ukha's sickle. The situation was deteriorating and it seemed that there would be firing soon. Intimidated by the gravity of the situation, the DC had fled and taken shelter in a nearby ladies beauty parlour. Seeing him enter the parlour, however, the protesters surrounded the place (Ms Sewali Neog, 2012, pers.com, 10 October).

Durga Dutta from Kenduguri did not take part in organizing the event, but on that day he went to the blockade venue to see the happenings, as well as with the intention of helping in controlling the crowd to keep it peaceful. When the DC got trapped inside the parlour, he sent a message to Durga Dutta through somebody and Dutta slipped into the parlour too. The DC asked Dutta to do something to control the situation. Finally, on Durga Dutta's advice, the DC came out to talk, though he was still visibly frightened, but they were quickly surrounded by people shouting slogans. Durga Dutta tried to calm them down by asking them to at least listen to the DC, even if they did not agree to what he said. Somebody from the crowd shouted, '*Apunak kinile neki?*' (Have you been bought over?). Somebody else said, 'Who is asking you to mediate?' (Mr Durga Dutta, 2012, pers.com, 9 April).

Despite the initial heat and anger, after a while the crowd settled down and they sent Durga Dutta, Sewali Neog, and two more people to talk to the DC, it a forest department building named Nahor Bhavan in Makum. In this meeting, the demands of the people of Lakhipathar were placed before the DC. These were, first, to arrange for replacing the Bihar Regiment with another regiment, and second, to arrange compensation to the people for bamboos, palm leaves, and free labour forcibly taken by the army. The DC promised to come to Lakhipathar and hold a public meeting the next day to discuss these issues (Mr Durga Dutta, 2012, pers.com, 9 April).

On the decided day, the DC Lohia came, and the meeting was held in the high school field. Durga Dutta presided over the meeting and Lohia sat next to him. The commander of the army unit stationed at Lakhipathar was also seated in chairs along with them.

This meeting was highly publicized and local leaders of various political parties and student organizations came and spoke. The army jawans were criticized while the officers, Commander Mahaveer Singh and Captain Ahluwalia, were sitting there. At one point, the people sitting on the ground got agitated and stood up shouting slogans demanding that the army commander offer a public apology.

Finally an agreement was reached. It was promised that attempts would be made to change the regiment. Further, as it was difficult to calculate and pay individuals for the bamboos taken from them, a lump sum amount would be given to the people of Lakhipathar as a whole, which they could use as they wished.

Later, about Rs 25,000 according to one account, and Rs 42,000 according to another account, was given out, out of which allegedly about Rs 35,000 was spent in buying a mike set, which is now lying somewhere, in someone's house, falling out of use, bearing the marks of an exchange of labour, goods, and suffering with a compensation (Mr Durga Dutta, 2012, pers.com, 27 April; Mr Deepak Gogoi, 2012, 22 May).

In this episode of display of public anger and mobilized opposition to the army, while in itself being quite notable and exceptional in the context of Lakhipathar, one thing that was really striking was the demands made by the people. Given the more than a decade long history of violence by the army in Lakhipathar, one expected that the prime demand of the people would be the removal of the army from the area. However, surprisingly the army was not asked to be removed, and only a specific regiment, the Bihar Regiment which the people identified as barbaric, was asked to be replaced. The second demand that was made was about compensation, and not about justice in terms of setting up any inquiries or imposing legal/penal action against the tormentors.

## Past Experiences and Everyday Living

The army's position in Lakhipathar at the present seems to be almost uncontested, despite the fact that people from some communities and villages engage with it less than the others. No one from Biren dai's family went to either of the events of Lakhipathar organized by the army in the spring and summer of 2012: the Bihu function and the football match respectively. Their staying away from these activities while most other people were so enthusiastic was curious. The Sonowal family did not have apparent 'political' reasons or affiliations to reject such functions. However, the politics of their daily life itself seemed to be a peculiar combination of strategic involvement. While they fully participate in every function of their village community, they do not take much interest in the matters of the Lakhipathar panchayat or the army functions. At the same time, Biren dai's son Latu had strong affiliations with the ruling Congress party; Biren dai is very proud of his job in the public sector company and regrets that he could not get a similar job for any of his sons. Bou works in the government Anganbadi centre in Laupoti which her younger daughter also attends.

While the ULFA operated uncontested in Lakhipathar before the Operation Bajrang came, after the Operation, Laupoti being the closest village from the main road, the rebel cadres gradually found it inconvenient to come to this village. Having easy access and being small in terms of population, the Indian army very soon established full surveillance over this village. Thus, in the later years after Operations Bajrang and Rhino, there were not many cases of police or army torture in the everyday lives of the people of this village.[2] The army and the people of Laupoti cohabited with a level of mutually accepted distance. That is despite the fact that they remember the days of Bajrang often and the understandings of army atrocities have become part of the familial world in such a way, that the threat of army is used even to frighten children refusing to eat and sleep.

When the people of Laupoti now talk either of the army or the ULFA, it seems that they look at both the army and the ULFA more in terms of valiance. Personal experiences of suffering take a back seat in considerations of good and bad, and chivalry and heroism draw more attention. In the discussions of the past, the more important question always becomes who fought that war better, the army or the ULFA, how the ULFA cadres fled, or how the ULFA roamed around in the villages before the operation. The narratives of violence were often spoken in a light hearted manner. Laughter may be a strategy to mend the old wounds, but an aspiration for justice interpreted in terms of revenge or punishment, or even in terms of needs of compensation and apologies were not visible.

They also seemed to be a bit complacent about happenings such as houses being burnt in the Moran villages a few years back, the Makum *path abarodh* (road blockade), or even the fact that the army is still there, from the least amount of interest they showed when these issues were brought up. It appeared that their past and contemporary lives have a clear break, in terms of experiences. Their present lives apparently give out an impression of a 'politically disinterested' or 'indifferent' people: not taking interest in what is happening in the state or the country on a larger scale, but concerned only with the smaller everyday issues of going to work, or seeing a doctor, or preparing the haaj in time.

In some ways it seemed that they have been successful in keeping the state out where they do not want it, and accepting it where they need it. In Kenduguri, on the other hand, where the army took some time to reach, and thus the atrocities began later than in the easily accessible

[2] Such an observation is in agreement with Stathis Kalyvas's (2006) argument that when a political actor has complete control over a territory and population it does not need to use violence. This argument is discussed in more detail later in the chapter.

villages of Laupoti or Dhonda Nahar, violence gradually escalated beginning from 1991. The memories of violence in this village are fresh, as appeared from the involved and very sentimental manner in which events of Bajrang as well as those of following years such as torture in the name of being SULFA or just for being Assamese were narrated. The injuries were still new, and it still affects their everyday lives.

Despite this, it is intriguing to note, the people from this village work in greater interaction with the army unit in Lakhipathar. The Bihu function organized by the army was held in a public ground near the Kenduguri village, and people from most of the nearby villages including Kenduguri participated enthusiastically. Chandrakanta Koch, who could not be stopped from working for ULFA during ULFA's reign in Lakhipathar despite him being the son of the gaon burha, now works for the army and appreciates the presence of army in Lakhipathar. Rather than shutting out to a violent state, over time, the state has been allowed in to penetrate more and more in Kenduguri.

Both these reactions to state violence comes in contrast to a sense of resignation that we see in the case of Sewali Neog. Sewali moved from being a suffering villager to a politically motivated activist of the ULFA and then back to a life of non-eventful normality. Sewali became well known in and around Lakhipathar after her name was published in the media after her interaction with Hiteshwar Saikia in the relief camp in Digboi. After coming back from the relief camp, and Operation Bajrang subsided, Sewali soon joined the xangathan. However, after spending some time in hiding in several places in Assam, she returned to Lakhipathar in the decade of 90s itself. Upon return, however, she kept working as an over-ground sympathizer for the xangathan till early 2000. She, however, surrendered at a formal ceremony at the Rong Ghar bakori in Sivasagar on 4 April 2000, after all the other members of Sewali's small cultural–political group were killed by state-sponsored armed groups. This was the time of what was known as *gupta hatya* or secret killings: the state was using surrendered ULFA cadres to engage in killing of suspected ULFA cadres and their relatives with complete impunity. One day Sewali too was picked up. She was kept blindfolded with her hair tied to a rope hanging from the ceiling, and was asked questions about links to the xangathan. Her neck was squeezed as if to strangle, releasing a sound about which she had heard before: the kind of sound that secret killers get released from one's neck! While she escaped what seemed to be impending death, she went out straight for a formal surrender after that.

These days she keeps a low profile, living in a small temporarily built structure in the suburb of Digboi with her husband and son. Some people in the village also make suggestive comments about her inactivity, but she has decided to focus on her family life rather than the political past. Though she works in the ME school in the village, a job which she believes she secured because of the goodwill of some AGP leader of that time, her salary is not regular. At times, she goes unpaid for months at a stretch. Neela, her husband, does not have any regular job, and works on temporary contracts whenever he manages to get one.

The Makum path abarodh was the last of her active political involvements. These days her most politicized acts are watching news in TV with her husband and discussing them with him. She seems to have developed a frustration with the overall turn of events. So many young men and women had given their lives, so many had sacrificed their most valuable years, all these seem to have been wasted when the pro-talk leaders are now not able to even secure a job for the ones who deserve. Neither is she very hopeful that the talks would achieve much. Paresh Baruah, no matter whether he could do anything about an independent Assam, she wishes stays back in the forests, if only to keep the honour of the Assamese people, if only to make an example to show the future generations, that not everyone compromises, that Assamese people are capable too.

## The Ceasefire, Peace Talks, Relief, and Betrayal

In 2012, when I lived in Lakhipathar and talked to people, people described their lives as normal and peaceful. They often attributed this time of peace to the nature of the Gorkha or Nepali people, who they feel can understand many of the Assamese ways. Some of them also talk of the cease-fire and the peace-talks that began in 2011 between a faction of the ULFA with many of its major leaders and the Indian state. However, when people talk of this, they do not use the nomenclatures of 'peace-talks' or 'pro-talks faction' that one can find in the media in Assam. They rather refer to it as Jiten Dutta's decision, the leader of ULFA hailing from Digboi who led the most potent strike group the Alpha company of the 28th battalion. Names of the organization's top leaders such as Arabinda Rajkhowa, or Chitraban Hazarika are not taken.

Jiten Dutta was the general secretary of Digboi College before joining the xangathan. Everyone, including teachers in Digboi College remembered him as a very bright and popular young man. After he joined the xangathan his sojourns in hiding in Lakhipathar started on and off. People in the villages of Lakhipathar remember him as a very good orator. He would collect around him young boys and girls and talk of ideals. Coming to this part of the story, people often become sceptical: 'What happened now to all those big talk, now he is sitting with property and does not care for anyone' (Deepak Gogoi, 2012, pers.com, 20 June).[3]

After the ceasefire was declared, he once came to Lakhipathar to speak in a public meeting, but never after that. The families of young men who died as activists of the xangathan speak bitterly about Jiten Dutta's inability to reach out to them. Medini Gogoi from Kopohua joined the xangathan influenced by Jiten Dutta, who later died in the hands of the army in the forests of Pengeri in Tinisukia. His body was found with a bullet which pierced him from behind. After the ceasefire, Medini Gogoi's mother invited Jiten Dutta to come and meet them twice, but he did not come. When he offered a *gamosa* (a traditional Assamese towel offered to elders and to show respect) to Medini's father in the public meeting at Lakhipathar, naming him the father of a martyr, the father refused to accept it. Now Medini's elder brother Deena lives with his parents and his wife and children, and ekes out a livelihood from daily wage labour, as the land he owns is very little to sustain all of them. While I was talking to Deena and the mother, the ailing father was coughing away in his bed.

The mother of a young boy in the Rangsangi Moran gaon who died after joining the xangathan also cried about her ill fate and how Jiten Dutta and others had really failed them. She held Jiten Dutta responsible for the death of her son, accused them of deciding to come out for talks too late. Had they decided to come out a little earlier, her son could have been saved.

[3] Jiten Dutta now lives in Ramnagar area of Digboi in a large and beautiful house. On the days when Jiten Dutta is at home, one would see four to five fancy vehicles parked on the porch. He divides his time between a camp of pro-talks faction cadres at Kakopathar and home. My attempts to meet him for an interview were futile.

Khirod Gogoi of Maj Kopohua has a case against him under several sections of IPC, Arms Act and under sections 10 and 13 of the UAPA. What he did was giving shelter to Jiten Dutta and his group on a night when they killed a Nepali man named Raju Chetri in suspicion of being an army informer and then ambushed an army vehicle the next morning. He was forced by the group to give shelter, Gogoi says. Now he does not have enough money to pay the lawyer, but asking Jiten Dutta to help him out has been useless. In addition, 'Jiten Dutta, who killed so many people, is now talking of good things; it does not suit him', Gogoi vented out his anger (Mr Khirod Gogoi, 2012, pers.com, 24 May).

Sewali Neog also feels that leaders like Jiten Dutta and Mrinal Hazarika, the commander of the whole 28th battalion, have not taken proper note of her sacrifices. They had invited her and had thanked her for her support all through after they came over-ground, but had not offered anything concrete in terms of improving her life, while they themselves are getting everything.

Those who had suffered personal losses, will always have their grudges: other people in Lakhipathar say. They say that whatever the personal opinion of those whose sons and daughters have died, one must admit that the situation in Lakhipathar has improved a lot in the last few years, and that the people of Lakhipathar must thank Jiten Dutta for that. Now that the fear of the army, the ULFA, and the police is away, people can breathe in peace. Earlier all their concerns were centred around how to keep themselves safe, now they can divert their energies to more productive issues (Deepak Gogoi, 2012, pers.com, 14 October; Biren Sonowal, 2012, pers.com, 20 June; Durga Dutta, 2012, pers.com, 28 May; Jotin Koch, 2012, pers.com, 10 April; Pobin Bora, 2012, pers.com, 23 May).

These days the visits of the army jawans to the villages and to families to make various inquiries do not offend them. Their activities like health camps and cultural functions are attended by people. The Gorkha regiment is now accepted almost as well-wishers of the people. They are invited to take part in the affairs of the village, and are talked of in a positive manner, commending their activities in social policing.

In the last 10 years or so, the army has seeped in to form a part of the regular and even necessary part of life in Lakhipathar. The ULFA on the other hand, gradually seem to have become irrelevant. Either they are remembered as characters from a distant past in the pre-Bajrang era, or they are remembered for how they had betrayed the people of Lakhipathar in later years.

A brief interview with the commander of the army unit stationed in Lakhipathar, however, did not give out exactly the same impression of familiarity and trust that people of Lakhipathar expressed towards the army. The commander was a captain, who joined the Indian army as a lieutenant. He is a young Nepali man, who grew up in Assam itself, in the army sites in Sonapur near Guwahati, his father being in the Gorkha regiment of the Indian army too. He, however, was not happy to entertain an interviewer, and repeatedly kept asking what I was up to. The only things that he happily divulged were the community relation programmes that they organize. He said that the Lakhipathar people are not afraid of the army any more, and that people come to them with land disputes, husband–wife quarrels, and cattle fight cases, expecting the army to sort those out.

When I asked if the army unit is still needed to be based in Lakhipathar given the fact that the ULFA has more or less come to the talks tables,[4] and the people do not seem to be in support of the xangathan any more, he said that the situation has not changed: 'Everyday boys are going to ULFA.' He also justified the presence of the army rather than the state police force or the CRPF, on the grounds that whoever opposes the state is an 'outsider', they are not rightful 'citizens', and thus justifiably needing to be fought by an army which is kept for the purpose of fighting external enemies (2012, pers.com, 22 May).

## The Turned Tables: Authority and Legitimacy in Lakhipathar Over the Years

In an interview with Chitraban Hazarika, the Finance Secretary and one time AGS of ULFA, now one of the prominent leaders of the pro-talks

[4] This interview was conducted towards the end of May 2012, when the situation seemed to be calm, the anti-talks faction of the ULFA lying low. Since then there have been isolated news reports on the capture of suspected ULFA cadres in parts of upper Assam, but the portrayal by the army captain of a situation of the ULFA growing daily, appeared to be largely out of place.

faction, I asked him about the nature and level of political consciousness of the people of Lakhipathar when the ULFA had the camp there, and of common people in Assam in general. Hazarika talked about the meetings organized by the 'boys' in the villages of Lakhipathar to make people politically aware. However, he qualified this statement by adding, 'You need to remember that the political consciousness of the leaders or learned people will be different from that of the villagers. It was not that they understood everything about politics. But the most important thing was: they *loved* Assam immensely.'[5] According to his beliefs, that is why the ULFA could win them to their side.

Looking at how common people in Lakhipathar responded to and engaged with varying contexts and life-experiences since the times of ULFA's dominance into the present times, it seems that Hazarika in a way underestimated and misjudged the masses. It does not appear that they were moved merely by an abstract 'love for their motherland' when they were living at peace with the ULFA. Neither does it appear that they preferred a relation with the ULFA in the name of 'love of their motherland' at the cost of their personal peace and security. While Hazarika may be correct in saying that they were not fully aware of the political ideology, methods and goals of the ULFA, the reasons for their support to the xangathan appear to be their own, and different from what Hazarika believed. While the powers-that-be always attempt to and do penetrate with their versions of political theology, the common people do not merely *receive* them, but interact with those in their own imaginative ways and rationales.

When we analyse the role and status of both the army and the ULFA in Lakhipathar over the period of last two and a half decades, a Machiavellian logic of a good army leading to good laws seem to work in explaining the shifts. Stathis N. Kalyvas (2006) in his comparative study of civil wars, finds that a political actor is most likely to act violently on civilian populations when its control over it is *almost near* hegemonic, or when it has *near* complete control over the given territory and population. Where it has full control, it does not need to use violence. Where it has no control, in such a context due to lack of information, it cannot use selective violence, and indiscriminate violence is often counterproductive. Where it shares control equally with a rival

[5] C Hazarika, 2012, pers.com, 10 June, emphasis added.

group, there people will not collaborate with any of the political actors due to fear of retaliation from the opposing actor (Kalyvas 2006: 12).

Kalyvas also finds proof supporting the related argument advanced by the 'security thesis'—which says that the barbarism and violence of political actors in a civil war is related to the degree of insecurity faced by the armed actor. The more insecure an actor is, the more prone the actor is to act violently. This is related also to the problem of identification. If an actor is unable to differentiate between who is an enemy combatant and who is a civilian, or when the line between these two is blurred, then it is more prone to use pre-emptive violence (Kalyvas 2006: 84–5).

While having no control at all might dissuade a political actor to act violently in fear of producing adverse results, when the actor is the state, and the issue involved is the territorial unity and integrity of the 'nation-state', having no control at all might result in indiscriminate violence from the state-agent. This is facilitated by several factors. First, the state is already in a privileged position due to the de jure recognition of the territory as belonging to the given nation-state in question. To make this strategy work, the state-agent will also have to ensure that it is militarily much stronger than the opposing actor, and that the opposing actor cannot offer security to the people. In this way, if the state-actor can make the war unbearable for the common people, in such situations the people themselves will start collaborating with the state-actor and raise against the weaker actor so that the stronger political actor stops violence towards them in suspicion of their collaboration with the opponents. The stronger army is believed to be capable of giving better protection and thus leaving less space for lawlessness.[6]

In the context of Lakhipathar, the late 1980s was the period when the ULFA enjoyed what could be perceived as complete control over the people of Lakhipathar. It reached its unquestionable stature by making clear to the people its unchallengeable coercive power—which could not even be challenged by the state police forces—by an open display of their capacity for violence and also through their actual physical violence. They established an order of social morality and ethics through the use of punishment, and through this morality confirmed and firmly

[6] The law that is talked about here is not about normative legal standards, but about what stands as laws in a given situation.

established their authority. Such a foundation was then further consolidated by cultural and social means.

ULFA's challenge to the claimed monopoly of violence of the Indian state in such a way, however, was responded with greater violence. For the state at that moment, when the ULFA already had established a firm presence amongst the people under its influence, it was not an easy task to reverse the loyalties of people and make them support and recognize the authority of the state. In such a situation, persuasion was not easy, and violence showed to be more effective than persuasion. Such violence was often indiscriminate, prompting many to join the ranks of ULFA in the early days of Bajrang. But following Kalyvas's (Kalyvas 2006) argument, the experiences of Lakhipathar also show, that the loyalties of people, in terms of observable behaviour is endogenous to the war, and does not precede it.

In the context of Lakhipathar, the loyalties of people were shaped through the experiences of violence. It was not denied by anyone that the army was brutal. However, in the present when people talk about it, the blame for such violence is often put on the xangathan, for not being able to protect and care for the people, or for not being able to choose peace-talks when it was not too late yet.

For people, the initial observable support for any group may be due to a variety of reasons: security considerations, economic considerations like need of work, to avenge personal rivalry with other people, social status that comes with being a member of a particular army, etc. While in the context of support and mobilization for ULFA in Lakhipathar in the late 1980s, it was a combination all these listed factors, the allegiance to the army was initially a response to violence upon the body. Effective use of violence replaced other material and nonmaterial benefits inducing people to collaborate with ULFA. Violence may not *alone* suffice to sustain regimes in the long run, and other techniques are evolved once the control is gained. Long lasting physical control also spawns robust informational and cultural monopolies that socialize populations accordingly. From the predominant role that the army had started to play in the socio-cultural spheres—as exemplified by the Bihu functions, the football matches, the demand that interpersonal disputes be resolved by the army—such a socialization is visible, which took place over a period of time since the army fist came to Lakhipathar.

# Conclusion

## Produced Belongings, Imagined Geographies

In this research, I raised questions about legitimacy and authority in the context of a state which is—being a democracy—supposed to be based on popular consent, but appears to be 'torn between the ideals of non-violence and the practice of extreme violence' (Austin 1994: 30). My attempt has been towards a re-conceptualization of the relation between the state, specifically the modern territorial nation-state as a political entity, its practices of violence, and how notions of citizenship and identity get influenced by it. Through ethnographic explorations of the experiences of and responses to violence by power-holders, mostly state institutions of police and the Indian army, but also the not-yet-state institution of ULFA in the context of Assam, my attempt has been to develop a narrative of how the violence of power holders and the image of a territorial nation-state interact with each other to produce legitimacy. The specific vision that the nation-state is, marked by geographical boundaries and internal sovereignty often need to use violence to legitimize its existence. What is, however, notable is that such use of violence does not appear to be leading to a disillusionment with the form or the institutions of the state.

Being a study of violence of power holders upon the same constituencies from which it seeks legitimacy, it is also a study of the margins of the state—both territorial and conceptual. It is a study of sites which are often seen as that of disorder, of danger, to both the national-body and the citizen-self. And following Das and Poole (2004) I observe that in attempts to re-found 'order' in these spaces, the state uses its violence on an everyday basis. We see a continuous recurrence of what Benjamin (1999) called the 'foundational' violence, because the state that is imagined here, the modern-territorial nation-state with *monopoly* of violence and clearly demarcated *boundaries* of inside and outside, is always an ongoing project, making its practices of violence part of its continuous foundational process. The continuous foundational violence, in turn, I argue, generates bases for legitimacy.

As we have seen, the nature and pattern of the violence in Lakhipathar and Delhi differ based on structural and institutional differences and distinct targets, but the experiences of violence in both cases seem to have stabilized authority structures of the state. While such an argument may sound counter-intuitive, I argue that there is a need to engage with such counter-intuitive field insights, for the purpose of a critical examination of the nature and logic of the dominant political community of our times, that is, the nation-state. To pan out these ideas further, I attempt to highlight some major conceptual themes that emerged from the field-narratives of this research, which form the basis of the larger arguments that I make.

## Experiences of the State

The narratives from the field that we find in the preceding chapters portray that the category of the state is not understood in a uniform manner across contexts. Depending on how the state is imagined and experienced in a specific context, expectations from and relations to it are also variedly shaped. In the case of Delhi, the people who are most often the target of police violence accept or invite police into their lives. This is because those who are sufferers of police atrocities can also use police to serve their personal agendas. The acts of torture and killing by the police on the other hand, act as a double-sided sword. While a large majority of dominant sections of people who are not targets of police violence expect police to use such means and encourage them, those in the margins who are targeted in their day-to-day lives through discursive productions of crime and criminality, often expect such acts and overlook the trauma from personal loss, to save themselves from everyday harassment and hassles. What is even more revealing is that in the context of hard everyday lives, wounds of such violence, even of deaths, are suppressed and force-healed.

In the context of Lakhipathar on the other hand, the role of the state was played by the ULFA and the Indian army at various points of time, by exerting more or less control and authority. During the reign of ULFA, it had achieved acceptance on several fronts, but when the Indian state entered the scene in the form of the Army, which outsmarted the contesting power locus presented by the ULFA, the people of Lakhipathar gradually shifted their expectations of good governance to the Indian army. The army, which entered through violence to enforce complete domination, through its presence in Lakhipathar over a period of time, gradually facilitated the return of the 'regular' life, or rather, the regularization of a particular way of life, where the armed forces of the state became the repository of all kinds of authority. Its uncontested power at the moment of entry brought in stability and security, which gradually gave way to acceptance. What is striking in both the field sites is the blurring of boundaries between what is 'normal' and what is 'extraordinary' or 'violent', over years of experiencing the state.

Such normalization of violence is not only seen in the form of helpless acceptance, but also displayed by the value that is attached to acts and capacities of violence. In both Delhi and Lakhipathar, the violence wielded by the police and the army are valued, though the individuals doling out such violence are looked at in different ways. Unlike in Delhi where the police is perceived by the targets of its violence as corruptible and unethical, useful at times, and unavoidable at other times, the army in Lakhipathar has been shrouded in a characteristic awesomeness. While people are bitter about the violence inflicted upon their bodies by the army, their superior physical qualities, skills related to intelligence and planning, as well as role as protectors were not questioned. To add on to that characterization of a strong presence, it has now come to enjoy an amount of trust as a fair dispenser of justice and maintainer of law and order.

It is evident from the institutional structure, nature and mode of work of the police and the Indian army respectively that despite being institutions identified with state violence, they have different logics of operation. One looks for disciplining criminality to protect civil society, whereas the other looks for disciplining political imaginations to protect the sanctity of the nation-state. However, it appears that both these disciplinings merge at a point where it attempts to produce people that 'belong'.

## 'Other'ing and Conservation of the Self

While violence was accepted, and the violent actor was often lauded for its acts of violence, in both Lakhipathar and Delhi, this was made possible by the specific vision of the political community within which these institutions worked. The model of the nation-state works by including some and excluding others. This was the vision upon which the political movement of the ULFA was based, of developing a homeland/state for Assamese people exclusively, for economic, social, and political purposes. This vision required an othering of not only the institutions of the Indian state, but an othering of anyone who seemed to represent the dominant Indian nation, such as Marwari business families who were made to pay taxes or the Bihari migrant labourers who were attacked.

The response of the Indian state to this vision of ULFA was not by developing an institutional mechanism wherein the aspirations of the Assamese nationality politics could be accommodated and nurtured within that of a larger Indian identity, but by crushing the movement through violence, upon those who have been 'misguided', or those who have become 'traitors', thus producing a new 'other'. This 'other' is refused space within the category of Indian citizen body, both at the early moment when Operation Bajrang was sent in by declaring a state of emergency, and at the present, as one could read from the statement of the commander of the army unit stationed in Lakhipathar, that whoever opposes the state is an 'outsider', they are not rightful 'citizens'.

In both the instances, the identities of the 'self' in contrast to the 'other' were also constructed through regular enactments, such as display of armed strength by ULFA by establishing check posts and deploying armed guards lining village roads when there were no imminent threat to the organization, and patrols and march pasts by the army, torture in their respective camps by both ULFA and the Indian army, and expressions of charisma and camaraderie through mythical stories and friendly popular sports events. In both stints of operations of power, attempts at constructing a 'moral self' was also presented in forms of policing of social behaviour of people.

While the 'self' and the 'other' at this site were demarcated mostly based on ethnic identity and political aspirations, the othering that is visible in the context of policing in Delhi is based on an intersectional line of class, caste, gender, habit and religious preferences. The poor of the city, who often also belong to depressed castes and minority religions, are systematically 'other'ed by production of categories such as Bad Characters (BCs), ruffians, 'Bangladeshis', 'criminal tribes'/'ex-criminal tribes', etc. These othered people are then surveilled, restrained, tortured, and occasionally killed, in attempts at securing the citizen 'self' of the city.

At both these sites, however, the process of othering is intricately linked also to the marginalization or an othering of geographical space and claims of territory. The secessionist movement of ULFA was based on a premise of the 'colonial attitude' of the Indian state towards the region. It was alleged that the resources of the region are extracted by the Indian state, without sharing the benefits of these resources with the ethnic Assamese people. The movement was projected as an assertion of territorial claims over the lands and resources of Assam by the ethnic Assamese. The Indian state in response, stuck to its claims of territory too, over these lands, while imposing extra-ordinary laws like AFSPA upon its people. Exercise of such extraordinary laws further marginalized these spaces in the geography of the Indian state, as spaces of exception.

Policing in Delhi, on the other hand, produced marginal spaces within the centre that is the capital of the Indian state, of slums placed next to middle class gated societies. These spaces are marginal in a conceptual sense, in that they are marginalized by the dominant understandings of civil, modern, national life-spaces. These are margins that do not lie in the territorial peripheries, but run through the centre of our nation-state. These are the spaces which are marked out as 'filthy', and as 'breeding ground for criminals'. These spaces are seen as requiring cleaning up, but not as requiring protection. The filth in these spaces is seen as both physical and psycho-social, as kids from these localities were seen as requiring special training so that they do not (if left untrained by police) become criminals. The construction of these 'other's, whether in the context of Assam or in Delhi, appears to be a continuous process. In addition, as the opposite to this 'other', the citizen 'self' needing protection from the state through its means of violence is continuously sustained.

While I argued in an earlier chapter on policing in Delhi that the state constantly requires an 'other' to sustain a legitimate ground for its own existence, we also see that there is a ceaseless attempt on part of the 'other' to cross-over and to become 'selves' worthy of protection by the institution which wields power within the given discourse of othering. Thus we see that the same people in the villages of Lakhipathar who accepted ULFA as a legitimate authority offering them their taste of 'freedom', gradually reached a stage when they participate in activities organized by the army, want the army to settle personal disputes, and consider them responsible for maintaining peace. The slum dwellers in Delhi call upon the police to 'teach' someone 'a lesson', while seeing themselves being promoted to the status of 'protected' citizens. Still others, who have experienced personal loss in the context of police custodial deaths, stay silent and cooperate, because the only way to 'protect' oneself is to stay silent. The protection here is offered by the police against their own acts of violence, in return for acceptance and cooperation. And this need for protection not only results in stifled voices of resistance, but in a thriving arena for production and reproduction of stories of those who do not belong, that is, the BCs, and the ruffians, in opposition to those who consistently struggle to get included.

## Protection Racket?

Such a scenario of self/other and security/surveillance, reminds one of Charles Tilly's (2002) theorizations on state. Tilly compares states with protection rackets, as according to him, states tend to monopolize violence, and thus, offers protection to its citizens from threats which are often imaginary or their (states') own consequences. He argues that the states perform four different activities: war-making or eliminating rivals outside territories over which they have clear control; state-making or eliminating rivals inside territories in their own control; protection or eliminating enemies of their clients inside their territories; and extraction or acquiring of the means for carrying out the first three activities. He further argues that the modern states are a result of combined effect of all these four functions. In fact, to the extent that states claim to offer protection from local and external violence, and command people thus 'protected' to pay a price for this, in a context where states themselves commonly simulate, stimulate or even fabricate threats, they act as protection rackets.

This is a theoretical point, where my two distinct field-sites seem to offer a merger of arguments. In the case of Delhi, societal violence often feeds into the violence that is perpetrated by police, and police violence does not always work as an antithesis to violence from other sources. But despite this, due to its officially sanctioned capacity to use violence, it is seen as having a greater effect than other societal violence. This is one reason why police violence is sought after both by people at the margins and by the dominant sections. And a state, which may not otherwise seem too attractive, becomes attractive in its capacity to provide security in de facto and de jure ways, that is, by fulfilling the second and the third functions of a state in the Tillian schema.

In the context of Lakhipathar, where there is a clear conflict over people and territory between two groups and two contesting formulations of nation-states, the logic is even simpler. When both the contending actors have the capacity to act violently, and people have experienced that, they would choose the more competent group in a deal for protection.

This is apparent that in such a situation, it is a deal that people strike with the wielder of violence. However, what is crucial here is, can such a state which acts as a protection racket be legitimate?

## Legitimacy, Violence, and Creation of *Nationalized* Space

The fact of violence practiced by the states, and its role in the development of the state form that is present today, is well documented in both conceptual and historical works on the state. The issue of legitimacy as noted in the introduction, has not been adequately studied in a sociological manner. If the state in democracies like India engages in violence, then is this state still accepted by the people?

My observations in the field offer an image, where the people who suffer in the hands of state institutions also often value these institutions. This attitude was indicated by the way people engage with the institutions in question. The police is called in to the slums of Delhi to resolve petty disputes, to take action against someone with a personal enmity, and as an observer to play a role much like a referee. This is in a context where police violence is rampant towards slum dwellers, which is also justified through various discursive classifications and idealized goals. Similarly, in the context of Lakhipathar, the people have a relationship with the army that is marked by unforgettable pain but also feelings of safety and stability. Despite the pain that they remember, the 'peace' and the stability which is allowing them to hold Bihu functions, and to play friendly football matches with the army, is considered invaluable. The army is approached in instances of disputes to play the role of a resolver. It is asked and expected to act in a certain way.

This may appear to be a pessimistic view of human nature, of accepting as authorities those power holders which are violent, rather than rising in revolution against them. But this could also be read as a practical choice made by the people. Legitimacy as studied in this work is about observable behaviour, about if and why people accept power holders as authority, and not about whether it is the ideal way to engage with violent power holders within the discourses of normative political theory. And what we see in both the contexts studied in this work is acceptance, though it may be slow and appear flickering or contextual at time.

It would perhaps be pertinent to tease out into view here a question that lingers on. Why do people often come to believe that acceptance of the violent political wielder is the best choice they have? A crucial element in researching this question appears to be the structure of political communities that we imagine. When the state is imagined as a community of the nation, it leaves out many who are not part of that nation. Such considerations of insiders and outsiders are the first steps towards violence. A state that is bound by such an identity of self and other, is bound to physically enforce these classifications while producing newer 'others' on a daily basis. This appears to be applicable to both the established states like the Indian state as well as state-aspirants like the political formation of the ULFA in late 1980s, which routinely marked out *deshdrohis* (traitors) and punished them.

When the state is imagined as the political community of the nation, it also requires that the national space is free of contestations. The transition from an era of frontiers to that of bordered nation-states, is achieved by a process of exclusion: exclusion of those who do not share the same vision of the national space, exclusion of those who do not live up to the idealized ways of being a citizen.

In the context of states sponsoring migration to a frontier region in attempts at nation-building and this leading to conflicts, political scientists Fearon and Laitin (2001) argue that nation-building has a 'gory character'. It appears from this study, that while attempting to create spaces that belong to the *national* state, violence is used regularly. While the ideals of a territorially integrated India are utilized to militarily suppress the alternative territorial claim by the 'sons' of 'Assamese soil', the image of a 'civic' citizen marked by education, wealth, and status is protected as the ideal national person living in a legitimate legal space of the nation in contrast to those who live on the fringes, their claims to rights of citizenship rendered meaningless.

The idea of territoriality, as much as it is attached to the imagination of the nation-state, stands in the way of imagining territorially overlapping nations. Thus those who are 'outsiders' or 'others' within the territorial bounds of the nation, are required to be either overthrown, controlled, or won over through reformation of their minds. To sustain the form of state that is also a territorial nation with specific 'imaginative geographies' (Said [1984] 1998), violence is thus a necessity. To add to that, the very imagination of this specific political form composed of insiders and outsiders, at times encourages people to be insiders rather than outsiders, when they are trapped within its territorial limits, thus producing practices that mark the consent of the governed, such as voting, participating in activities of the rulers, looking up to it for their own needs, and harbouring expectations from it.

# Glossary

| | |
|---|---|
| *Aai* | a word of respect for motherly figures |
| *Aghon* | a winter month in the Assamese calendar roughly falling between mid-November to mid-December |
| *Bai* | elder sister |
| *Bandh* | strike or close down |
| *Bazaar* | market |
| *Been* | a wind instrument played by snake charmers in the Indian subcontinent |
| *Bhaat* | cooked rice |
| *Bhai* | an address for a brother, but often also used by unrelated acquaintances |
| *Bidroh* | rebellion |
| *Bihu* | major Assamese festival |
| *Borma* | wife of paternal uncle but used as an address by unrelated acquaintances too |
| *Borta* | paternal uncle but used as an address by unrelated acquaintances too |
| *Bou* | wife of elder brother but used as an address by unrelated acquaintances too |
| *Chaador* | an unstitched piece of long cloth generally wrapped around the upper body by men and worn with a skirt called *mekhela* by women |
| *Chittha munshi* | a lower level police personnel who is assigned the job of assisting the SHO in working out duties and shifts |
| *Daftar* | office |

| | |
|---|---|
| *Dai* | paternal uncle but used as an address by unrelated acquaintances too |
| Dharna | Protest rally |
| *Gamosa* | a traditional Assamese towel offered to elders and to show respect |
| *Gaon* | village |
| *Gaon burha* | Village headman of Lakhipathar appointed by the Forest Department, most often on hereditary basis |
| *Haaj* | alocoholic liquor made from fermented rice |
| Jawan | an armed forces personnel |
| *Jethai* | Father's elder sister but used as an address by unrelated acquaintances too |
| *Jhagra* | quarrel |
| *Juddha* | War |
| *Khuri* | Wife of paternal uncle but used as an address by unrelated acquaintances too |
| *Lakh* | a hundred thousand |
| *Lathi* | Wooden or bamboo stick used by police personnel |
| *Laupani* | a locally brewed alcoholoic liquor |
| *Maalkhana* | store room |
| *mama* | Maternal uncle |
| *Mekhela* | a traditional Assamese skirt worn by women together with a chaador |
| *Mukhia* | unelected chief of urban villages in Delhi |
| *Namghar* | halls for collective prayers in villages, used by various sects of broadly Hindu communities in Assam |
| *Paakghar* | kitchen |
| Panchayat | an institution of local self-governance |
| *Path abarodh* | road blockade |
| *Pathar* | field or ground |
| *Patila* | a cooking pan with a wide bottom |
| *Patta* | legal document certifying ownership or entitlement of land |
| *Pira* | low wooden stool |
| *Poduli* | entrance to a traditional Assamese home's compound leading to the dwelling house |
| *Pradhan* | unelected chief of urban villages in Delhi |
| *Rawangi* | the act or time of leaving the police station |

| | |
|---|---|
| Roti | Chapati |
| Saadhu | holy man |
| *Sarkar* | government |
| *Sipahi* | constable |
| *Swadhin Axom* | independent Assam |
| *Thana* | police station |
| *Tiniali* | an intersection of three roads |
| *Wapsi* | the act or time of return to the police station |
| *xangathan* | literally organization; used to refer to the ULFA in common parlance |
| *Xibir* | relief camp |

# References

## Books and Articles


Abrams, P. 1988. 'Notes on the Difficulty of Studying the State (1977)', *Journal of Historical Sociology* 1(1): 58–87.

Agamben, G. 1998. *Homo Sacer: Sovereign Power and Bare Life*, trans. Daniel Heller-Roazen. Stanford: Stanford University Press.

Ahmed, F. 1991. 'Assam: Pushed to the Brink', *India Today*, 30 September. Available at http://indiatoday.intoday.in/story/ulfa-killing-spree-compels-government-to-take-tough-stance/1/318852.html (accessed 5 May 2017).

Alavi, H. 1972. 'The State in Postcolonial Societies—Pakistan and Bangladesh', *New Left Review* 74 (July–August): 59–81.

Althusser, L. 1971. 'Ideology and Ideological State Apparatuses (Notes towards an Investigation)', in *Lenin and Philosophy and Other Essays*, trans. B. Brewster, pp. 127–86. New York and London: Monthly Review Press.

Amin, S. 1976. *Unequal Development: An Essay on the Social Formations of Peripheral Capitalism*. New York: Monthly Review Press.

Austin, D. 1994. *Democracy and Violence in India and Sri Lanka*. London: RIIA/Pinter Publishers, London.

Bailung, S. 2005. 'Lakhipathar: Prem aru Preronar Utsa' (Assamese). *Prerona* 1(September): 5–6.

Bamat, T. 1977. 'Relative State Autonomy and Capitalism in Brazil and Peru', *Insurgent Socialist*, vii(Spring): 74–84.

Bardhan, P. 1987 [2005]. 'The State as an Autonomous Actor', in *Political Economy of Development in India*, pp. 32–9. New Delhi: Oxford University Press.

Barker, R. 1990. *Political Legitimacy and the State*. Oxford: Clarendon Press.

Barpujari, H. 2007. *The Comprehensive History of Assam*, Volume II. Guwahati: Publication Board Assam.

Baruah, C.N. 2009. *Assamese Response to Regionalism*. New Delhi: Mittal.

Baruah, S. 1999, 4th impression 2008. *India against Itself: Assam and the Politics of Nationality*. New Delhi: Oxford University Press.

———. 2005 [2007]. *Durable Disorder: Understanding the Politics of Northeast India*. New Delhi: Oxford University Press.

Baviskar, A. 2003. 'Between Violence and Desire: Space, Power and Identity in the making of Metropolitan Delhi', *International Social Science Journal* 55(175): 89–98.

Baxi, U. 1982. *Crisis of the Indian Legal System*. New Delhi: Vikas Publishing House.

Beetham, D. 1991. *Legitimation of Power*. Basingstoke: Macmillan.

Benjamin, W. 1999. 'Critique of Violence', in *Violence and its Alternatives: An Interdisciplinary Reader*, edited by Manfred B. Steger and Nancy S. Lind, pp. 57–69. London: Macmillan.

Blom Hansen, T.B. and F. Stepputat. 2001. *States of Imagination: Ethnographic Explorations of the Postcolonial State*. Durham: Duke University Press.

Boo, K. 2012. *Behind the Beautiful Forevers: Life, Death and Hope in a Mumbai Undercity*. New Delhi: Hamish Hamilton.

Bowden, M. 2003. 'The Dark Art of Interrogation', *The Atlantic Monthly* 292(3): 51–76.

Boyes, D.G. 1993. 'From Assaye to "the Assaye": Reflections on British Government, Force, and Force in India', *Journal of Military History* 65(3): 643–68.

Branch, J. 2014. *The Cartographic State: Maps, Territory, and the Origin of Sovereignty*. Cambridge: Cambridge University Press.

Burman, A. 2010. 'Legislative Brief: The Prevention of Torture Bill, 2010'. Available at http://www.prsindia.org/uploads/media/Torture/Brief%20%20Prevention%20of%20Torture%20Bill%202010.pdf (accessed on 24 June 2013).

Butler, J. 2004. *Precarious Life*. London: Verso.

Chakrabarty, D. 1992. 'Of Garbage, Modernity, and the Citizen's Gaze'. *Economic and Political Weekly* 27(10/11): 541–7.

———. 2007. '"In the Name of Politics": Democracy and the Power of the Multitude in India', *Public Culture* 19(1): 35–57.

Chandavarkar, R. 1998. *Imperial Power and Popular Politics: Class, Resistance and the State in India, 1850–1950*. Cambridge: Cambridge University Press.

Chappel, B. 2006. 'Rehearsals of the Sovereign: States of Exception and Threat Governmentality', *Cultural Dynamics* 18(3). Available at http://cdy.sagepub.com (accessed on 8 October 2010).

Chatterjee, P. 2004. *The Politics of the Governed: Reflections on Popular Politics in Most of the World*. Delhi: Permanent Black.

———. 2012. *The Black Hole of Empire: History of a Global Practice of Power*. Princeton: Princeton University Press.

Coady, C. A. J. 1998. 'Violence', in *Routledge Encyclopedia of Philosophy*, general editor E. Craig, p. 615. London and New York: Routledge.

Commonwealth Human Rights Initiative (CHRI). 2010. *Prevention of Torture Bill: A Critique*. New Delhi.

Corrigan, P. and D. Sayer. 1985. *The Great Arch: English State Formation as Cultural Revolution*. Oxford: Basil Blackwell.

Das, B.M. 2007. 'Sonowal Kacharir Nrigosthiyo Porichoy' (Assamese), in *Sonowal Sourav Smarak Grantha*, edited by M. Sonowal. Dibrugarh: Sonowal Kachari Autonomous Council.

Das, D. (under pseudonym Banasur). 1969. 'The Moamoria Peasant', *Shillong Observer*, Sunday, 1 June (reprinted in Guha 1993, pp. 103–9).

Das, V. 1997. 'Language and Body', in *Social Suffering*, edited by V. Das, A. Kleinman, and M. Lock, pp. 67–91. Los Angeles: University of California Press.

———. 2007. 'The Event and the Everyday', in *Life and Words: Violence and the Descent into the Ordinary*, pp. 1–17. Berkeley: University of California Press.

Das, V. and D. Poole. 2004. 'State and its Margins: Comparative Ethnographies', in *Anthropology in the Margins of the State*, edited by V. Das and D. Poole, pp. 3–35. Santa Fe: School of American Research Press.

Davis, M. 2006. *Planet of Slums*. London and New York: Verso.

Derrida, J. 1999. 'Excerpt from "Force of Law: The Mystical Foundation of Authority"', in *Violence and its Alternatives: An Interdisciplinary Reader*, edited by M. B. Steger and N. S. Lind, pp. 77–83. London: Macmillan.

Dershowitz, A. 2002. 'Want to Torture? Get a Warrant', *San Francisco Chronicle*, 22 January: A19.

Dhareshwar, V. and R. Srivatsan. 1996. '"Rowdy-sheeters": An Essay on Subalternity and Politics', in *Subaltern Studies IX: Writings in South Asian History and Society*, edited by Shahid Amin and Dipesh Chakrabarty, pp. 201–32. New Delhi: Oxford University Press.

Douglas, M. 1966 (2002 reprint). *Purity and Danger: An Analysis of the Concepts of Pollution and Taboo*. London: Routledge.

Dutta, U. 2008. *Creating Robin Hoods: The Insurgency of the ULFA in Its Early Period, its Parallel Administration and the Role of Assamese Vernacular Press, 1985–1990*. New Delhi: WISCOMP, Foundation for Universal Responsibility of His Holiness the Dalai Lama.

Eckert, J. 2004. 'Urban Governance and Emergent Forms of Legal Pluralism in Mumbai', *Journal of Legal Pluralism* 36(50): 29–60.

Fanon, F. 1963 [1991]. *The Wretched of the Earth*. New York: Grove Press.

Fearon, J.D. and D.D. Laitin. 2001. 'Ethnicity, Insurgency and Civil War'. Paper presented at the 2001 Annual Meeting of the American Political Science Association, San Francisco, CA, 30 August–2 September. Available at https://web.stanford.edu/group/ethnic/workingpapers/apsa011.pdf (accessed on 22 May 2017).

Fereira, A. 2010. 'An Act of Torture: A Critical Appraisal of the Proposed Prevention of Torture Bill 2010'. Available at http://www.countercurrents.org/ferreira120510.htm (accessed on 10 March 2011).

Finer, S.E. 1975. 'State and Nation-building in Europe: The Role of the Military', in *The Formation of National States in Western Europe*, edited by C. Tilly, pp. 84–163. Princeton, NJ: Princeton University Press.

Frisch, M. 1990. A *Shared Authority: Essays on the Craft and Meaning of Oral and Public History*. Albany: State University of New York Press.

Gait, S.E. 1926 [1981] [2012 reprint]. *A History of Assam*. Guwahati: EBH Publishers.

Giddens, A. 1985. *The Nation-State and Violence*. Berkeley: University of California Press.

Gogoi, M.K. 2004. *Kene Ason Mok Nusudhiba* (Assamese). Dibrugarh: Kaustuv Prakashan.

Gooptu, N. 2001. *The Politics of the Urban Poor in Early Twentieth-Century India*. Cambridge: Cambridge University Press.

Goswami, U. 2014. *Conflict and Reconciliation: The Politics of Ethnicity in Assam*. New Delhi: Routledge.

Gross, O. 2004. 'The Prohibition on Torture and the Limits of the Law', in *Torture*, edited by S. Levinson, pp. 165–82. Oxford: Oxford University Press.

Guha, A. 1993. *Baishnavbaador pora Mayamoria Bidroholoi* (Assamese). Guwahati: Students Stores.

Hall, S. 1984. 'The State in Question', in *The Idea of the Modern State*, edited by Gregor McLennan, David Held, and Stuart Hall, pp. 1–28. Bristol: Open University Press.

Hazarika, S. 1994 (2011). *Strangers of the Mist: Tales of War and Peace from India's Northeast*. New Delhi: Penguin.

Held, D. 1992. 'The Development of the Modern State', in *Formations of Modernity*, edited by Stuart Hall and Bram Gieben, pp. 71–126. Cambridge: The Polity Press with the Open University, Cambridge.

Hillyard, P. 1993. *Suspect Community*. London: Pluto Press.

Hope, D. 2004. 'Torture'. *The International and Comparative Law Quarterly* 53(4): 807–32.

Hussain, J. n.d. 'Xironama Nai' (Assamese). *Panthaxala* 1(1).

James, L. 1997. *Raj: The Making and Unmaking of British India*. London: Little and Brown Co.

Jauregui, B. 2015. 'Just War: The Metaphysics of Police Vigilantism in India', in *Conflict and Society: Advances in Research* 1(1): 41–59.

Kalyvas, S.N. 2006. *The Logic of Violence in Civil War*. Cambridge: Cambridge University Press.

Kavanagh, D. 1972. *Political Culture*. London: MacMillan.

Kaviraj, S. 1991. 'On State, Society and Discourse in India', in *Rethinking Third World Politics*, edited by J. Manor, pp. 72–99. Harlow: Longman.

———. 1997. 'Filth and the Public Sphere'. *Public Culture* 10(1): 83–113.

Khanikar, S. 2016. 'Women Police in the city of Delhi: Gender Hierarchies, "Pariah Femininities" and the Politics of Presence'. *Studies in Indian Politics* 4(2): 159–77.

Kleinman, A. and J. Kleinman. 2009. 'Cultural Appropriations of Suffering', in *Cultures of Fear: A Critical Reader*, edited by U. Linke and D.T. Smith, pp. 288–303. London: Pluto Press.

Kristeva, J. 1982. *Powers of Horror*, trans. L. S. Roudiez. New York: Columbia University Press.

Legg, S. 2008. *Spaces of Colonialism: Delhi's Urban Governmentalities*. Malden: Blackwell Publishing.

Leys, C. 1981. 'The "Overdeveloped" Post-Colonial State: A Re-evaluation'. *Review of African Political Economy* 3(5): 39–48.

Linke, U. 2006. 'Contact Zones: Rethinking the Sensual Life of the State', *Anthropological Theory* 6(2): 205–25. Available at http://ant.sagepub.com (accessed on 8 October 2010).

Lipset, S.M. 1959. 'Some Social Requisites of Democracy: Economic Development and Political Legitimacy'. *The American Political Science Review* 53(1): 69–105.

———. 1984. 'Social Conflict, Legitimacy, and Democracy', in *Legitimacy and the State*, edited by W. Connolly, pp. 88–103. Oxford: Basil Blackwell.

———. 1994. 'The Social Requisites of Democracy Revisited: 1993 Presidential Address'. *American Sociological Review* 59(1): 1–22. Available at http://www.jstor.org/stable/2096130 (accessed 25 May 2009).

Lokaneeta, J. 2011. *Transnational Torture: Law, Violence and State Power in the United States and India*. New York: New York University Press.

Luban, D. 2005. 'Liberalism, Torture and the Ticking Bomb', *Virginia Law Review* 91(6): 1425–61.

Mahanta, N.G. 2013. *Confronting the State: ULFA's Quest for Sovereignty*. Sage: New Delhi.

Mann, M. 1988. *States, War and Capitalism: Studies in Political Sociology*. Oxford: Basil Blackwell.

———. 1993. 'A Theory of the Modern State' in *The Sources of Social Power (Volume II): The Rise of Classes and Nation-states, 1760–1914*, edited by M. Mann, pp. 44–91. Cambridge: Cambridge University Press.

Marcus, G.E. 1998. *Ethnography through Thick and Thin*. Princeton: Princeton University Press.

Marston, D. P. and C.S. Sundaram. 2007. 'Why This Book?', in *A Military History of India and South Asia: From the East India Company to the Nuclear Era*, edited by D.P. Marston and S.S. Chandar, pp. xi–xii. Bloomington: Indiana University Press.

Marx, K. 1970. 'Theses on Feuerbach', in *The German Ideology*, K. Marx and F. Engels, edited by C. Arthur, pp. 121–3. London: Lawrence and Wishart.

Marx, K. and F. Engels. 1932. *The German Ideology*. Institute of Marxism–Leninism of the Central Committee of the CPSU.

Mbembe, A. 2001. *On the Postcolony*. Berkeley: University of California Press.

McCarthy, A.C. 2005. 'Torture: Thinking about the Unthinkable', in *The Torture Debate in America*, edited by K.J. Greenberg, pp. 98–110. Cambridge: Cambridge University Press.

Menon, N. and A. Nigam. 2007. *Power and Contestation: India since 1989*. London: Zed Books.

Merelman, R. 1966. 'Learning and Legitimacy'. *American Political Science Review* 60(3): 548–61.

Migdal, J. 2001. *State in Society: Studying How States and Societies Transform and Constitute One Another*. New York: Cambridge University Press.

———. 1999. 'Society, Economy and the State Effect', in *State/culture: State Formation after the Cultural Turn*, edited by G. Steinmetz, 76–97. Ithaca: Cornell University Press.

Nagengast, C. 1994. 'Violence, Terror, and the Crisis of the State'. *Annual Review of Anthropology* 23: 109–36. Available at http://www.jstor.org/stable/2156008 (accessed 22 June 2009.)

Nettl, J.P. 1968. 'The State as a Conceptual Variable'. *World Politics* 20(4): 559–92.

Nordstrom, C. 2004. *Shadows of War: Violence, War and International Profiteering in the Twenty-first Century*. Berkeley: University of California Press.

Parry, J.T. 2005. 'Pain, Interrogation and the Body', in *Evil, Law and the State, Perspectives on State Power and Violence*, edited by J.T. Parry, pp. 1–16. Amsterdam: Rodopi.

———. 2008. 'Torture Warrants and the Rule of Law', *Albany Law Review* 71: 885.

Perks, R. and A. Thomson. 1998. *The Oral History Reader*. London: Routledge.

Poggi, G. 1990. 'The Nature of the Modern State', in *The State, Its Nature, Development and Prospects*, edited by G. Poggi, pp. 19–33. Cambridge: Polity Press.

Poulantzas, N. 1980. *State, Power and Socialism*. London: Verso, New Left Review.

Prabhakara, M.S. 2003. 'Outrage in Assam', *Frontline* 20(25). Available at http://www.frontline.in/static/html/fl2025/stories/20031219006800800.htm (accessed on 9 May 2017).

Ramanathan, U. 2005. 'Demolition Drive'. *Economic and Political Weekly* XL(27). Available at http://www.ielrc.org/content/a0507.pdf (accessed on 28 July 2014).

Rammohan, E.N. 2005. *Simply Khaki: A Policeman Remembers*. New Delhi: Indialog Publications.

Rejali, D. 2007. *Torture and Democracy*. Princeton: Princeton University Press.

Riches, D. 1986. 'The Phenomenon of Violence', in *The Anthropology of Violence*, edited by D. Riches, pp. 1–27. Oxford: Basil Blackwell.

Rudolph, L.I. and S.H. Rudolph. 1987. *In Pursuit of Lakshmi: The Political Economy of the Indian State*. Chicago and London: The University of Chicago Press.

Said, E. (1984) 1998. 'Orientalism Reconsidered', excerpt from *Europe and Its Others*, Volume 1, reproduced in *The Geopolitics Reader*, edited by G.O. Tuathail, S. Dalby, and P. Routledge, pp. 256–61. London: Routledge.

Saikia, P. 2015. 'The ULFA Insurgency in Assam', in *Ethnic Subnationalist Insurgencies in South Asia: Identities, Interests and Challenges to State Authority*, edited by J.S. Chima, pp. 41–60. New York: Routledge.

Sarat, A. and T.R. Kearns. 1995. 'Introduction', in *Law's Violence*, edited by A. Sarat and T.R. Kearns, pp. 1–22. USA: University of Michigan Press.

Scarry, E. 1985. *The Body in Pain: The Making and Unmaking of the World*. New York: Oxford University Press.

Scheper-Hughes, N. 1993. *Death without Weeping: The Violence of Everyday Life in Brazil*. Berkeley: University of California Press.

Schmitt, C. 2005. *Political Theology, Four Chapters on the Concept of Sovereignty*, trans. George Schwab. Chicago: University of Chicago Press.

Sethi, M. 2012. 'Delhi Police Special Cell—Encounters, Frame-ups, Impunity', guest-post at www.kafila.org. Available at https://kafila.org/2012/02/21/delhi-police-special-cell-encounters-frame-ups-impunity-manisha-sethi/ (accessed 23 August 2016).

Sherman, T.C. 2010. *State Violence and Punishment in India*. New York: Routledge.

Shue, H. 1978. 'Torture', *Philosophy and Public Affairs* 7(2): 124–43.

———. 2006. 'Torture in Dreamland: Disposing of the Ticking Bomb', *Journal of International Law* 37(2): 231–9.

Sim, J. and S. Tombs. 2009. 'State Talk, State Silence: Work and "Violence" in the UK', in *Violence Today: Actually Existing Barbarism, Socialist Register 2009*, edited by L. Panitch and C. Leys, pp. 88–104. New Delhi: Leftword Books.

Singh, U.K. 1998. *Political Prisoners in India*. New Delhi: Oxford University Press.

———. 2007. *The State, Democracy and Anti-Terror Laws in India*. New Delhi: Sage.

Skocpol, T. 1979. *States and Social Revolutions*. Cambridge: Cambridge University Press.

Skocpol, T. 1984a. 'Sociology's Historical Imagination', in *Vision and Method in Historical Sociology*, edited by T. Skocpol, pp. 1–21. Cambridge: Cambridge University Press.

———. 1984b. 'Emerging Agendas and Recurrent Strategies in Historical Sociology', in *Vision and Method in Historical Sociology*, edited by T. Skocpol, pp. 356–91. Cambridge: Cambridge University Press.

Sundar, N. 2001. 'Beyond the Bounds? Violence at the Margins of New Legal Geographies', in *Violent Environments*, edited by N. Peluso and M. Watts, pp. 328–53. Ithaca, NY: Cornell University Press.

Sundaram, C.S. 2002. 'Reviving a "Dead Letter": Military Indianization and the Ideology of Anglo-India, 1885–1891', in *The British Raj and its Indian Armed Forces, 1851–1939*, edited by P.S. Gupta and A. Deshpande, pp. 45–97. Delhi: Oxford University Press.

Talukdar, M., U. Borpujari, and K. Deka. 2008 (2011). *Secret Killings of Assam: The Horrific Story of Assam's Darkest Period*. Guwahai: Nanda Talukdar Foundation and Bhabani, Guwahati.

Talukdar, M. and K.K. Kalita. 2011. *ULFA* (Assamese). Guwahati: Nanda Talukdar Foundation and Bhanbani.

Tarlo, E. 2003. *Unsettling Memories: Narratives of India's Emergency*. Delhi: Permanent Black.

Taussig, M. 1989. 'Terror as Usual: Walter Benjamin's Theory of History as a State of Siege', *Social Text* 23(Autumn–Winter): 3–20.

Therborn, G. 1980. *The Ideology of Power and the Power of Ideology*. London: Verso and NLB.

Tilly, C., ed. 1975. *The Formation of National States in Western Europe*. Princeton: Princeton University Press.

———. 1992. *Coercion, Capital and European States: AD 990–1992*. Cambridge: Basil Blackwell.

———. 2002. 'War Making and State Making as Organized Crime', in *Violence, A Reader*, edited by C. Besteman, pp. 35–60. New York: Palgrave.

Trimberger, K.E. 1977. 'State Power and Modes of Production: Implications of the Japanese Transition to Capitalism', *Insurgent Socialist* 7(Spring): 85–98.

Trautmann, T.R. 1979. 'Traditions of Statecraft in Ancient India', in *Tradition and Politics in South Asia*, edited by R.J. Moore, pp. 86–102. New Delhi: Vikas Publishing House.

von der Dunk, H. 1997. 'The Formation of Modern States in Europe', in *Dynamics of State Formation, India and Europe Compared*, edited by M. Doornbos and S. Kaviraj, pp. 56–73. New Delhi: Sage.

Walzer, M. 1974. 'Political Action: The Problem of Dirty Hands', in *War and Moral Responsibility*, edited by M. Cohen, T. Nagel, and T. Scanlon, pp. 76–82. Princeton, NJ: Princeton University Press.

Wantchekon, L. and A. Healy. 1999. 'The "Game" of Torture', *The Journal of Conflict Resolution* 43(5): 596–609.

Weber, M. 1978. *Economy and Society: An Outline of Interpretive Sociology*. London: University of California Press.

———. 1984. 'Legitimacy, Politics and the State', in *Legitimacy and the State*, edited by W. Connolly, pp. 32–62. Oxford: Basil Blackwell.

———. 2002. 'Politics as a Vocation', in *Violence: A Reader*, edited by C. Besteman, pp. 13–18. New York: Palgrave.

Weiss, L. and J.H. Hobson. 1995. *States and Economic Development: A Comparative Historical Analysis*. Cambridge: Polity Press.

Young, I.M. 2005. 'The Logic of Masculinist Protection: Reflections on the Current Security State', in *Women and Citizenship*, edited by M. Friedman, pp. 15–34. Oxford: Oxford University Press.

Zizek, S. 2002. 'From Homo Sucker to Homo Sacer', in *Welcome to the Desert of the Real! Five Essays on September 11 and Related Dates*, pp. 83–111. London: Verso.

## Reports, Documents, and Web-pages

Almitra H. Patel and Anr. Vs Union of India and Ors. 2000. Available at https://indiankanoon.org/doc/339109/ (accessed 21 October 2012).

ashis2k. 2013. 'Beggars and Louts in Uniform Empowered by CM'. Available at http://www.mouthshut.com/review/Delhi-Police-review-utootusnlm (accessed on 3 January 2013).

Code of Criminal Procedure. 1973. (No. 2 of 1974 dated 25 January 1974).

*Dainik Asam*. 29 November 1990. 'Axomor khetrat dillir xiddhanta' (Assamese), p. 1.

———. 2 December 1990. 'Lakhipatharot obhijan aru keibadinu solibo' (Assamese), p. 1.

———. 4 December 1990. 'Lakhipatharei ULFAr prodhan ghaati buli xenar xondeh', Guwahati, p. 1.

———. 17 December 1990. 'Atixorjyor biruddhe writ abedan: Ekoish decemberot poroborti xunani' (Assamese), p. 1 continued on p. 6.

———. 7 January 1991. 'Abhijukta jowanak xashti biha xomporke' (Assamese), Letter to Editor by Sri Nagen Saikia, p. 4.

———. 13 February 1991. 'Xenai hospital sofa kore kiyo?' (Assamese), p. 1.

———. 6 March 1991a. 'Kahudi' (Assamese), p. 1.

———. 6 March 1991b. 'Uccha nyayalayat bibhinna abedan: Xenar paxobik atyacharor biboron' (Assamese), p. 1 continued on p. 6.

———. 16 March 1991c. Letters to Editor by Sri Dhiraj Kumar Das, Sri Sangram Baruah, Sri Rituraj Burhagoahain, and Sri Biplob Gogoi, p. 4.

Delhi Police Website. 2013. Available at http://www.delhipolice.nic.in/ (accessed on 31 January 2013).

Facebook. 2013. Available at https://www.facebook.com/delhipolice4u/posts/475159332530184 (accessed on 31 January 2013).

FIR 373/87, Shahdara Police Station, date and time of incident 23 August 1987 & not known. Record Room, Shahdara Police Station, Delhi.

FIR 89/05, Shahdara Police Station, 19 March 2005, Record Room, Shahdara Police Station, Delhi.

*Hindustan Times*. 30 November 1990. '48 Captured in Army Swoop on ULFA Camps', report by Sachin Barooah, p. 1.

———. 14 December 1990. 'Camps Reveal ULFA plot', report by Deepak Joshi, p. 7, Delhi.

———. 2008. 'The Rise and Fall of ACP Rajbir Singh'. Available at http://www.hindustantimes.com/India-news/NewDelhi/The-rise-and-fall-of-ACP-Rajbir-Singh/Article1-284306.aspx (accessed on 11 April 2013).

*India Today*. 1 August 2013. 'Delhi Police withdraws controversial ad on street children'. Available at http://indiatoday.intoday.in/story/delhi-police-withdraws-controversial-advertisement-street-children/1/297458.html (accessed on 15 September 2015).

India, Delhi Police. 2010. *Annual Report 2010*. New Delhi: Delhi Police.

———. 2011. *Annual 2011*. New Delhi.

———. 2012a. *Annual Report 2012*. New Delhi.

———. 2012b. *Annual Review 2012*. Delhi.

———. 2013. *Annual Review 2013*. New Delhi.

———. n.d.b. *Parivartan: A Campaign for the Safety of Women in Delhi*, Delhi.

———. n.d.c. *Delhi Police Manuals*. Available at http://www.delhipolice.nic.in/home/rti/rti.aspx (accessed on 11 October 2011).

India, Delhi Police. Rejoinder, No. 271/PRO/PHQ dated Delhi 6-8-2009. Available at http://www.delhipolice.nic.in/home/press/27106082009.pdf (accessed on 15 December 2011).

Lakhipathar Central Rongali Bihu Organizing Committtee. 2012. *Rongali Bihu Xanmilon—2012*. Lakhipathar, booklet.

Law Commission of India. 2003. *Review of the Indian Evidence Act, (Part II)*. Available at http://lawcommissionofindia.nic.in/reports/185thReport-PartII.pdf (accessed on 21 December 2011).

Letter to the DCP North West District from the Assistant Registrar (Law), Case No. 2386/30/2000-2001-CD, dated 28 July 2008, accessed through an application under Right to Information Act, 2005.

Malabika, M. 2011. Comment to article by Nivedita Menon, 'I'd Rather Die than Clean Your House', *Tehelka* 24 (8). Available at http://www.tehelka.com/id-rather-die-than-clean-your-house/ (accessed 11 August 2014).

NCRB. 2013. *Crime in India, Annual Report of the National Crime Records Bureau*. Available at http://ncrb.nic.in/ (accessed on 22 May 2017).

PUDR. March 1998. *Capital Crimes: Deaths in Police Custody, Delhi 1980–1997*. New Delhi.

———. October 1989. *Invisible Crimes: A Report on Custodial Death 1980–1989*. New Delhi.

———. March 1992. *'Escaping' Death: Death in Custody at Budh Vihar Police Chowki, Sultanpuri Police Station*. New Delhi.

———. April 1993. *A Cover-up that Failed: Death and Protest at Najafgarh Police Station*. New Delhi.

———. August 1996. *A Tale of Two Cities: Custodial Death and Police Firing in Ashok Vihar*, Second Edition. New Delhi.

———. February 1998. *Last Stop: Custodial Death at New Delhi Railway Station P.S.* New Delhi.

———. March 1998. *Capital Crimes: Deaths in Police Custody, Delhi 1980–1997*. New Delhi.

———. 2000. *Dead Men's Tales: Death in Police Custody, Delhi 2000*, pp. 10–11, December. New Delhi.

———. February 2002. *Deaths in Police Custody, Delhi, 2001*. New Delhi.

———. 2003. *Courting Disaster: A Report on Inter-caste Marriages, Society and State*. New Delhi.

———. 2011. *A Story of 'Suicide' and Survival: Death in the Custody of Vijay Vihar Police Station*. Available at http://www.pudr.org/sites/default/files/Vijay_vihar_Report_2__1_.pdf (accessed on 21 February 2012).

———. 2014. *Crimes of Habit: A Report on Custodial Torture in Vijay Vihar Police Station*. New Delhi.

———. n.d. 'PUDR Condemns Death Sentence Awarded to Police Officer for Custodial Killing: The Death Penalty is No Answer to Custodial Violence!', available at http://pudr.org/?q=content/pudr-condemns-death-sentence-awarded-police-officer-custodial-killing.

*Sadin*. 7 December 1990. 'Axomor akaxot kolia dawor: Lakhipatharor ghatanar xobixex' (Assamese), report by Dilip Chandan, p. 1 continued on p. 4.

———. 7 December 1990, 'Hiteshwar Saikiak hudu kheda' (Assamese), p. 1 continued on p. 14.

———. 14 December 1990. 'Congress I r roxat Sadin' (Assamese), p. 1 continued on p. 4.

*The Assam Tribune*. 8 March 1991. 'Army Can't Defy Court Order', p. 1.

*The Delhi Police Act, 1978* (No. 34 of 1978 dated 27 August 1978).

*The Telegraph*. 25 July 2009. 'Morans mull shield to stop felling of hollong'. Available at http://www.telegraphindia.com/1090725/jsp/northeast/story_11230750.jsp (accessed on 28 August 2016).

*The Times of India*. 2011. 'Midnight Police Swoop on Baba Ramdev Ends Protest'. Available at http://articles.timesofindia.indiatimes.com/2011-06-05/india/29623134_1_baba-ramdev-yoga-guru-yoga-camp (accessed on 11 April 2013).

*TNN*. 2012. 'Confidence Deficit: Most Residents feel the Cops have Failed Them'. Available at http://articles.timesofindia.indiatimes.com/2012-12-21/delhi/35952577_1_delhi-cop-city-cop-south-delhi (accessed on 31 January 2013).

ULFA. 1989. *'SangjuktaMukti Bahini Axom' or Doxom Protishtha Divas, 7 April, 1988, Bixex Prochar Patrar Prakax*. Booklet, reprinted by M. Talukar & K. K. Kalita 2011. Guwahati: ULFA, Nanda Talukdar Foundation and Bhabani.

———. 1992. 'Ahombashi Purbabangiya Janaganaloy', trans. Bibhu Prasad Routray. Available at http://www.satp.org/satporgtp/publication/faultlines/volume13/Article6.htm (accessed on 23 May 2017).

## Archival Source

File No. AFR 119/53, Agriculture Department Forests Branch, Secretariat, Military Secretary's Office, 1953, Assam State Archives, Guwahati.

# Index

# About the Author

**Santana Khanikar** teaches political geography at Jawaharlal Nehru University, New Delhi, India. She has a PhD in political science from the University of Delhi, and had worked previously at University of Delhi and the Centre for Women's Development Studies, New Delhi. She grew up in a small town in Assam witnessing both insurgent and state and state-sponsored violence from close quarters, where presence of armed forces was a routine part of daily life, Independence Day or republic day celebrations were marred by ULFA calls of bandh every year, and school children were on roads participating in movements led by AASU regularly. The areas of her research interest are practices of violence of the state, territoriality and identity, politics in northeast India, and feminist studies. She has published research articles in journals *Studies in Indian Politics* and *Pratimaan*.